ROUTLEDGE LIBRARY EDITIONS:
SOCIAL THEORY

Volume 38

LEGITIMACY AND THE POLITICS OF THE KNOWABLE

LEGITIMACY AND THE POLITICS OF THE KNOWABLE

ROGER HOLMES

Routledge
Taylor & Francis Group
LONDON AND NEW YORK

First published in 1976

This edition first published in 2015
by Routledge
2 Park Square, Milton Park, Abingdon, Oxon, OX14 4RN

and by Routledge
711 Third Avenue, New York, NY 10017

Routledge is an imprint of the Taylor & Francis Group, an informa business

British Library Cataloguing in Publication Data
A catalogue record for this book is available from the British Library

ISBN: 978-0-415-72731-0 (Set)
eISBN: 978-1-315-76997-4 (Set)
ISBN: 978-1-138-78424-6 (Volume 38)
eISBN: 978-1-315-76354-5 (Volume 38)

Publisher's Note
The publisher has gone to great lengths to ensure the quality of this reprint but points out that some imperfections in the original copies may be apparent.

Disclaimer
The publisher has made every effort to trace copyright holders and would welcome correspondence from those they have been unable to trace.

MIX
Paper from responsible sources
FSC® C013604

LEGITIMACY AND THE POLITICS OF THE KNOWABLE

ROGER HOLMES

ROUTLEDGE DIRECT EDITIONS

ROUTLEDGE & KEGAN PAUL
London, Henley and Boston

First published in 1976
by Routledge & Kegan Paul Ltd
39 Store Street,
London WC1E 7DD,
Reading Road,
Henley-on-Thames,
Oxon RG9 1EN and
9 Park Street,
Boston, Mass. 02108, USA
Manuscript typed by Jacqueline Bayes
Printed and bound in Great Britain
by Unwin Brothers Limited,
The Gresham Press, Old Woking, Surrey
A member of the Staples Printing Group

ISBN 0 7100 8351 3

CONTENTS

	FOREWORD	v
	ACKNOWLEDGMENTS	viii
	INTRODUCTION	1
1	FREUD AND SOCIAL CLASS	9
2	FREUD, PIAGET AND DEMOCRATIC LEADERSHIP	29
3	THE OWNERSHIP OF WORK: A PSYCHOLOGICAL APPROACH	46
4	THE UNIVERSITY SEMINAR AND THE PRIMAL HORDE	60
5	THE NATURE OF MORALE	75
6	MARXISM AND THE NATURE OF GROUPS	91
7	THE POLITICS OF THE KNOWABLE	103
8	THE TRANSIENT AND THE SUBSUMED: SOME EPISTEMOLOGICAL IMPLICATIONS OF CROSS-CULTURAL RESEARCH	118
9	THE ORGANIZATIONAL AND THE SCIENTIFIC: TWO LEVELS OF DISCOURSE	124
10	A NOTE ON THE DEFINITION OF SYSTEMS	134
11	EMPIRICISM AND PSYCHOANALYSIS	138
	Empiricism and psychoanalysis	138
	The Piagetian resolution	144
	Two forms of knowing	148

The approach adopted here 155
Objects 156
Numbers 158
Structures 164
The relevance for psychoanalysis 166
The nature of the social psychological 171
Psychoanalysis, empiricism and the social psychological 172
The social psychological and the revenge of the mythological 181
INDEX 189

FOREWORD

Donald G. MacRae

Few things are more unfashionable than thought - thought which is of its nature unmediated as regards experience, elliptical in its modality, bothered therefore by the conventions of received accounts of reality and by the convenient lies wherein we have our personal and social being. It seems to me that Roger Holmes is guilty of thought of this kind, and that it is this which makes his collected papers worthwhile and, more than that, which makes them a unity. I do not wish when I call his thinking unmediated to suggest that it is not learned - which it evidently is - but to stress his sensory and intellectual nakedness, his candour towards matters which are repressed by the customary decorum of academic discourse, of the rhetorical forms which facilitate the polite conduct of academic teaching and research, and the scientistic apparatus by which psychology is customarily conducted in Britain and North America.

When Holmes asked me, a sociologist, to introduce his book I was both flattered and puzzled. True some of his earliest work had been published in the 'British Journal of Sociology' during my period as its editor. I had welcomed these pieces because of their intrinsic merit and excitement and resonance, and also because the 'Journal' had from its foundation on been intended to be ecumenical, spanning a related group of studies to which sociology was central, but which extends to anthropology, social psychology and philosophy. On the whole this catholic intention had been but partly achieved: here now was work by a psychologist which was relevant to all who were concerned to understand and explicate those devices by which social and personal life are made possible and even tolerable, but which was clearly work which only a psychologist could have done. It is only with reflection that I see why a sociological journal with the charter of the 'B.J.S.' seemed to him an appropriate medium for what he had to say.

Two things appeared to be involved - and perhaps Holmes would repudiate them both. One was the criterion of relevance, of the question to whom his concerns might matter. The other was the constrictive nature of psychology which in the silent, deadly struggles of the world of learning had taken on a hard carapace of scientism - which is far from being the same as rigour - in order to protect itself from the jealous predation of the life sciences, of medicine, of statistics as an end - not a means - in itself. Perhaps we sociologists, whose need of work like his was obvious, would also receive what he had to say without such constriction.

Put it another way: to an observer the situation in social psychology was not so much that of the hermit crab using the shell of a dead mollusc for protection as that of Oscar Wilde's happy hypocrite who, donning a mask, found his face moulded to that mask. Only, in Wilde's fable, the mask was indeed a happy assumption and aided its wearer to the winning of his beloved, while the mask worn by the psychologists had, though instrumentally successful enough, also left them with features capable of but a narrow range of expression, essentially unsocial. This range meant that the psychologist confronting existential realities might do best to mingle with the scaramouches of sociology and not merely instruct them but also learn himself a new freedom.

The paradoxes of our lives are very familiar but, out of habit or fear of pain or effort, very seldom explored. The self is contingently the victim and creature, patient not agent, of social and physical reality; it is also the maker of reality. We cannot say that this is a world we never made, but each of us may say this is a world I never made and would not will. Holmes approaches this paradoxical state with the help of great men. They are a Freud (who I do not quite recognize as the Freud most of us read), a Piaget who is very clearly the Piaget with whom I have argued and who is still in old age a creator and magus as well as a scientist, Marx and a Durkheim (to whom Holmes perhaps should pay more attention). But more important than these influences is Holmes's sensitivity to experience and the contingencies, organizations and structures which we in part make and which in part are imposed on us by our life in time. 'Awareness', says Holmes, 'of the public present, then, the starting point for the empiricist and the end point for Piaget, is re-adapted biology.' Our lives are a losing struggle for successful homeostasis, for equilibrium. The central trick in this, a kind of Hegelian 'cunning of reason', is that if we won the struggle we would not be: quite literally, would not be be; not merely would not be human in a human society.

The journey to this destination, itself open to its own potentialities and the contingencies of things, is by way of our biology, our infancy, our socialization, our reflexive relation to society. It is, like all novel thought and as I said at the beginning, elliptical. Spelling Holmes out in full would perhaps be to falsify him but would certainly involve an elaboration of exposition which these tight papers, inter-woven as they are, do not possess. This seems to me merit but of course it could be taken as defect in terms of customary rhetoric. I shall, however, be most surprised if others do not spell him out, follow, and sometimes go further than he does. I hope that they do so with due acknowledgment, even in disagreement, to his work. I hope even more that he will himself continue to develop and extend what he gives us here.

After all there is no one path to follow in these matters, no one legitimation of the knowable. To a sociologist the excitement and strength of this work is that we are called to pay attention to the immediate things which we have neglected, that we are shown that the apparent dead ends of investigation are in fact gateways which can be unlocked, that the structures of 'every-day life' are not trivial nor ungeneralizable, and that thought matters. In the sense that politics is about power, the capacity to do and have done, this book is more than a recognition that the art of the possible is not merely the affair, as Holmes says, of politicians, but of all living and of all inquiry.

ACKNOWLEDGMENTS

The author and publishers are grateful to the following for kind permission to reprint material in this volume:

'British Journal of Sociology' for Freud and Social Class, first published in vol. 16, no. 1, March 1965; Freud, Piaget and Democratic Leadership, first published in vol. 16, no. 2, June 1965; The University Seminar and the Primal Horde, first published in vol. 18, no. 2, June 1967; Marxism and the Nature of Groups, first published in vol. 21, no. 3, September 1970; and The Politics of the Knowable, first published in vol. 23, no. 2, June 1972.

'British Journal of Industrial Relations' for The Ownership of Work: A Psychological Approach, first published in part in vol. 5, March 1967.

Penguin Books Ltd for The Nature of Morale, first published in Denis Pym (ed.), 'Industrial Society: Social Sciences in Management', Pelican Library of Business and Management, 1968, copyright © Penguin Books Ltd, 1968.

'Comparative Education Review' for The Transient and the Subsumed: Some Epistemological Implications of Cross-cultural Research, first published in vol. 14, no. 1, February 1970.

The British Psychological Society for The Organizational and the Scientific: Two Levels of Discourse, first published in the Society's 'Bulletin', vol. 24, April 1971.

INTRODUCTION

At first sight, this set of papers, published over the years, appears to belong to two categories. On the one hand there appear to be 'social' papers, dealing with such matters as social class, leadership, University seminars, morale and the sense of ownership, on the other hand there are the 'theory of knowledge' papers, dealing with the usefulness of cross-cultural data, the definition of that much used term 'system', the scientific nature (or otherwise) of organizations and the problems of reconciling empirical and psychoanalytic approaches.

These two sets appear distinct. What, it might be asked, has the problem of leadership to do with the difficulties of reconciling empiricism and psychoanalysis? Surely the first is the practical concern of the industrial and social psychologist and the second the abstract preoccupation of the philosopher or the guilty-minded psychoanalyst? How, it might be asked, can the lion lie down with the lamb? (The reader may choose for himself which one is which.)

To this (very reasonable) question, two points can be made. In the first place, any clear-cut division into categories like 'social' and 'theory of knowledge' is misleading, whatever the titles may suggest. It is misleading since these two aspects - the nature of the people involved on the one hand, and the nature of what they assume as 'knowledge' on the other - are not kept distinct. If we take a 'social' paper like The University Seminar and the Primal Horde, for instance, it is not only concerned with the relationship between audience and speakers at a university seminar, but also with the reciprocal effect these relationships have with that which is professed as 'knowable'. Again, if we take a 'theory of knowledge' paper such as Empiricism and Psychoanalysis, we find that the whole concluding section is concerned with the knowable in social situations. Indeed, it can be argued that, of the eleven papers in this collection, at least seven can be looked on as covering both aspects.

In some cases this is clear from the title and in some cases it is determined by the subject matter. An example that should be clear from its title is The Politics of the Knowable, an example that is determined by the subject matter is Marxism and the

Nature of Groups. (Marxism is both a social and a theory of knowledge package-deal; hence, of course, much of its attractiveness.) But even when it is not obvious, either from the title or subject matter, the actual content of the paper will, often as not, be found to face in both directions. This is the case, for instance, with A Note on the Definitions of Systems, a paper that outlines a possible infrastructure (elaborated, although, it must be admitted, not explicitly and at much greater length in the subsequent Empiricism and Psychoanalysis) of both the social and the known. Both of these papers (A Note on the Definitions of Systems and Empiricism and Psychoanalysis) are theory of knowledge papers and both of them have a social content, whether explicit or implicit. Indeed, all the theory of knowledge papers have distinct social implications in their conclusions. This is not adventitious but a valid reflection of the approach taken, an approach that holds whatever the subject matter might be.

This move from the nature of the subject matter itself to the nature of the approach taken towards the subject matter, brings us to the second, and more substantive, underlying coherence of these papers.

These papers are frankly psychological, psychological in that they are concerned not really with the known and the social at all, but with the knower - the individual who knows - and the actor - the individual who participates in society. This is the common point that these papers share. Whatever the sociological or philosophical implications may (or may not) be (for instance, the derivation of social class on the one hand or the nature of empiricism on the other), these papers are frankly psychological at base. Whatever is known or done is known or done by someone. And it is that 'someone' that is the central point of interest. It is the concern with the individual that gives these papers any coherence they may have.

This in spite of - or rather, because of - the fact that the two main theoretical influences are Freud and Piaget, and that the influences of each is largely (not wholly) restricted to one of the two sections (Freud being the main influence in the social papers and Piaget in the theory of knowledge papers). This does not sound so terrible until we remember that Freud and Piaget, if not totally distinct (Piaget is so encompassing that he can hardly be 'totally distinct' from anyone) are at least highly incompatible.

To show how this circle can be squared, how the two sets - which anyway, as we shall see, have a certain internal coherence - can be integrated into what might pass as a reasonable whole, the reader will have to turn to Empiricism and Psychoanalysis, not only the last paper to be written but also by far the most ambitiously integrative in intent. This argument will not be repeated here. What will be done, though, is to take each section separately and show its central point of interest and then, having done that, show in bald terms how these two sets could lead to a more general conclusion. This way of proceding will have the advantage of treating each section in its own right as well as showing its interrelatedness with the other.

The social papers are very social indeed, for they deal with the derivation of formal social structures and of values. By 'formal social structures' is meant a position or an institution (like 'being a Queen' or an 'organization') that exists in its own right independently of its occupant(s). These 'structures' are closely related to 'values'. 'Values' bespeak a 'higher reality' we should endeavour to maintain (or attain, according to our political orientation). They can clearly be built into formal structures. When this happens, they are often called 'duties'. 'As a foreman', for instance, one has certain 'duties'. One also has certain 'rights' - 'rights' are 'legitimate' powers - powers sanctioned by values.

Now the main point of interest in these papers is the relationship between the individual and these impersonal, formal structural aspects of society. This relationship is discussed in Freudian terms. The individual is looked on much as Freud saw him, quite narcissistic at birth, driven by instinctual impulses (that are referred to in Empiricism and Psychoanalysis as the 'will'), impulses that assert with an insistence that precedes reason and so determine their own private known. A private known that, we may fairly say, has no room for social structure and social obligations. How the child learns of the latter (social structure and social obligation) and how he comes to accept external demands upon his self-justifying 'will' (that is, his impulses that justify themselves) and accept them as 'legitimate' - the reflection of a valid outer source - is the central concern of these papers.

And not just among children. The most 'complete' paper - the one that most clearly presents the approach in all its detail - is perhaps The Ownership of Work, and this paper deals with the emergence of structure and value amongst those adult interest/value groups, the professions and the trade unions.

The Ownership of Work begins with competing adults, unstructured in their relationships, and argues the development of structure and commitment. Other papers also reflect this preoccupation with emergent structure and value. The first paper of all, for instance, Freud and Social Class, is concerned with the derivation of that most pervasive of structures (informal, though, rather than formal), social class (the message, by the way, is that, unless countervailing forces operate, we are all of us going to end up - not in our life time, of course - not just in a class, but in a caste society) and a somewhat later paper, The Nature of Morale, discusses the very different issue of the maintenance of that fragile social commitment known as 'morale'.

And, throughout, explanation is rooted in the individual. The critical question always is - how can the private, inner 'will' (self-sufficient in its conviction, narcissistic, even anarchic) somehow or other accept an outer, social 'will', a social will that is then - once the individual has been influenced - seen as legitimate and so not resented by those within its power.

This progression, it must be admitted, is viewed with jaundiced eye. In almost every social paper it is contended that we accept that which is outside ourselves as legitimate because we have come to see that 'outside' as an extension of ourselves. Social love is a form of extended self-love, in other words. Self-sufficiency is squared with outer ethic by accepting that ethic as a form of property - it is 'our own'. (Not that another, albeit somewhat secondary, ethic is also thought possible. See, for instance, the end of Freud, Piaget and Democratic Leadership.)

But even then - with all our ability to rationalize and to come to see as 'our own' values which were clearly imposed upon us - this progression, any more than true love, does not run smooth. Indeed, a whole paper, Marxism and the Nature of Groups, discusses the derivation of what might be called a 'negative ideology' - the value system of those who reject the established value system. This paper relies heavily (as do two others, Freud and the Social Class, The University Seminar and the Primal Horde) on the pessimistic myth of the Primal Horde. This is not treated (like Freud himself did) as something that actually happened, but as a parable that explicates the explanatory potential of such simple assumptions that we are, all of us, suspicious of our 'brothers' (those 'like us') and resent as much as revere our 'fathers' (those who are superior and apart).

So much for the social development, seen in Freudian terms. The theory of knowledge papers also assume the relevance of early childhood, only in quite a different way. While Freud was interested in the persistence of the childish in adulthood (the immature impulse in the mature form), Piaget, quite differently, saw childhood not as a source of persistent relevance, but as a baseline from which we can escape - escape, furthermore, through an acceptance of what cannot, not can be helped. This 'cannot be helped' can either be the inevitability of 'fact' or the extended inevitability of 'inference'.

Piagetian development, unlike Freudian development, involves an acceptance of reality on its (reality's) terms, not ours; no longer can we redefine outer reality to suit the narcissistic presumptions of our self-sufficiency (as we do, of course, when we come to accept the erstwhile alien value as our own).

The acceptance of both fact and inference is argued, in other words, to be learned, and learned in a Piagetian way. Piaget has shown how the child gradually attains the awareness of external 'fact' (and hence increasing sensory mastery of the here and now) and then later comes to develop the complex 'conservations' of intelligence. 'Intelligence'is seen as the ability to accept the inevitabilities we are confronted with by our ability to infer - inevitabilities that, whether we like it or not, converge in their implication, and so result (when implication is turned upon itself and explicated in its operation) in 'logic'. Intelligence - the manipulation of inferences - in consequence, lies in the ability to see similarities where earlier we saw differences; logic, intelligence in action, is a procedure by which we can persuade ourselves that nothing has changed.

All four of the theory of knowledge papers here are concerned with the relationship between these two achievements - the gradual acceptance of the immediate disciplines of fact and of the extended, self-conscious disciplines of logic. And the critical point argued throughout is that these two achievements - that of the recognition of facts and of logic - are not, in the last resort, distinct.

This is not common sense. Nor, come to that, is it common theory. Common sense argues that 'facts' are 'facts' (and, common theory adds, the basis of empiricism) and that the manipulation of symbols (as in logic and the use of numbers) is the manipulation of symbols (and, common theory would add, are 'tautologies' and so have the ambiguous status of being inevitable or 'irrefutable').

All four papers are concerned with refuting this distinction, explicitly in the case of Empiricism and Psychoanalysis and implicitly in the case of the earlier three papers. The Organizational and the Scientific argues that an insistence on 'facts' as being 'facts' and so quite separate from 'theories' or the way that 'facts' are manipulated, is to indulge in Platonism. Not, of course, that Platonism is a bad thing. It is just that one should be aware of one's own identity.

As it would appear too many scientists are not. The paper The Transient and the Subsumed, for instance, discusses the confusion arising through the failure to distinguish between what is called 'news' and 'science' - between the 'transient' news that never will be repeated and the 'subsumed' science of the causal laws that underlie - a 'science' that owes its distinctiveness from 'news' through the admixture of inference or logic. (Extended far enough, this subsuming of the transient fact leads us to the phenomenon of 'structuralism'. Structuralism can be looked on as the elaboration of really wide order subsuming constants or generalities. So wide order, indeed, and so far removed from the factual here and now, that the very distinction between fact and logic becomes blurred. Conventional science - 'normal' fact multiplied by 'normal' inference - hovers somewhere in between.)

Thus, extremely briefly, the scope of the two sets of papers and the influence of Freud and Piaget - Freud being used to show that society's values and formal structures can be explained by recourse to instinctual impulses (or what is called the 'will') and Piaget to show that the concrete and inferential awarenesses we experience are learned and interrelated.

Now what, it might be asked, can be inferred from these two sets of incompatibles - on the one hand the enduring relevance of the instinctual 'will' and, on the other, the totally opposite emergence of the factual and the inferential 'inevitabilities'?

And the answer is that they imply that these two - fact and value - having a common source are not distinct. In other words, when put together, they undermine the conventional idea of truth speaking with its own insistent voice, a voice that will, in the end, prevail and, by the same token, the complementary notion of the scientist pursuing truth in a spirit of dispassionate inquiry.

And this depressing conclusion is arrived at by taking Freud and Piaget seriously and then taking the fact that they are being taken together seriously. Freud showed, or can be argued to show, that men's motives underlie the values they profess and the social structures they acknowledge, and Piaget showed that the motives cannot be ignored.

Let us begin with Freud. Scientists are people too, scientists also have their impulses and desires. They too, if the horrid truth were told, are trying to get their PhDs, or Nobel Prizes, or trying to put that young upstart back in his place. And when it comes to scientists in a group rather than by themselves, then, just as a paper is included in this collection (The Ownership of Work) that argues the development of a profession or trade union, so one could write a very similar paper outlining the development of a corporate scientific discipline - the emergence of similar rivalries, ethics and sense of group identity could be plotted. And, just as in Freud and Social Class, the emergence of social class was discussed in Freudian terms, so one could talk about the development of the ideal of the academic as being someone apart, spared the humiliation of showing he was some use, his work being value free, or valued for its own sake. Given the same status as play, in other words.

In The University Seminar and the Primal Horde paper, I have tried to show in a half humorous, half serious way just how distant a university seminar can be from any idea of 'play'. Rather than being enjoyable, it can produce a degree of jealousy and terror that renders the subsequent behaviour as 'unscientific' as one could imagine. The enactment of stereotyped behaviour - ritual - no less.

But the fact that scientists are frightened of one another, and spend a great deal of their time putting each other down, need not argue that their findings are thereby suspect. After all, one can be right for the wrong reasons. Copernicus may have thought that he was vindicating a Hermetic view of the cosmos but this did not invalidate his heliocentric theory.

The intellectual integrity of science has always depended on this assumption - that the knower can be irrelevant to the known. And the knower can be irrelevant to the known because the known can have its inherent validity - a validity that can have a logical or a sensory base. Thus 2 and 2 make 4, whatever the time of day - or whatever the attempt to mislead. Again, four of Jupiter's moons could be seen through Galileo's telescope (the example used in Empiricism and Psychoanalysis) whatever the reigning ideology. In Galileo's case, indeed, this 'fact' won through to acceptance in the teeth of the accepted ideology.

This is where the work of Piaget comes in. For Piaget showed that, despite all common sense and aesthetic force, the visual and logical self-evidence were not independent of the observer but were in some measure - a measure that in the long run is unknowable - the product of that observer. We participate, in other words, in what we know and we can no more declare ourselves irrelevant than we can declare ourselves non-existent. Those that live in the sea will willy nilly displace water.

But, even if we do displace water, do we displace enough to make any difference? And not so much logically - logically we can never escape our influence - but practically? After all, the sciences have done quite well! And the answer suggested here is that it does very much. And it does so for various reasons - certain of which are advanced in these papers (particularly in The Politics of the Knowable where it is argued that it renders the social sciences different in degree from the natural sciences) and one of which will be pursued here in this introduction. This is the conclusion arrived at in the last - and most lengthy and most integrative - paper of all, Empiricism and Psychoanalysis (a paper that attempts to sum up in one statement the interrelationship between the social and theory of knowledge considerations constantly adumbrated in the earlier papers). And this conclusion at the end of Empiricism and Psychoanalysis argues the possibility of a new and more sinister relationship (at least by current standards) between science and society.

And this is that society may subsume science. Even to make this statement at all today sounds not just illogical but slightly absurd. And this not just because science would appear logically inviolate but because we live in an age of scientific imperialism. Nothing, but nothing, cannot be studied. Including, of course, society itself. Society too can reveal its laws - values and structures, for instance, can emerge under determinate conditions just like anything else. Science, in other words, can subsume society - the known can subsume the knower (society being but an association of knowers).

But, once we accept that the known and the knower are not categorically distinct, then the converse becomes equally possible - the knower can subsume the known; society can subsume science.

Science is based on fact and inference - those 'outer' realities we must come to terms with. Science, in other words, from the point of view of the instinctual 'will' can be looked on as the codification of failure, the spelling out of what cannot be helped. Not so society. In society we can succeed! (And politics, it might be added, is the activity of those who persuade each other how.) Impulse in society can justify itself - indeed the whole fabric of society, the laws and structures that give it form, are the result of a co-operation (or, to the jaundiced, a collusion, or, to the misanthropic Platonist, a conspiracy) in which we persuade each other what is 'there'.

In society we can act like God and 'create', at least at the level of discourse where we can exist as separate individuals, formal structures of all kinds; we can 'set up' organisations (indeed, like Cavour, a whole nation) and endow our work with 'powers'. The ultimate redundancy that science seeks (the notion of 'power' or 'cause') can be promulgated by legislative decree. (This point, the dramatic distinction between 'powers' in society and 'power' in science, is argued at some length in The Organizational and the Scientific.)

In society we can succeed: and, of all the successes in society, the most cogent for this introduction and that which is implicit throughout these papers and becomes explicit at the end of the last one of all - Empiricism and Psychoanalysis - is the success of society over science itself. The importance of the observer participating in the observed will have come home to roost.

And this will come about, not because of the failure of science but because of its success. For the argument advanced, the reader will have to refer to Empiricism and Psychoanalysis. Suffice it to say that it hinges on the assumption that a 'truth' that does not speak with its own voice (in the 'self-evidents' of fact and logic) but must be learned, can equally well (under a reversal of the conditions that made learning possible - or necessary) lose its integrity and be reabsorbed. And when this happens, we shall see the return of the self-sufficient Freudian 'will', the impulse that, as already said, justifies itself in its own insistence. This already happens in society - society as noted above (and as suggested in The Ownership of Work, Freud and Social Class, Freud, Piaget and Democratic Leadership) is a venue where we can provide each other with the reality, 'owned' by those with power, that each of us must then accept.

In other words, the victory of the social over the scientific will take the very form that the social papers have been at pains to analyse, namely the emergence of legitimacy. Knowledge, too, will become differentially valued, the knowable considered legitimate or illegitimate by those who have lost the ability to doubt. And science will lose the innocence of its amorality and become the prey of those who act out their instinctual 'will' in social terms. A new morality will arise, clad this time in the impenetrable armour of scientific rectitude.

Whether this will happen - whether society will absorb science or whether science will continue to modify society - is, of course, unknowable to us. But, once it is granted that we participate in what we know, and once it is accepted that awareness of the outer inevitabilities of fact and logic are achievements to be treasured, not baselines to be taken for granted - and so forgotten, as is the fate of baselines - then the danger is there. And the greatest threat is surely the possible growth of consensus and unanimity; those who act in concert need not, as argued in the primal horde papers, feel guilt. Perhaps, indeed, the best we can hope for (since there will always be a social dimension to the known) is that an overpowering consensus will not arise and that, through the continuation of conflict inherent in 'politics', some 'knowable' will remain possible.

Chapter 1

FREUD AND SOCIAL CLASS

This paper attempts to resolve a contradiction in Freud's view of the position of the leader. On the one hand he claims that a leader must exist for a group to exist at all (in 'Group Psychology and the Analysis of the Ego'), on the other, that the followers kill the king and destroy the very source of their unity (in 'Totem and Taboo'). A suggested resolution of this contradiction is presented. A 'third force', here termed 'Authority', is invoked which makes it possible for the leader to be both 'qualitatively distinct' from his followers (with a consequent right to an unrivalled position) while remaining 'qualitatively the same' (and thus not so exceptional that the envy of his followers becomes uncontrollable).

A group is seen as being polarized not, as with Freud, around a leader, but around an 'Authority' - an Authority to which the leader is himself subordinated. It is further contended that, not only will the nature of the Authority existing in any group or society be a prime determinant of the kind of group or society it will be, but that certain forms of Authority will be more likely to eventuate and will be more inherently stable than others. In particular the Freudian position would suggest that a class society based on birth will be the most likely to supervene.

Freud appeals to what he calls the 'scientific myth' of the Primal Horde to account for the development of groups. Before the dawn of history, the father 'absolutely narcissistic, self-confident and independent', (1) kept the women for his own use and excluded his sons and rivals. These sons, forced into abstinence, developed emotional ties with their father. He became their ego-ideal, both because of the idealism, that, with Freud, derives from aim-inhibited libido, and also because they 'identified with the aggressor' and prevented retaliation by internalizing the source of vengeance. It is out of the awareness of their common lot, that the sons identify with one another and form the first group. 'A primary group of this kind is a number of individuals who have put one and the same object in the place of their ego ideal and have consequently identified themselves with one another in their own ego.' (2)

Group psychology is here an extension of individual psychology. A single son can internalize his father and install him as his ego ideal. This is no more than occurs in that other example of aim-inhibited libido - renunciation of the mother by the boy with the passing of the Oedipus complex. The Victorian family is, indeed, almost a little 'horde' in itself. This development could be called 'fear of the father' and can be expressed schematically as shown in Figure 1.1.

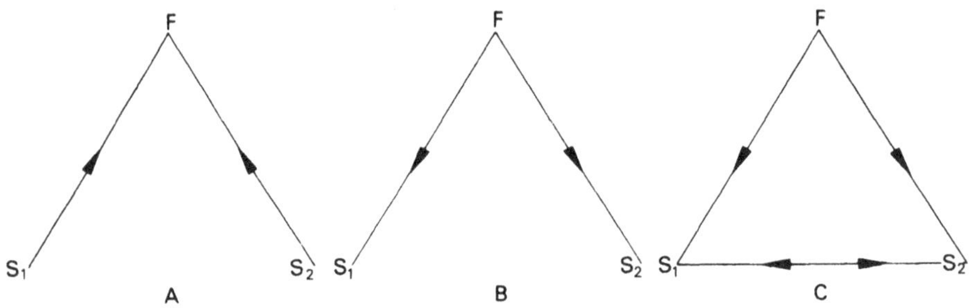

FIGURE 1.1 Fear of the father

Two sons (S1 and S2) independently resent their father, F, (in A), and so come to internalize him (B). Out of their awareness of their common subordination, they identify with one another and become fellow 'group members' (C).

The second mechanism of group formation is based not on mutual fear but on mutual jealousy. This mechanism (not explicitly distinguished by Freud from 'fear of the father') may be called 'love of the mother'. Thus, two sons both want to possess the mother but each renounces his claims to prevent the other: 'Social justice means that we deny ourselves many things so that others may have to do without them as well.' (3) This can be schematically represented as in Figure 1.2.

The first son renounces the mother (M) because the second son also has aspirations. This renunciation becomes an ideal forceful enough to command universal obedience: 'This demand for equality is the root of social conscience and the sense of duty.' (4) Unlike 'fear of the father', identification of group members with

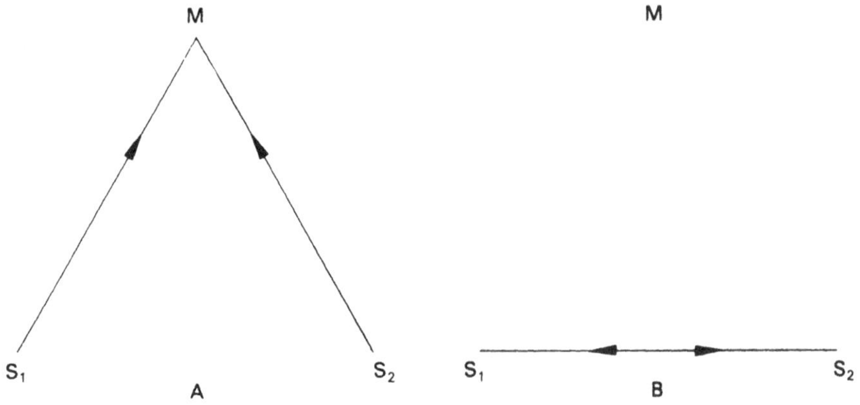

FIGURE 1.2 Love of the mother

one another through what I have called the 'love of the mother', is purely the product of social situations. Where there is no rival, renunciation and the growth of belief are unnecessary. What it does do is to provide a rationale for the development of norms as an emergent property; there is no need, as with 'fear of the father', to postulate a pre-existing loyalty. Thus, common subordination (whether imported from the past or developed in the present) is the basis of that identification with one another we understand by 'group membership'. To Freud, a group is polarized around its sources of authority.

But if in 'Group Psychology and the Analysis of the Ego', from which the above quotations have been taken, Freud stresses the need for a group to have a common object of loyalty for it to exist at all, in 'Totem and Taboo', (5) written some eight years earlier, he spelt out the intolerability of this very yoke. The sons eventually banded together to kill the father. Not only was the father killed, but no one was allowed to take his place even though each secretly wished for sole power: 'None of the group of victors could take his place or if one of them did, the battles began afresh until they understood that they must all renounce their father's heritage.' (6) If the rule of the father was intolerable, the rule of a fellow son was even more intolerable.

This is the dilemma taken from Freud: some of its consequences will be expanded in the rest of this paper: on the one hand a leader is necessary for social living, on the other such a leader cannot exist. Such a leader cannot exist for we all wish to be leader ourselves. The thought of another leader - whether he be the father, or, worse still, a rival who is 'no better than we are' - is intolerable. Each with his individual aspirations would kill the very force that unites them. This built-in disintegration might be called a kind of homeostasis in reverse. (In extrapolating somewhat from Freud, one might say that social living witnesses the constant struggle of each to gain control over all.) In the last chapter of 'Totem and Taboo' and at the end of 'Group Psychology', Freud deals with this problem in some detail, discussing in this context 'the beginnings of religion, morals, society and art', (7) all of which converge in that latter-day miniature dilemma, the Oedipus complex. Rather less ambitious, I shall content myself here with abstracting one conclusion. This conclusion is not explicitly stated by Freud but may none the less be worth pursuing.

Two facts stand out from the above discussion. The leader must be qualitatively different from his followers, for only thus can he insulate himself from the jealousy of those whose rival claims are 'as good as his'. (The prototype of the Freudian leader is the nineteenth-century parent - remote, distinct, unchallenged.) But he must not only be qualitatively distinct, he must also be qualitatively the same, for in no other way is the leader tolerable. Those with exaggerated pretensions are killed, the leader must be 'one of us'; those with insufficient pretensions cannot validate their claim to privilege. The implications of this dilemma form the subject of this paper.

The only possible resolution - and here the reader is warned, I am going beyond what Freud actually wrote - is for the leader to be both - both 'one of us' and 'one of them'. This consummation devoutly to be wished, can in turn be effected only by introducing a third party into the two-part relationship of leader and follower. If an 'Authority' is postulated that at once unites leader with follower and yet, by its very existence, endows the leader with a 'right' that his followers cannot hope to possess, then the circle is squared. This solution is not only logically convenient but also has much to commend it in practice. The mediaeval king had a special relationship with the deity that ensured his 'Divine Right' and yet was but a fellow mortal. The Pope is in the same position. Hitler, to take a different case, had a special relationship to 'Germany' and was yet content to find his ultimate honour in being a 'good German'. A religious leader who claims to be more than a prophet is very rare, even Jesus Christ (and the Christian religion is, in some ways, nearer to God than others) did not claim to be more than the son of God.

Assuming that his notion of the 'special relationship' to an 'Authority' is correct (and that assumption is made here), two requirements must be met for this relationship to be effective. In the first place, clearly, this sanctifying 'authority' must be believed in by the followers. The followers must accept the validity of something bigger than the leader - they must believe in 'God' or 'Germany' - for only thus can the leader gain their consent. (8) For this belief in the eyes of the subordinates not only endows the leader with the 'right' to lead but also ensures that the leader, subordinated as he is to the same object of reverence, is ultimately 'one of us'. Not only must the follower believe in the Authority, but the leader must believe in himself. The sheer logic of the Freudian position would demand that the leader be subordinate as well, however extraordinary he be, for he must not be (or at least he must not appear to be) self-sufficient and narcissistic in an idiosyncratic way. He, too, must pay the price, a price we all have to pay when very young, and internalize a set of values. Once he pays this price, he can reap his reward, for by his special relationship with that which he values as greater than himself, he can gain that self-enhancement that is so often necessary for those who are alone in authority and must forgo the direct support of their fellows.

What I have said so far can be expressed in schematic form as in Figure 1.3. The leader directs the follower and is in turn

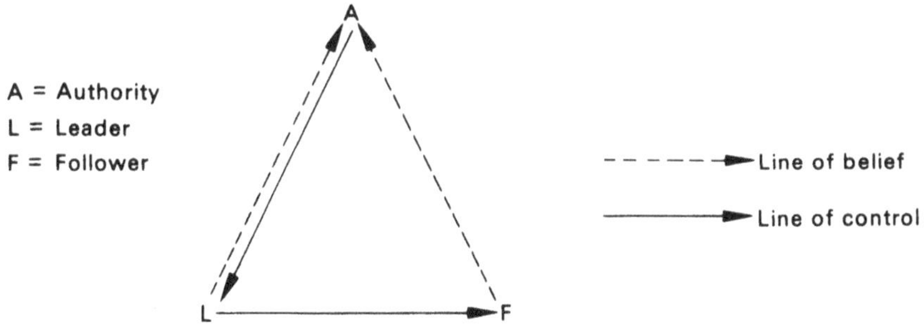

FIGURE 1.3 The leader-follower relationship

directed by the 'Authority' - an 'Authority' that owes its validity to the beliefs of both. The leader and follower are put in what can be called a latter-day 'social contract'. If either refuses to believe, the other withdraws his consent. Then only sheer force or 'power' can fill the void: the leader will 'punish' the follower who does not believe what he should, the follower will withdraw in horror from a leader who does not venerate the source of his legitimacy. Clearly, according to this analysis, the central feature of any leader-follower relationship is the nature of the 'Authority' and, indeed, it is the consequence of two different kinds of Authority that I am here concerned with. But before resorting to thesis and evidence, two somewhat extended observations must be made.

In the first place, I am driven by what I have said so far, to make a radical distinction between two kinds of unfairness - unfairness in the sense of inequality and unfairness in the sense of inconsistency. The latter is always intolerable since it assumes that the law, which should be consistently imposed, is arbitrarily imposed. Where it is consistently imposed the leader, too, is subordinate; where it is arbitrarily imposed, the leader is above the law. The leader who is above the law has broken his relationship with that which legitimizes his position; a leader who subordinates himself to the law - however unequal or inequitable that law may be - has paid the price his followers demand. The leader must buy consent with anonymity. This is tantamount to saying that almost any form of social group is self-validating. To the extent that discriminations are made, so will those who are discriminated against come to believe in the basis of these discriminations. While the Freudian position would seem to argue that this is true, yet certain bases of discrimination (i.e. certain kinds of 'Authority'), will tend to be inherently more stable than others.

Second, 'Authorities' can somewhat arbitrarily be divided into two kinds: sociological and psychological, or put another way, what a man is and what a man does. Thus a man can be revered because he is old, young, his father's son, white, British, male or alternatively because he is intelligent, cruel, industrious, brave or pious. The former, what a man is, I shall call 'social attributes', the latter, what a man does, 'behavioural attributes'. Either of these attributes can be used as a basis for an 'Authority'. Thus the ruling class can be based on birth, skin colour, nationality or can be chosen from those most valiant in battle, best able to pass examinations or solicitous in attending party meetings - in principle, one form of legitimizing privilege is presumably as good as another. In principle, perhaps, but not, I hope, in practice.

Social attributes differ from behavioural attributes in two fundamental respects. In the first place, they cannot be helped - they can neither be gained nor lost. This does not always apply, of course. One can change one's nationality and one's religion, for instance, but, by and large, being white, male or short, is just something given. In a society based firmly on that most important of all social attributes, birth, success cannot come by 'trying harder' - joining the right clubs, wearing the right dress or disapproving of the right scapegoats. Second, social attributes are more clear cut - they tend to be all-or-nothing categories rather than dimensional categories. Thus one is either one's father's son or one is not, one is either in general terms male or one is not. The same does not apply to being industrious or patient - one can be 'more or less' industrious in many different ways at once.

Relating this to the two kinds of 'unfairness', it seems that while discrimination on the basis of social attributes has the disadvantage of being 'unfair in the sense of inequality', it has the great advantage of usually not being 'unfair in the sense of inconsistency'. With the behavioural attributes this is reversed. The possibility of gradations implicit in the word 'effort' makes judgment more difficult.

Now I can state the main thesis of this paper: namely that Freudian views on formation of groups would lead us to expect that (1) human societies would be articulated into strata, certain members being accorded more worth, value and influence than others (put in terms used above, they will be 'qualitatively different') and (2) that this articulation will be based on a social attribute that is clear cut and unfair rather than a dimensional and fair behavioural attribute.

Having stated this baldly, I must make clear that I am not asserting that wide and clear-cut differences in status will characterize all societies. What I am saying is that the 'natural' state of man is one in which subordinates can use their 'betters' in order to keep each other under control, that the simplest problem is why there should not be such a society rather than why there should. A 'class' society not only more plausibly satisfies these 'Freudian presuppositions' but (and this is a much more ambitious statement) is in accord with much of the evidence - evidence that has been gained from real life situations and so missed by those psychologists who are restricted in their thinking to the results of laboratory findings. This may seem an unduly harsh conclusion, but with Freud, autocracy springs from below. A follower is primarily concerned with dispossessing the father and, since that is not possible, of preventing anyone who is 'as good as him' from doing so either. This follows from both mechanisms of group development. In the case of 'fear of the father', the son is unable, in his jealousy, to tolerate his peers succeeding where he has failed. Further, to the extent that he resents his own submission, so will he have the temptation to 'identify with the aggressor' against those who set a bad example in their insubordination. (All this is familiar in the psychoanalytic view of the criminal and of the nature of 'retributive punishment'.) (9) In the case of 'love of the mother', the basic anti-egalitarianism of the Freudian position is even more clear, the whole purpose of veneration is control - the leader is set apart so that others may not reach him.

A class society not only ensures that those previously dubbed inferior will remain inferior, thus satisfying the jealousy of these very inferiors, it also offers three very substantial further advantages. First it provides a leader class that can be idealized. The need to have someone to over-estimate, that heritage of our Freudian childhood, can be instantly satisfied. Heroes are provided ready made; they are born with medals on, like Balkan kings. Second, the inferior, although lowly in estate, has an unchallenged 'right' to the position he does occupy. It will be unchallenged because it will be based on a 'social attribute'. Lipset has described the advantages in general unselfconsciousness and spontaneity that follow when behaviour is considered less important than birth in assessing merit. (10) This he compares to our own society where there are so many opportunities to succeed (or, relatively, to fail) that we have to behave ourselves in almost every direction at once. We even have to make friends with unpleasant people. The third advantage, which is really the same as the second - is the opportunity it provides for those who would have failed in open competition to feel self-righteous in their enforced lack of assertion; they can feel meritorious in their smugness and conventionality. It is difficult to imagine the possibility of greater built-in stability.

This last point is the key to the kind of society it will be. If there are sufficient opportunities for advancement, what I have said above will not hold because the followers will be divided amongst themselves: there will not be a large enough number with interests in common and they will be unable to impose on others the sacrifice they have made.

Later, I shall argue that such an 'open society' (as, indeed, we enjoy today) is a transitory phenomenon and cannot be expected to last, since it is the result of social change. For the moment I admit that it is possible that the class society I have described will all too readily be able to degenerate into tyranny, with the rulers firmly ensconced, indifferent to the consent of their followers. This is quite possible, though even in these days of secret police, more difficult than it sounds, for the leaders too have their jealousy problems; they will either have their own legitimizing 'Authority' or not, and in either case they may have difficulty. If they have their own Authority, their own alien code, the leaders will squabble amongst themselves and may be tempted to appeal to the common people in an attempt to legitimize their position.

The task I have set myself is, in principle, not as difficult as might be thought. It seems so obviously 'right' that all men should be treated equally, that we forget - not only that the notion of 'equal treatment' is very frequently absent in past history or, indeed, today - but that any criticism of other beliefs as 'obviously wrong', begs the question in that it involves the invocation of standards which are themselves the topic of discussion. To say that 'inequality is wrong' is, of course, the reader's - or anyone else's - privilege, but to say that 'other people say inequality is wrong' is exactly what is being disputed.

For how can we assess worth? There are two main reasons for valuing something. One is that it has good or bad consequences; we can value a tin opener because it helps us to open tins, or we can value a driver's skill because it enables him to drive us where we want to go. The other is that we value something because it is good in itself; thus we like watching television because we like watching television and that is all there is to it, we think a girl looks beautiful because we think a girl looks beautiful. Of course, there are reasons why we like watching television and think the girl is beautiful, but these reasons are different in kind from what might be called valuing something for 'instrumental' reasons. Despite the enormous importance in human affairs of actions that appear to be their own reward (although, of course, they do have their antecedents) we often feel rather shamefaced about them. We may pretend, for instance, we look at television as a means to an end, rather than as an end in itself. We may even maintain, in the case of the girl, that we say we think she is beautiful in order to seduce her (whereas we really want to seduce her because she looks beautiful).

These two reasons for valuing something - as a means to an end or as an end in itself - I shall call 'extrinsic' reasons and 'intrinsic' reasons. They closely resemble behavioural attributes and social attributes. If we value someone for some behavioural attribute, because he is brave or hardworking, we are valuing him for his 'extrinsic' qualities - his qualities can lead to certain consequences. If we value someone for some social attribute, because he is white or male, we are valuing him for 'intrinsic' reasons - his qualities are their own justification, validated by repetition. As such they may be no 'better' or 'worse' than a host of other 'intrinsic' values - including, be it said, the value that all men are 'intrinsically' equal.

If Freud is right in arguing that jealousy is the first social emotion, it follows that any system is self-perpetuating, since it is equal treatment or continuity that is valued. Once the values are fixed - that men are 'good' and women are 'bad' for instance - they will remain fixed. All men will be determined to be rated as 'good' along with other men, and all women will be determined that other women will be rated as 'bad' along with them too. Thus jealousy can endow any system with intrinsic value, since the value will lie in the continuity itself. Having shown that there is no reason in principle why men should all consider themselves 'equal', I must now turn to evidence. This evidence will not be sufficient in itself to establish the argument, but at least it may show that certain necessary features of any future class society do, in fact, lie within us all.

In order to establish my argument - that the lower orders will keep each other under control and so the 'natural' state of man is a class, if not a caste, society - I shall have to show (1) that we deny ourselves so that others be denied as well, (2) that we have a concept of our 'due' that gives us a feeling of 'right' to some limited share of the returns and (3) that this notion of 'due' is more 'readily' or 'naturally' based on the unfair clear-cut social attributes than on the more egalitarian ambiguous behavioural attributes.

The first crucial postulate - we deny ourselves so that others be denied as well - is straightforward. To the extent that there are formal sanctions, such as restrictive laws, and, to the extent that these restrictions are supported by at least some of the population, it is reasonable to assume that this part of the population is prepared to accept the restriction imposed by these laws, for the sake of the restrictions they impose on others. Thus, the most physically powerful member of a tribe is unlikely to vote against indiscriminate use of physical force; rather it is more plausible to assume that it is the weaker brethren who will combine to impose sanctions on those more powerful than themselves. What is gained - freedom from being assaulted - is greater than what is forgone - the problematic ability to assault. Indeed, it was a mechanism such as this that Freud presumed to underlie the beginning of morality - each son, weak as he is, renounces his claim to his father's old pre-eminence and the rule of law was established over all.

Not only is it possible that we are prepared to renounce our individual freedom in order that others be deprived as well, but the converse may also be true: we may be anxious to deprive others of what we have already been deprived. This, indeed, is the more usual course of events. By our earlier upbringing we have been taught to control ourselves in certain ways, to go to church on Sundays, not to drink alcohol, and the like, and we then later insist that others make the same sacrifice. Those who do not drink insist on early closing hours. That this should happen is not surprising if we follow the above logic. Having made our sacrifice before the event, what we ourselves further forgo is zero. The result of the extension of our sacrifice is control over others. So can we wield power - vicariously and piously.

This does not only happen on a large, historical scale - it is not only heathens and heretics who are persecuted - it happens in more workaday and contemporary circumstances as well. Sayles (11) in his study of industrial groups has related the emergence of group norms (particularly those concerned with group output) to the power structure of the group. He has shown that norms arise where a powerful enough faction has a common interest in curbing the freedom of others. If the method of payment is such that the 'average' worker (who is, of course, in the majority) would lose if the behaviour of others were not controlled, then the behaviour of others will be controlled - an unofficial norm will evolve which it will be treasonable to break. (A 'black-leg' after all is someone who puts his individual advantage before the 'common good'.) As norms are made by power, so can they be broken by power. If management does not like this collusion among its workers, the moral is clear - divide and rule. If it can hold out a large enough number of individual rewards then it will be to the benefit of enough of the energetic and skilful to brave the displeasure of others less energetic and gifted. The companionship that comes from solidarity and belief will be broken, the workers will be divided, ruled by their individual hopes. (12) This may seem too cynical and pessimistic, but it is, after all, no more than very often happens in the managerial class itself. Those who have hopes of individual advancement have less incentive to impose restrictions upon their colleagues if they will also be expected to abide by them themselves.

I have at least adumbrated the possibility that norms can be seen as a political weapon, a form of control by the majority (or at least the most powerful), and it is clear that an important feature - almost a 'dimension' - of any society is the degree to which behaviour is controlled by norms. Certain societies will specify much more precisely than others what should be done. These societies will value conformity rather than individualism. This problem of the 'degree of required conformity' will be taken up later. (13) I can now return to the second criterion - that we have a concept of our 'due' and that this 'due' is finite.

Before beginning this section, we can note that it is not unreasonable to expect an adult to see someone as a reflection of his erstwhile parents, qualitatively distinct, whom it is hubris to challenge. We can further note (and this, being an extension of the argument above, is of somewhat more weight) that an insistence on 'due' reward is but part of a general insistence on the supremacy of norms. As such, it offers the advantage I have already mentioned - the control of others vicariously. When we are content with our 'due', we give our consent to the validity of a code that controls others besides ourselves. We cannot (oh fortunate world!) make an individual sacrifice.

My first examples will deal with that prime bone of contention, money. Whatever the working population of this country may secretly want, in practice it contents itself with insisting on adequate differentials being maintained. (14) This is made explicit in job evaluation schemes where such factors as length of training, degree of skill, amount of responsibility held, etc., are combined to show how much a man should be paid. Note that these schemes, despite their meticulous arithmetic, only work to the extent that they are accepted, i.e. are seen to be just. The skill in devising a job-evaluation scheme indeed, consists in measuring those items that are taken to be relevant by those concerned. What is relevant may not be self-evident; thus Elliott Jaques has recently argued that the basis of 'felt equity' in payment is the 'time span of discretion', that is how frequently one's performance is reviewed. (15) Indeed, considering how very little industrial strife there is in a country such as Britain, where such very great differences in rewards exist, contentment with wage packet looks as if it is based on something other than the employer's ability to resist demands.

This line of thought has recently been developed as the 'theory of distributive justice'. (16) This theory assumes that felt satisfaction with one's 'rewards' is proportional to one's 'investments'. The nature of the rewards and the investments may vary from society to society (although rewards will usually be some sort of differential monetary payment or some sort of differential prestige rating and investments will be some sort of behavioural attribute or some sort of social attribute), but however they may vary, there remains a felt need for the 'reward' to be commensurate with the 'investment'. Zaleznik and his co-writers spell out what they assume will happen when rewards do not meet investments. (17)

1 When the investments of a member of a group are greater than those of others but his returns are less, a condition of felt injustice exists.
2 When the investments of a member of a group are less than others but his returns are greater, a condition of 'guilt' is likely to be felt.

This can be elaborated as follows - the individual whose investments are not being met will make complaints; the individual who is getting more than his deserts will not complain, but will feel guilty none the less. Those who feel hard done by will become touchy and exacting in their social due; they may even attempt to 'shed the load', decrease their investments 'goof-off on the job'; those who are unduly favoured may take on further work, even assume informal responsibility and try to help out others. And the others? They will be sorry for those who are being sold short and envious of those on the gravy-train, an envy 'mingled with admiration for what they are able to get away with'.

This general thesis has some confirmation both from the Zaleznik study just quoted (as they themselves put it, 'The data corroborated the idea in the theory of distributive justice that individuals will actively compare their degree of reward, in relation to their perceived investments, with other individuals in their immediate groups or in the groups in which they aspire to become members' (18)) and also from Nancy Morse who studied the satisfactions of clerical workers in a large American company. (19) She found, against expectation, that the greater the intrinsic satisfaction with the job, the less the satisfaction with the pay. Those who admitted their work was dull were more content with their pay than those of higher rank who enjoyed their work for its own sake. Any hopes that the idealist or the money-minded accountant may have had that satisfaction in the work itself would take the employee's mind off lower things (i.e. money) were dashed. Not only did the high-level technical worker feel his job was 'worth' more than he received (the very complexity of his task increasing his satisfaction with the work itself and decreasing his satisfaction with the pay), but, conversely, the repetitive clerical worker disliked what he did but admitted his pay was fair. (20)

So much for my second contention - that we all have some concept of our 'worth', and satisfaction (at least financial) with our reward depends on whether or not this sense of 'due' is met. Before proceeding to the third contention, I must of course admit that sheer grabbing for reward can occur. When it does, it is known as 'anomie'. This happens less often than might be supposed since the decay of normative forces may affect only one particular group; there may still remain a second group that will take up the individual's emotional slack. Thus, a thief may appear to be unaffected by society's values but may acknowledge the psychological importance of his own group. His 'group' may have values which are no less forceful for their being unorthodox. This is not true normlessness. True normlessness, such as panic, probably only occurs where the situation is so unusual as to be outside the repertoire of the group. The whole purpose of fire drill is to bring the situation within the repertoire of the group, to convince (to use the language I have used above) each individual the other is also 'playing his part' and that no-one is attempting an illegitimate short-cut to escape by ignoring group sanctions.

I now come to the third, and must the most contentious, assertion - that the concept of our 'due' is more 'readily' or 'naturally' based on the unfair and clear-cut social attributes than the more egalitarian and ambiguous behavioural attributes.

I will begin with the fairly modest assertion that behaviour can be a dependent variable, the product of one's position in society, not its cause. This point need not be laboured - after all, flattery does exist and a courtier who is wise may not only magnify his monarch's prowess (thus according it 'social reality'), but may be careful to lose at chess. Even in less exalted circles, it may not do to be cleverer than one's boss. A well-known example of the effects of social standing on behaviour, is that of W.F. Whyte in his 'Street Corner Society'. Here is Doc, the leader, discussing bowling scores with Long John, his lieutenant, and Whyte himself:

> Long John: I only wanted to be sure that Alec or Joe Dodge didn't win. That wouldn't have been right.
> Doc: That's right. We didn't want to make it tough for you (Whyte) because we liked you, and the other fellows did too. (21)

Whyte was popular and well treated, but others who attempted to do too well at bowling were not so fortunate. As Long John said to one of these: 'You think you could beat us, but under pressure you die.'

From this it can at least be inferred that behaviour used as an index of worth (that is the behaviour that is important for my argument) can itself be influenced by the amount of worth previously accorded. This provides the complementary statements - that if status depends on a particular item of behaviour, then behaviour can also depend on status. If we are as good as our table manners, our table manners may be as good as we are.

A further source of behavioural variance, perhaps unexpected, is the consistency (rather than, as discussed so far, the value) of an individual's investment. Those whose investments are 'in line' have what Zaleznik and his co-writers call 'social certitude' (and others call 'status equilibration', 'status crystallization', 'status congruence'), (22) those whose investments are 'out of line' do not. The young and uneducated negress who has recently joined the firm, and the old, educated, male, white employee of great seniority have social certitude. They are both 'all of a piece'; in one case all the investments are low, in the other case all the investments are high. In this they are unlike the much-publicized Angry Young Man. The Angry Young Man has risen out of his class, he is high on education, but low on social background. He does not fit into a society that does not know how to behave toward him.

The effects of social certitude, summarized by Zaleznik and his colleagues, suggests that those with social certitude will be more likely to:

1 show greater participation in non-work activities;
2 be more amenable to group norms;
3 be more conservative;
4 be less concerned to achieve prestige through greater competence and skill.

Those without social certitude will be more likely to:

5 show less participation in non-work activities;
6 assert the ideal over the norms of behaviour;
7 have more liberal social views;
8 seek to excel in technical competence and skill;
9 but be more formal in their relations with others.

Thus, on the one hand, a picture of someone who accepts the value of his society, who is not ambitious but is content with his lot and sees no great need for a change in the scheme of things. On the other hand, the individual who does not fit in, who rejects the values of his society, uses his idealism aggressively, and seeks to excel individually. This strongly suggests that those without social certitude use their behavioural ambitions as a make-weight - they are driven to excellence. (23)

So far I have argued firstly and crucially (for on this must all else depend) that we restrict ourselves that others be restricted as well and that the emergence of norms in groups can in part at least be seen as the attempt of certain group members to control others; I have then shown that satisfaction with reward is not an absolute but depends upon 'felt due'; and finally noted that what we have called the social attributes of what a person is (i.e. his skin colour, race, sex, etc.), as opposed to the behavioural attributes of what a person does (i.e. his abilities and his degree of law-abidingness, etc.) - can underlie both of the above: social attributes can account for both 'felt due' and behaviour.

Here are what might be called the 'building blocks of caste', I have shown what can happen, how 'unfair' attributes can become self-validating. But to show what can happen, is quite different from showing what actually will happen in any particular situation. Many more things are possible than likely. It is at this point that outright speculation becomes necessary.

So far an attempt, at least, has been made to shore up the discussion with specific evidence. This is no longer possible, and assumption and assertion will have to fill the vacuum. It is hoped, though, that these assumptions, even if arbitrary, are not wholly implausible. They will be four in number and will run as follows:

First assumption: that parents will do the best they can for their children.

Second assumption: that progressively fewer skills will be necessary to run any unchanging administrative or technical unit or work.

Third assumption: that change will not constantly breed further change.

Fourth assumption: that any activity that is frequently repeated with considerable lack of variation will become hallowed by custom and dignified by ritual.

With these four statements I hope to show how articulation by class will supervene. This paper will then end with the attempt to outline just how strong are some of the forces that can inhere in a structured society.

FIRST ASSUMPTION: THAT PARENTS WILL DO THE BEST THEY CAN FOR THEIR CHILDREN

This statement is probably unexceptionable. What could be more unnatural than the parent who did not foster and cherish his children to the best of his ability? Natural or not, the implications of such a simple statement can very well be momentous - it suggests that, unless there are influences that are constantly and actively reasserting what I might call the 'rights of the people', (24) the influence of hereditary factors (those simplest of all social attributes) will emerge. This will happen, not because any law enjoins it (indeed, 'the law' will follow and sanctify it) but just because some fathers will carry more weight than others. Those who have good social connections will not need so much ability. Rulers will first look amongst their own for their own replacements.

Later, I shall argue that not only is it more likely that the son of an influential man will be preferred to the son of an uninfluential man, but also that the greater opportunities awaiting those with influence can be justified on the ground that they make more satisfactory replacements. The son of the boss will make a better boss than the son of the subordinate would: provided that one all-important condition is met - that the son of the boss has sufficient ability.

If this thesis even begins to be true, then of great importance in any society are the number and types of skills needed for its perpetuation: the fewer the skills necessary, the less will the ruling class need to look elsewhere. At this point I come to the second assumption, no less unexceptionable I hope than the first.

SECOND ASSUMPTION: THAT PROGRESSIVELY FEWER SKILLS WILL BE NECESSARY TO RUN ANY UNCHANGING ADMINISTRATIVE OR TECHNICAL UNIT OF WORK

The essence of the managerial role is often considered that of 'decision making'. What, then, is a 'decision'? When can a conclusion be deemed a 'decision' and when can it be seen as 'inevitable'? Surely this depends on the knowledge of the outcome of a course of action. Where the outcome is not known, where there is an element of risk, we speak of a 'decision', but this term is hardly used, at least in the same sense, on the second and subsequent occasions when the situation is met. If the result of the first occasion was satisfactory then a repetition of the action 'suggests itself' unless it is thought that still further improvement is possible, that is, that there is still further ignorance to explore.

The term 'decision' implies risk and individual choice - there is no decision where there is no choice. The quality of a decision is radically affected by the intellectual powers of the decision maker, in particular by his powers of analysis and extrapolation. Indeed, since a 'decision' is the child of ignorance, the lower the intellectual calibre of the person in question and the greater his ignorance, the more decisions he will have to make. A central feature, then, in the analysis of work lies not only in the complexity of the task but also in the degree to which it is liable to change. Some highly complex tasks can be learned once and for all, they can be learned, as is said, 'by experience'.

Other tasks have been in existence so long that there is not even the need for the individual to learn it for himself. The expertise becomes embodied in a 'procedure manual', which 'serves as a substitute for personal experience' in the words of Blau and Scott. (25) These authors quote Michael Crozier's view that 'the expert's success is constantly self-diminishing' and then continue themselves to elaborate this thesis. To quote them at some length:

> As the knowledge of the experts increases, it transforms areas of uncertainty into areas that can be routinely handled (for example, advances in medicine enable nurses to perform tasks that previously required the judgment of physicians). The expert's own success, therefore, reduces the base of his power or, at least, shifts its base to a new area of uncertainty. (26)

Provided they can retain their power, though, the expert (and the specialist) may well resist innovation. Burns and Stalker (27) in an extended study of the effects of innovation in the electronics industry to which reference will be made again later, found that innovations were so frequently and so strenuously resisted, not merely because a change of any moment disrupted the prestige and the status balance of the concern (although it did), but also for the simple reason that periods of transition make much greater demands on the staff - they require harder work and greater ability. An interesting experimental verification of this line of thought is seen in a paper by R.L. Hamblin, entitled 'Leadership and Crisis'. (28) Hamblin set his three-man groups problems, and, at a certain point in the series, some of the groups, called 'crisis groups', had the rules they were working to arbitrarily changed. Introducing a 'crisis' of this sort had two effects. In the first place, a leader (i.e. the most influential group member) gained more influence, and secondly, was more likely to be replaced. The leadership stakes were raised. Where there is no change the leader is not needed, since the followers know what to do, but neither is he threatened, since his status has attained its own inertia.

For the skills necessary to run society even to remain the same, then, that society must be constantly evolving - new challenges will have to be met and new problems must require codification. Whether or not this will happen in the future is, of course, any one's guess, and my own third assumption:

THIRD ASSUMPTION: THAT CHANGE WILL NOT CONSTANTLY LEAD TO FURTHER CHANGE

This, of course, is an outright assumption with nothing like the same degree of plausibility as the first two. Since, however, it is being made, there remains some onus on me to account for the degree of change there has been in the recent past. This will somewhat arbitrarily be assumed to be due to conflict - whether in the form of economic competition or military warfare. That the former can lead to innovation is well known - indeed the firms studied by Burns and Stalker were undergoing the throes enforced upon them by the need for technical change. That warfare is also useful in this respect need not be any the less true for being an unpleasant truth.

However there is no reason in principle why conflict should be self-perpetuating. Indeed it can be expected to cease (either by the victory of one party or by mutual agreement of all parties) unless it is constantly recreated by the intervention of a third force, be that third force the monopolies commission or a new arrival on the market. This, of course, is specualtive. What is somewhat less speculative is that the forces required to raise a society from its sloth will be much greater than those needed to keep it from its sloth and if ever a descent is made into the 'static', very considerable forces will be needed to prevent a perpetuation of the static. The reason for this pessimism is given in the fourth assumption.

FOURTH ASSUMPTION: THAT ANY ACTIVITY THAT IS FREQUENTLY REPEATED WITH CONSIDERABLE LACK OF VARIATION WILL BECOME HALLOWED BY CUSTOM AND DIGNIFIED BY RITUAL

Actions can be performed for two reasons - either because they produce certain results or because they are 'good in themselves'. To revert to the distinction made earlier, the former are judged by their 'extrinsic' results, the latter by their 'intrinsic' qualities.

Actions designed to produce results can be said to be accompanied by some sense of 'purpose' on the part of the actor. They can therefore be said to be 'purposive'. To the extent that the aims of the behaviour can be held conceptually distinct from the means needed to attain it, will flexible 'means-ends', adaptive behaviour be possible. 'Purposive' behaviour is therefore only possible to any marked degree in a few of the higher species. (29) Actions that are 'good in themselves' on the other hand are independent of any separate 'purpose'. As a result they are inflexible, driven from 'behind' rather than from 'in front', and resemble a habit or even a reflex. What is odd enough is that this form of behaviour, characteristic as it is of the lower forms of life, should be indulged in by those humans who are defensive and afraid; but what is even more odd is that it should be engaged in by those who wish to assert their superiority.

The assumption made here is simply that, as actions cease to be experimental and become more and more the application of known techniques, so will the doubt over the outcome of the actions disappear. Where there is no doubt over the outcome there will be no 'decision' 'proprement dit' and behaviour will cease to be 'instrumental' and become 'expressive' and even 'ritualistic' in kind.

The pathology of bureaucratic behaviour (that is, behaviour in an ordered environment where there is no 'doubt over outcome' if certain procedural requirements are met) has been described by Merton as follows:

> Adherence to the rules, originally conceived as a means becomes transformed into an end-in-itself; there occurs the familiar process of displacement of goals whereby 'an instrumental value becomes a terminal value'.... This may be exaggerated to the point where primary concern with conformity to the rules interferes with the accomplishment of the purposes of the organization. (30)

This behaviour is interpreted by Merton as the result of excessive concern over the 'reliability of response' of the bureaucrat. As a result he may become overconcerned with conformity. However it is not immediately apparent whether this 'overconcern with conformity' is the cause or the result of the 'stereotyping' of behaviour. Does concern with conformity lead to stereotyping as Merton suggests, or can conformity itself be the dependent variable, a moral legitimation of habit? Here, for instance, the description by Burns and Stalker of a 'mechanistic' system of management, that is the kind of management structure that developed under 'static', unchanging conditions.

> The system of management within the factory was quite explicitly devised to keep production stable and production conditions stable.... Each working position in the hierarchy had its authority, information and technical competence specified once for all. (31)

Here, surely, the stress on conformity is the result rather than the cause of the standardization of behaviour. Whatever the cause, though, as the 'doubt over the outcome' recedes, so does the resulting standardization of behaviour become normative and 'ritualized', i.e. becomes 'good in itself'. It becomes 'morally encrusted'. A reason for this in Freudian terms will be given in a later paper. In the meanwhile I may perhaps mention a very much more mundance and almost adventitious reason for this 'displacement of goals' (whereby 'an instrumental value becomes a terminal value'), namely, that where the outcome is not in doubt, this is all that is asked from the subordinate. How can we control our inferiors if they do unexpected things in expected situations? In this, the attitude of a boss to his subordinate is similar to that of any group member to a fellow group member. Behaviour can become normative by an identical logic.

If these four assumptions, along with the earlier 'building blocks of caste', are taken seriously, what emerges? Fairly clearly, 'ritualization' or 'moral encrustation' of behaviour referred to above. More and more behaviour will become of 'intrinsic' rather than of 'extrinsic' value - an intrinsic evaluation that will extend to the a priori prescription of the necessary credentials of a role incumbent. Where the abilities required by the leader are few, the basis of his legitimacy must be more consistent and clear cut, for only thus can it become inviolable to envy. A class society will arise out of the very mediocrity of those who must be seen to be qualitatively distinct. Social attributes will not be just sufficient, they will be necessary.

In a subsequent paper it is hoped to spell out in greater detail how it is that a leader who cannot justify the tenure of his position on grounds of ability or personality, will become entrammelled by these very irrational or 'intrinsic' properties he must possess. It is then proposed to discuss the implications of this approach to the non-ritualistic leadership familiar in our society today. It is hoped to marry the ideas of Piaget to those of Freud in a discussion of 'democratic leadership'.

NOTES

1 Sigmund Freud, 'Group Psychology and the Analysis of the Ego', Hogarth Press, London, 1959, p. 56.
2 Ibid., p. 48.
3 Ibid., p. 53.
4 Ibid., p. 53.
5 Sigmund Freud, 'Totem and Taboo', Routledge & Kegan Paul, London, 1961.
6 'Group Psychology', p. 67.
7 'Totem and Taboo', p. 156.
8 It should be clear that, in this discussion, we are throughout only concerned with those who are freely accorded the right to their superior status. The man with a gun, the employer in times of unemployment who relies on unemployment, the prison warder with his bunch of keys, offer a simpler and less interesting (though none the less real) psychological problem.
9 See, for instance, 'Society and its Criminals' by Paul Reinwald (Heinemann, London, 1949), particularly the chapter on The Genesis of Punishment.
10 See Martin Lipset, A Conflict of American Ideals, 'Listener', 10 November 1960. In it he commends the suggested assumption that it 'is precisely because of the emphasis on equality and opportunity that Americans have been more status-conscious than those who live in the more aristocratic societies of Europe'.
11 Leonard R. Sayles, 'Behaviour in Industrial Work Groups: Prediction and Control', Wiley, New York, 1958.
12 On how to divide a group up, by promising individual rewards that conflict with the group expectations, see Carl Dreyfus in 'Reader in Bureaucracy', R.K. Merton (ed.), Free Press, Chicago, 1952, pp. 258-64.
13 We are for the moment leaving out of this discussion, for brevity's sake, the sheer effect of time upon the sanctity and 'honouring' of a norm. That a law or custom, however futile, can eventually come to be honoured for its own sake (since all those who do honour it, make sure that others honour it as well) need not belie the essential political origin of what has now become a religious belief. This point, amongst others, will be pursued in a subsequent paper.
14 'Differentials' implies a yardstick upon which payments should be made and suggests that factors other than sheer force act in the determination of wages.
15 See his 'Time Span of Responsibility', Tavistock Publications, London, 1956.
16 See A. Zaleznik, C.R. Christensen, F.J. Roethlisberger, 'The Motivation, Productivity and Satisfaction of Workers', Harvard Graduate School of Business Administration, 1958.

17 Op. cit., pp. 54, 55.
18 Op. cit., p. 321.
19 'Satisfaction in the White Collar Job', Ann Arbor, Michigan, 1957. See also G.C. Homans, 'Social Behaviour', Routledge & Kegan Paul, London, 1961, pp. 272-4.
20 Sayles, op. cit., has shown that the worst-paid workers need not give the most trouble. One reason being that they are the least qualified and they know it.
21 Quoted from G.C. Homans, 'The Human Group', Routledge & Kegan Paul, London, 1951, pp. 164-6.
22 See respectively, E. Benoit-Smullyan in 'American Sociological Review', 1944; G.E. Lenski in 'American Sociological Review', 1954; S.N. Adams, 'Social Forces', 1953. See also G.C. Homans, 'Social Behaviour', p. 248.
23 Consider in this respect the really remarkable record in the arts, sciences and commerce of the Jews.
24 That is, as is the case in this country today, where the less successful parents have been able to put some sort of a brake on the advantages the more successful parents enjoy.
25 Peter M. Blau and W. Richard Scott, 'Formal Organizations: a Comparative Approach', Routledge & Kegan Paul, London, 1963.
26 Michael Crozier, 'The French Bureaucratic System', Stanford University Press, quoted in Blau and Scott, pp. 175, 176.
27 Tom Burns and G.W. Stalker, 'The Management of Innovation', Tavistock Publications, London, 1961.
28 R.L. Hamblin, Leadership and Crisis, in 'Sociometry', 1958, 21, 322-35.
29 On this point see The Social Significance of Animal Studies by D.O. Hebb, and W.R. Thompson in G. Linzey (ed.), 'Handbook of Social Psychology', vol. 1, Addison-Wesley, New York.
30 See Bureaucratic Structure and Personality, 'Social Forces', May 1940.
31 Op. cit., p. 82.

Chapter 2

FREUD, PIAGET AND DEMOCRATIC LEADERSHIP

In an earlier paper (Freud and Social Class) it was suggested that the ambivalence that Freud maintained was felt to all leaders, necessitated for its resolution the assumption of a 'third force' or 'Authority' - an Authority that endowed a leader with a right to his position. It was further argued that the requirements of an adequate Authority would make a class society based on birth, rather than a democratic society based on ability, ultimately more probable. These assumptions were not fully spelled out. It now remains to show in greater detail how an 'irrationally' based leadership can become secure from resentment. In doing so I shall invoke an idea - that of the attitude of the leader to his position - which has so far been almost wholly neglected in the literature.

I shall begin with a discussion of the influence of the follower upon the leader. I hope to show how the leader may become entrammelled in the very source of his legitimacy. I shall then discuss the implications of this approach for an understanding of that most exacting and non-ritualistic form of leadership, sometimes known as 'democratic leadership'. In this second section I hope to show how the views, not only of Freud, but also of Piaget, lend support to the position presented here.

I will begin with formal leadership, not only because this form of leadership is much the most important in large-scale society, but also because informal situations are constantly hardening into formality by a process not unlike that of the development of ritual. Throughout the literature there has been an extraordinary neglect of what is surely the central feature of any formalized interaction - namely the attitude of the participants to their respective formal roles. Success in leadership does not merely depend on having certain abilities (mental powers or physical strength, etc.) nor does it depend only on having any very specific personality characteristics, but also on a third requirement, the leader's attitude to his own position. This is not unrelated to personality characteristics but differs in that an individual can perform well in a position that he feels he has a 'right' to, and yet badly in one he feels he has no 'right' to. (1)

The difference between these last two is brought out by what may well be considered a cautionary tale. Groups of four students (2) were observed in a discussion group situation and 'leadership' ratings were made for each individual. Before the second session started, the member who was 'most average' was told that he had the greatest 'leadership potential' in the group. As a result he asserted himself more in this second session; in my terms he had more of that desirable personality characteristic - self-confidence. At the third session he was 'appointed' leader in the presence of others. His 'leadership rating' went up again - this time because of my third rather than my second leadership requirement, namely that the leader believes in the legitimizing power of the role he occupies. This student felt that 'as somebody who had been appointed by a faculty member' he had the right to assert himself yet more. Alas, there is a sad ending to this story. At the fourth session the leader was given $13. $4 were for himself, and he was to distribute the remaining $9 to the other three group members as a reward for their 'contribution to the group's work'. $4 were to go to the member who had made the biggest contribution, $3 to the next and $2 to the last one. This request was made in the presence of the other group members. He did not take kindly to this enforced adjudication.

> He is usually first stunned, then irate, and then resistant, and retreats from the field to the extent of saying and doing considerably less than he has done in Session 3.... It is obvious that this increase in 'power' is more than one scale unit above public appointment, if indeed it is on the same dimension at all. (3)

Note that in the true tradition of American social psychology, 'public appointment' is treated as a unitary variable. What matters, of course, is who appoints to which position. This will be pursued in a moment. C.A. Gibb, in his account of this episode in the 'Handbook of Social Psychology', already referred to, draws the moral that the 'limit for the magnitude of the ordinary individual's desire for power over others' (4) is the cause of the odd behaviour in the fourth session. But what determines this 'limit for the magnitude of the ordinary individual's desire for power over others' except his ordinariness? This student said to himself, that 'as a fellow student, with the same status outside the experimental setting, of the same age and social class, etc. [i.e., having the same social attributes], I have not got the right to make invidious distinctions amongst my equals - even if I have been appointed by a faculty member.'

This cautionary tale brings out the whole crux of the leader's problem. For it is precisely the making of 'invidious distinctions' that all leaders have to do. The leader must adjudicate amongst his jealous followers, for it is he who must uphold the 'Authority', which is the basis of his legitimacy. This is why 'social distance' is necessary; it is necessary for the leader to be distant enough and hence self-confident enough not to be dependent on the very members between whom he must adjudicate.

'Attitude to the position' breaks down into two component attitudes - attitudes to the position itself and attitudes to one's right to occupy that position. The former is seen, for instance, when Elliott Jaques, in 'The Changing Culture of A Factory', (5) argues the need for joint consultation on the grounds that the managers felt that just 'as a manager' they did not have, in a democracy, the 'right' to implement a policy that had not been sanctioned by the work force at large. 'Being a manager' was not enough in itself, and it was on these grounds that he argued the necessity of joint consultation as a legitimizing agency.

The more impressive the position one occupies, the greater the enhancement. Elliott Jaques' managers did not think highly enough of 'being managers'. A king who genuinely believes in his divine right is in a totally different position psychologically from one who does not; here, as in loyalty to the institutions, or for that matter belief in one's God, the bigger the distance between the individual and the object of his reverence, the greater the benefit. To revert to my cautionary tale for a moment - the student's break-down in the fourth session is in a way no more than a demonstration of his attitude to the faculty member. He felt that 'being appointed leader by a faculty member' did not outweigh the social attributes he had in common with his fellows. Had the student been appointed by the President of the United States, or had the student managed to persuade himself that he heard the voice of God calling him, things might have been different.

The second component of 'attitude to position' is that individual's feeling of 'right' to occupy that position. Such a 'right' is nearly always granted on the ground of fulfilling certain requirements - a mediaeval king on grounds of primogeniture, a priest on grounds of ordination, which, in turn is based on having met certain attitudinal and other demands. Those who feel they have the 'right' to their position have a clear start over those who feel they are trespassing. Indeed, for the latter an attitude of reverence for the position will detract from their effectiveness. The trouble with Macbeth, for instance, was that he thought too highly of kingship and his trespass was all the greater in consequence.

The leader in the most favourable position, then, is the one who both reveres his position and believes in this right to his incumbency - the Sergeant Major who believes in the 'dignity of his rank' and who feels that appointment through the 'due' processes is itself enough to bestow the right - for frequently 'right' devolves from some cherished source. The leader in the least favourable position is the man who reveres his rank but who feels he has not got the 'right' to occupy it. Somewhere in the middle must come those who have no strong feelings about the position they occupy. Indeed, what might be called the 'ladder of effectiveness' could go like this:

1 High belief in the value of the position and belief in the right to occupy it.
2 Low belief in the value of the position and belief in the right to occupy it.
3 Low belief in the value of the position and no belief in the right to occupy it.
4 High belief in the value of the position and no belief in the right to occupy it.

Of course attitude to position is only one of three desiderata - the leader must also have the required ability and personality characteristics. If a mediaeval king such as Edward II was unable to keep order he was deposed even if his murder had to be camouflaged by a peculiarly atrocious crime. Indeed, it is possible that, as the demands on the leader become more arduous, so will the right 'abilities' and 'personality characteristics' become more important. In an emergency, birth is no substitute for ability; the army is more democratic in wartime and the warrior tribe will need a warrior at its head. The American Negro will be cheered on the international cinder track, in the boxing ring, and for that matter, in the jazz-band, (6) but once his distinctive skills have lost their appeal he will relapse into the limbo of second-class citizenship. (7)

All this is straightforward - but what is the implication? If abilities become more important in a leader when abilities are needed, abilities will also become less important when abilities are not needed. The army as we all know becomes less democratic in peacetime and concentrates on what really matters - the selection of 'gentlemen'; the Negro, once the acute need to win at an international sporting contest has passed, is gratefully relegated to where he belongs. The fewer the abilities needed the more must some belief in a more or less arbitrary 'right' supervene. This 'right' could be democratically or undemocratically based, but it is, of course, my contention that the latter is the more likely. Indeed, the whole thesis might be condensed into the assertion that the fewer the abilities needed to be a leader, the more exclusive a possession of a privileged class will it become. Where anyone could be a leader, leadership will be at its most irrational and most exclusive. This is, after all, no more than is summed up in this country by the position of the monarchy. For if we accept what, in the first paper, I called the 'building blocks of caste' - that we only expect our due, that behaviour and aspiration can be dependent variables, that our idea of due can itself be based on the social attributes of sex, age, birth, etc., then everything will depend on this last point, on whether the social attributes will indeed become the first basis of reward.

Once this is established, all will follow; once birth is seen as the criterion of worth, birth will perpetuate itself, since those who are controlled will identify with a force that allows them to keep their rivals (those 'as good as they are') under control. Indeed, the majority of the lower orders will be against the introduction of promotion possibilities - if these possibilities do not include themselves. Why should those 'as good as they are' be favoured? The establishment can only be overthrown if a large enough section of the subject population can hope to gain and if the reactionary, dog-in-the-manger attitude of what might be called the 'feeble lower orders' is sufficiently weakened.

It seems plausible to assume that such a class society would perpetuate itself, but why should it develop in the first place? Why should the social mobility of our own times congeal into the stagnancy of a system where merit is assessed on social attributes? In the first paper I assumed, of course, that change will cease to lead to yet further change. Given this flat assumption, I am left with the conclusion that less and less ability will be needed to act as a leader, and that more and more leader (and indeed follower) behaviour will become ritualized, stylized, 'good in itself' - a form of ceremony, the product, and the cause of continuity.

If this does occur, the leadership will cease to depend on exceptional abilities or personality characteristics - since these will be freely available and so will become irrelevant. Leadership, by the same token, will come to depend more and more on my third requirement - the leader's attitude to his own position and his right to that position. For, as leadership ceases to be 'instrumental', and as the leader finds it more and more difficult to justify his preferment on the grounds of the results he can attain through his exceptional endowment, so must a leader justify his actions and his position on irrational or, as I called it, on 'intrinsic', a priori grounds. A ritual act is an irrational act; it is the pure case of something that is believed in for its own sake, irrespective of the consequences it may have. It cannot, therefore, be refuted, but neither can it have a rational justification.

But how can a leader come to believe in the dignity of the irrational and the arbitrary - the value in being born British, for instance, in the need to take one's hat off in a lift, or in the evil of eating pork? The answer of course lies in the true source of all other beliefs held for their own sake - namely the upbringing of the individual.

At this point I must turn to another assumption made in the first paper - that parents will do the best they can for their children. Parents who are in a position of power will thus have the advantage of being able to grant their children earlier preferment and promotion, and they will also be able to inculcate the intrinsic value of certain activities. The irrational can be made self-evident to those who are caught young enough. A boy at public school in Victorian times could be made to believe that as an Englishman he had the 'right' as well as the obligation to direct the affairs of those lesser Indians and other colonials he had been called upon to 'serve'. There are none so self-confident as those that are blinkered or obtuse. The more one is aware of the claims of others, the more hollow do one's own pretensions appear - just as the more one is aware of the weaknesses of an argument, the more diffident will one be in outlining it. It may be that it is the relatively simple-minded preacher that communicates most efficiently. After all, as they say in the salesman's training course - one must believe in what one is selling. And does this not make good sense, too, in Freudian terms? What, after all, must underlie our relations with others but aggressions and guilt? What is important is to be at peace with oneself - however arrived at. Those who are not tormented by doubts will not only be able to act more effectively (that is self-evident) but will also be able to evoke a more effective response in others. To be led by someone who accepts his right to lead is to be led by someone who has withstood our aggressions. To be led by the emotionally crippled is to impose an intolerable load of guilt on the subordinate.

However, to return to my main contention: the more irrational and the more arbitrary, the more 'intrinsic', does the basis of leadership become (in that, for instance, it is based solely on birth) and the more irrational and the more arbitrary does the content of leadership become (in that it largely consists in the quasi-ceremonial implementation of preconceived actions), the more will leader effectiveness - and acceptability - become dependent on the past of the leader and follower alike - on earlier training and upbringing.

What protest will then be open to the aggrieved subordinate? How will he be able to gain the courage to attack what he has been taught to see as the source of his own enhancement? How, for that matter, can he gain a yardstick that will allow him to make a 'legitimate' complaint? The answer is, that - provided the society really is insulated from rival 'Authorities' - he cannot. In a society insulated from change there is only one yardstick - the existing set of values. Where there is only one set of values the only protest open to a subordinate is to attack the leadership because it does not conform enough, to claim that the rulers have abandoned the law, have betrayed the sacred trust, etc. The most likely attack on the establishment will be an ultra-conformist one. And why should the authorities provide cause for resentment? They may not, of course, but, equally well, they may - and the reason why they may provides us with the most ironic of all the consequences of the Freudian outlook on groups.

If the work of a leader in a static society becomes less and less exacting, by the same token it becomes more and more constricting. As ritual supervenes, as innumerable sequences of action become cut off from their extrinsic, instrumental purposes and enshrined in the tradition of the society, so will the leader find himself as much a slave to the values that are the source of his legitimacy as anyone else. In one sense, of course, the leader will have more 'power' than his subordinates but in another sense he will not. Has the actor who plays Hamlet more freedom than the actor who plays Fortinbras? Has the Sergeant Major more freedom - whether attitudinal or behavioural - than the recruit?

In my first paper the leader-follower relationship was schematically represented as shown in Figure 2.1.

The leader directs the follower and is in turn directed by the 'Authority', an 'Authority' that owes its legitimacy to the belief of both leader and follower. With the growth of ritual - or of any standardized behaviour - we arrive at something approaching Figure 2.2.

Here the 'Authority' directly affects the follower, as well as coming through the leader. The follower also knows what he is supposed to do, and the base of the triangle - the influence of the leader on the follower - becomes redundant.

And this, in Freudian terms, is as it should be - the 'Authority' must rule the ruler and the ruled. A leader can never be accepted who is not himself subordinate.

This revenge of the subordinate is subtle and difficult to escape. It may be the leader, who often enough will feel the

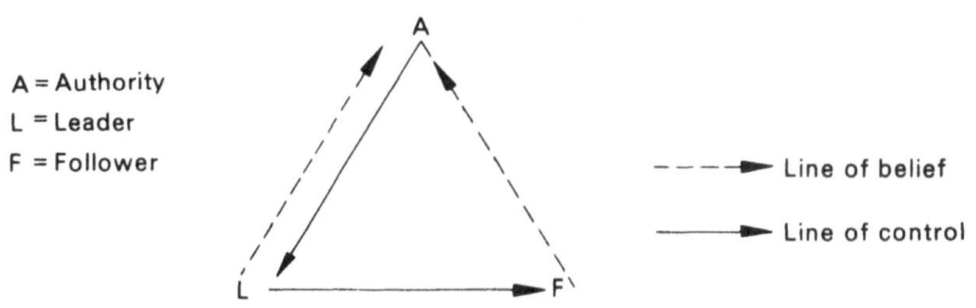

FIGURE 2.1 The leader-follower relationship

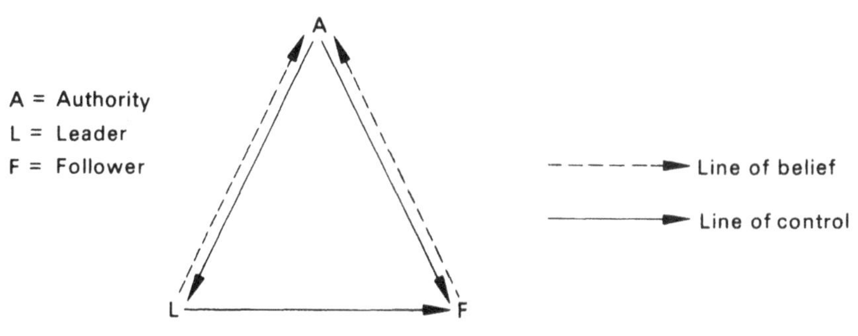

FIGURE 2.2 The leader-follower relationship: the development of ritual

need to break free; he will be both more constricted and yet less in need of emotional support. He will have greater leisure and better opportunities for education and discussion. No wonder he will be the first to treat the values of his society with detachment and even cynicism. It would not be too surprising if he reacted against the call of omnipresent duty and used his more advantageous position in the network of responsibilities, to express his personal cupidity, his private resentments and aggressions, his unauthorized (we might say, id-iosyncratic) assertions and cruelties.

This behaviour on the part of the leader would give the ruled a legitimate complaint - a complaint that the traditional values were not heeded by their 'betters'. This kind of complaint can be peculiarly difficult to ignore and even more difficult to refute. The trouble with Luther, from the Pope's point of view, was that he took Christianity too seriously - and continued to do so despite secular blandishments. And was not Luther quite right? After all, the purpose of all moral behaviour is control - and being moral and conformist is something anyone can be.

All this makes good sense in Freudian terms. The dilemma of social living, as stated in my first paper, was the problem of how to succeed without allowing others to succeed as well in one's wake. The son tries to usurp the father's place without the retaliation of the father, or (and this is more to the point here) from the other sons. Equally, the son tries to possess the mother without incurring his father's wrath and his brothers' competition.

The solution to this dilemma lay in subordinating oneself to a code (or 'Authority') that was equally binding on the self and others. 'Since I cannot succeed myself, no one shall be allowed to succeed as well.' At one blow one has both expiated one's own guilt and gained control: for, having subordinated onself to the current morality, one is then free to express one's aggression blamelessly, self-righteously - and anonymously. The 'law', 'God', 'public opinion', 'necessity' - or in whatever guise the 'Authority' may be found - can be evoked instead.

Whether or not the result will necessarily be a class society based on birth as argued here, is, of course, open to doubt. What is less in doubt, I think, is that, unless the process is arrested by (a) conflict or (b) the manifestly greater usefulness of one course of action over another (i.e. those factors that encourage means-end behaviour) more and more behaviour will become ritualized and 'morally encrusted' and 'leadership' will become absorbed into the system - a system that allows the complete control of everyone by all.

It will be a system in which the leadership will be used by the followers even more than the followers will be dominated by the leader. The leader will both provide that enhancement to the follower that only social distance can give and will act as a weighty weapon in the battle that really rages - the pre-occupation of each with the other's behaviour. Our leaders, like our gods, are created to enhance (the self) and to control (others).

Hence the enormous appeal of ritual to the subordinate. 'Ritual' is activity that is valued for its own sake - activity that is dominated by an 'Authority' and creates its own aura of veneration. We create an object of veneration that we may impress - and control. The leader becomes entrammelled in the very source of his legitimacy, he becomes emasculated by the basis of his stature. The creation of ritual, too, is a move in that warfare of power that must express itself 'legitimately'. To our democratic minds the existence of a parasitic elite that does nothing to 'deserve' its position is an anathema. Looked at from another point of view, they are the docile pawns of their followers' beliefs.

With my argument so clearly demonstrated, it seems sad to admit that it hardly ever applies; docile proletariats and ritualistic, or, for that matter, well-behaved leaders are not all that much in evidence. Why is this so? There are two reasons for this, of which only the second will be discussed.

The first reason is simply that the leadership may be strong enough to ignore the good will of those it controls. So far I have only been concerned with consent - the conditions under which a follower will accept his superiors as legitimate. If a leader is strong enough he can happily remain indifferent to such feelings, maintaining his position by a judicious use of force and patronage. This type of situation is perhaps not quite as important as might be expected, at least if the Freudian thesis is accepted, for if jealousy is the first social emotion and the prime pre-occupation of one and all is that others 'as good as them' are equally treated, there will be a constant drift from rule by force to rule by consent. It might be called a 'drift to legitimacy'.

This would occur, for instance, when subordinate 'A' suffers the rule of one he fears. Having suffered, he will insist that subordinate 'B' suffer in turn. Subordinate 'A', then, will come to believe in the rightness of a rule that will control others as well. This is no more, after all, than the basis of the evolution of group norms as described in my first paper. Further, the more subordinate 'A' has suffered, the more will he feel the need that subordinate 'B' should suffer too. This is no more than the self imposing on someone else the constraints that, in brainwashing, the self imposes on the self. This 'drift to legitimacy' - the acceptance of the right of the usurper to rule unless a large enough body can be got together (soon enough) to overthrow him - can act as a constant temptation on the ruler to abandon his distrust and to heed the good will of his people. Thus may he be seduced into a legitimizing conformity.

The second reason why my argument may be irrelevant is very different, and much more important. It is, of course, that the flat plateau of technical stagnation has not been (and will not be) reached and that the rule of the leader, far from being reduced to a recital of ceremonial legitimations, will involve exceptional abilities and exceptional personality characteristics. It is possible that new situations will continually have to be met; new decisions will have to be made without the crutch of precedent, but resting instead on the intellectual and nervous resources of the individual.

It is with the problem of leadership under these conditions that this section will be largely concerned. How, when his task is at its most arduous, can a leader justify his position? For, by a cruel paradox, he cannot rely solely on the social attributes of what he is if the result of his actions leave clearly and grossly much to be admired. It is only those who have no demands made upon them who have no need to justify themselves.

We have come back to the problem of 'extrinsic' and 'intrinsic' grounds for holding beliefs which has been discussed. The leader who has to make decisions is measured by results, by his effectiveness in a situation. It is the entry of the situation as a third force that completely alters the relationship of the leader to his followers. For the situation challenges the leader; it allows him to be shown up to the follower. The 'situation' may well become so challenging that it imposes severe demands upon him. To the extent that the leader becomes exposed to the sanction of 'failure', so does his entire relationship to his follower undergo a change.

For, if a leader fails, he reveals his qualitative similarity to other lesser human beings. The whole force of the leader resides in that in some way he is seen as larger than life. This is why he is accorded 'veneration' and 'respect'. This is welcomed by the follower for neither enhancement nor control can come from those that are no better than we are. If he fail, even the most desirable of social attributes may not save him. Indeed, if he is a 'gentleman' this need not prevent his incurring the odium of failure - on the contrary, 'being a gentleman' itself may become suspect. The capital of social attribute, rather than helping him, may itself be threatened. But the situation may be worse than this. The leader may not be a gentleman. In taxing times more leaders are promoted on merit than in calmer times, leaders tend to be without the prop of desirable social attributes at the time they need them most. What then can this leader do? How can he justify his position to those who were erstwhile as 'good as him'? The position of this leader is peculiarly difficult; not only does he very frequently not have the customary social attributes, not only must he use his abilities, but also, he may very well call from his subordinates activities without justification or legitimation in precedent. This does not apply, or not nearly to the same extent, to other kinds of leaders. Thus, a traditional leader, who is not called upon to meet a new situation, may very well be acceptable to the followers in that all that is asked of them is that they engage in prelegitimated acts. This the followers will welcome because it allows them to control the leader. But this does not apply to the leader in times of change; he may not only lack the right social attributes, but he may be forced to demand of his men actions that have not previously been accepted as 'right'.

Since a leader in this position cannot invoke the 'Authority' of precedent, or ritual or of custom, he is driven to invoke a new 'Authority' - an 'Authority' that does not owe its persuasiveness to the legitimacy inherent in sheer repetition. And what can this 'Authority' be? The leader must confront the root cause of his difficulties and invoke these same difficulties as a new and radically different form of legitimation - the leader must invoke the situation itself. This, surely, is the psychological justification for what is known as democratic leadership. The leader must say, 'Look, it is not I that ask this of you, but the situation that demands it.' In a sense the leader must never ask for obedience to himself alone - even the 'traditional leader' as we have seen, is not free, and must say that the 'law' or that 'custom' demands it. This is true enough, but there is still a considerable difference between the position of the leader who is a 'traditional leader', and the 'leader in times of change'. At least the 'traditional leader' is able to fuse into the custom he embodies, he can allow the 'Authority' to 'emanate' from him, thus confounding his personal aura with the aura he 'serves'. But the 'Authority' of the 'leader in times of change' has a different effect. To the extent that the situation is a reality that demands attention, so is the leader not separate from his followers like the King at the ritual of the coronation is separated from his subjects; he is, on the contrary, placed on the same level.

The whole force of the 'objective situation' lies in that it unites the leader and his followers. He must show his qualitative similarity, in that he demonstrates that he too is subject to harsh empirical laws - laws that, unlike custom, will favour no man. 'We are in this together; I, too, must work and suffer' - the similarity of the leader to his followers, not his difference, is stressed.

Whence, then, the leader's 'qualitative difference'? This too, as I have argued throughout, is necessary. He must, alas, earn this status, through his competence and through the help he can give his subordinates. In that his subordinates may very well need help, they may be the more open to gratitude, but the leader must earn it none the less. In particular he must help his subordinate against the outside forces that hinder and challenges his 'group', even if those 'forces' be the leader's own superiors.

It is not surprising, then, that the leader who doubts the adequacy of his abilities will attempt a retreat into the inscrutable; for if no reasons are given, the rightness of his actions cannot be gainsaid. Another way of concealing incompetence is to attempt to concentrate decision making into his own hands, thus again breaking the 'contract' with his critical and reluctant subordinates. For, by a final twist of the knife, the 'democratic leader' is not only expected to give reasons and show his dependence on the situation, he is also expected to delegate. Where the 'situation' rules as the legitimizing agency, it legitimizes one and all: it is the man who knows who should be consulted, the man who has special skills who must be trusted.

All this can arguably be inferred from Freud's views on groups, but it is none the less gratifying to find a psychologist with a completely different orientation substantially agreeing with this distinction between 'Authority based on precedent' and 'Authority based on the situation'. The psychologist is Jean Piaget; in my opinion the only figure in psychology of comparable stature to Freud. Piaget is more concerned with the development of the abilities than with the emotions, but in one book, 'The Moral Judgment of the Child', (8) he deals with the emotional growth of young children. In this book he argues that the transfer from the acceptance of an 'Authority' based on tradition to the acceptance of an 'Authority' based on situational factors is not just something that happens on a social scale, it is also something that occurs in the life of every individual.

The child's earliest morality is the 'morality of constraint'. The child accepts his ideas of right and wrong from the parent - a parent who is seen as omniscient and above circumstance. The environment in which the parent operates being outside the child's comprehension, the child is free to see the parent as an unmoved mover. The parent is indeed seen in some way as dominating and controlling the entire world - and as a result a two-part rather than a three-part relationship supervenes: the child-parent, not the 'child-parent-environment'. Since there is no 'environment' to act as a yardstick, the parent's pronouncements - whether on matters of value or on matters of fact - are judged by their source rather than their content.

From about the age of five onwards, the child begins to interact - or 'co-operate' - with equals. Dealing with equals is different in two important ways from dealing with parents or superiors. In the first place, there is no barrier of social distance, and secondly, since they share the same environment, the source of others' opinions and beliefs is understood: the fellow child is seen as a dependent variable. The position of the other is understood, because the forces acting upon him are understood. This introduction of the environment as the third force quite changes the relationship: it allows the child to assess the content of his fellow's communications, and also to identify with him on the basis of a perceived common lot. This 'taking the role of the other' is not only necessary for the development of intelligence (in that intellectual operations are based on the ability to see the same data from more than one point of view), but also allows the emergence of a new morality - the morality of 'good' rather than the morality of 'duty'. The morality of 'good' is based on an awareness of the meaning of the situation to another, on an appreciation of both the person and his circumstances. The morality of 'duty' is based on the acceptance of an external fiat, as binding as it is inflexible and arbitrary.

The similarity with the two kinds of leadership discussed in this paper should be immediately apparent. What should be equally apparent is why so many leaders prefer to replace the parent than to replace the colleague. How nice to be believed and obeyed for what one is, and not to have to give reasons! (Even if one has to be totally imprisoned within one's own myth as a consequence.) What a comedown it is for a leader to shed his pretensions to ontological superiority and allow himself to be seen as a fellow human whose powers are not qualitatively different from others!

A 'mature' individual, then, prefers an egalitarian leader; it is the adult who is still fixated at an early stage of emotional development who prefers his oracle intact. But how 'mature' are we? Piaget contends that this development from 'constraint' to 'co-operation' will not take place when the child (a) is not exposed to contrary information and (b) remains in awe of the source of truth. 'Co-operation' will only grow where there is a clash of opinions; if we are insulated from contrary currents, it will not occur to us to change our views.

> There can be no doubt that this phenomenon is peculiar to our civilization.... In our societies the child escapes from the family circle and comes in contact with an ever-increasing number of social circles which widen his mental outlook. Whereas in so-called primitive communities, adolescence is the age of initiation, therefore of the strongest moral constraint, and the individual, as he grows older, becomes more and more dependent. (9)

Second, the child must escape the awesome source. Boys can discuss the rules of marbles 'intelligently' only when there are no older boys who play marbles. We will believe unless our gods withdraw.

> And if, at a given moment, co-operation takes the place of constraint, or autonomy that of conformity, it is because the child, as he grows older, becomes progressively free from adult supervision. This came out very clearly in the game of marbles. Children of 11 to 13 have no others above them in this game since it is one that is played only in the lower school. (10)

But will our gods withdraw? Piaget contrasts our western societies, with their complex cross-currents of emotional belief and factual orientations, with the simpler, homogeneous savage societies where all believe the same truths and subscribe to the same code. It is competition and the clash of interests that has characterized our own society and led to such decay of the 'morality of constraint' as there has been. But this development could equally well be reversed, if, for any reason, conflict or competition ceased to be a live force and wider areas of social life become entrammelled with precedent and agreement.

Thus with Piaget, directly, and with Freud, by inference, a society structured by social distance is seen as the 'natural society': the state to which society will return unless there are forces that constantly reassert equality and doubt. Whether or not the social distance be based on birth rather than merit, lot or conviction is, of course, another matter. In the 'first assumption' given here I have assumed that it will be. This is perhaps not so important. What may be more important for this argument is not the origin of any ruling caste there may be, but how secure and unchallenged it can manage to become and how 'socially distant' it remains. The importance of the leader remaining secure and retaining at least some 'social distance', even in the egalitarian society of today, will be the last point taken up and will, it is hoped, form a fitting coda.

Neither of the two descriptions of leadership given so far fits the actual kind of leader who appears to be appreciated in western industry today. What a worker wants from a 'good boss' has been summarized (11) and fits neither the picture of the remote socially distant parent nor that of the egalitarian colleague. The crude fact would seem to be that many subordinates, when it comes to their leaders, want to have their cake and eat it. They want someone who is secure enough and distant enough to act as a reasonable source of psychological support, to be strong enough so that he remains above the fray which he must adjudicate, and yet, at the same time, they want someone who is 'democratic', who consults and gives reasons.

But he need not always consult or delegate - only if the subject matter is new (as is evidence by the 'resistance to change' studies) (12) or is within the abilities of the subordinate. If the topic is too difficult for the subordinate, delegation is, not surprisingly, unwelcomed, and if the topic (or something like it) has been met before, the subordinate may very well be willing to grant his leader his trust. The leader may gain a 'zone of indifference' in Barnard's term (13) and so will be free to take his onerous decisions in solitude. The subordinate, in other words, wants it both ways. He wants someone to take the difficult decisions and to leave him a voice in the easier ones; he wants someone who is strong enough to be an effective protector and judge while remaining approachable enough to understand his point of view. The leader must be both parent and servant.

Who is most likely to fill this exacting role? Who will be grand enough to enhance and control while yet remaining human enough to consult and to understand? Who will value his subordinates and yet not be dependent upon them? It is perhaps the last and cruellest paradox of the entire discussion that it is arguable the 'non-democratic' leader who is most likely to be 'democratic' in his behaviour. This is possible because the word 'democratic' has two meanings - meanings which seem directly antithetical to one another. On the one hand, a 'democratic' leader can be one who has been promoted on merit, and who does not owe his position to privilege; on the other, a 'democratic' leader can be an approachable leader, a leader who accepts the need for his instructions to be understood, a leader who asks for contributions and gives reasons for praise and blame. One leader is democratic by derivation, the other is democratic by behaviour. The assumption being made here is that, provided he is sufficiently competent, the leader who is undemocratic in the first sense will be the more democratic in the second sense - the man of privilege will be the man of the people.

'The man of privilege' may well be superior to the 'man of the people' on three counts. In the first place he will be in a better position to support his own subordinates, for the purely fortuitous reason that his own superiors will be more likely to take him seriously than they would someone who is not 'one of them'. (14) Second, he may be the more ready to delegate and consult. Since he cannot be dispossessed by his subordinates, he will have nothing to fear from them. Rather than worry unduly about being 'shown up' by their competence, he will welcome their contributions. He can afford to co-operate since there is no need to compete.

Finally and crucially, such a leader, particularly if his leadership has been foreseen and the right steps have been taken, may well accept his own right to lead. He is less likely to be trammelled by doubts over the legality of his position, and he will therefore attain that independence from his subordinates that all who occasionally have to take unpopular decisions must have. As a result he will be free to implement dispassionately what is after all the source of his subordinates' consent - the law, the 'Authority'.

And what is the lot of the 'democratically elected' leader, the leader who has no edge of intrinsic social superiority over his followers? Attempting to deal with subordinates who want both a protector and a servant, dominated by a 'situational authority' that may very well reveal the weaknesses of the only qualities on which he can base his claim to a higher status, the leader may well become little more than the hardest working and the most harrassed member present. Some may attempt a retreat into dignity, leaving themselves open to the danger of the industrious subordinate who, like a latter-day mayor of the palace, may gain real power. Others may abandon the sacrifice necessary to gain the consent of their followers and attempt to manipulate them by an appeal to the wholly extrinsic incentives of money and fear.

And what is the result of this 'extrinsic manipulation'? If it fail, the followers will unite against their leaders, impose, by restricting output, their own local norms and evolve their own 'unofficial' leaders. In brief, they will attain their own 'Authority'. The 'official leadership' (namely management) will now be outside the moral orbit of the followers, their status will be that of an enemy in wartime - the enemy that it is meritorious to attack. The followers, with a scapegoat to hand on which to blame each other's shortcomings, may at last attain that harmony of group life and lack of social distance between leader and follower we are so often assured is the basis of mental health in industry. And if it succeed? Success is particularly likely where, by instilling strong competition, the followers are pitted one against the other. Where the rewards and penalties are high, each follower threatens the other, and the leader can withdraw, allowing his subordinates to pace one another.

It is not within the purview of this paper to discuss the advantages or disadvantages (from the leader's point of view) of encouraging such competition in subordinates, but, what can be said (and what forms an amusing conclusion to the whole discussion) is that rather than leading to democratic, egalitarian or 'spontaneous' behaviour, in some ways it resembles in its effects the very worst forms of an unduly rigid class structure.

For what happens? Wispé and Lloyd have described the effects of such competition in the relations between life insurance salesmen. (15) Here all are 'equal' and yet all are a possible help or hindrance to the other. As a result, beneath the friendliness, a formality and a rigidity of behaviour is found that serves to keep the salesman distant from one another rather more effectively than would be a barrier of rank. There was a desire for formalized structured relationships, for only then could they allay the 'permeating anxiety which results from the intense competition through which the agents must live and their inability to meet it efficaciously'. The authors continue, 'the desire for structured personal interaction is thus a defence mechanism which attempts to control the behaviour of these individuals in the system who have the authority to initiate negative sanctions'.

Put in another way, the salesman do not form a 'group', they do not identify with one another because they cannot control one another. They cannot control one another because the 'natural' source of control, namely the leader, has abdicated his responsibilities. In playing off one against the other, the leader loses all claim to the loyalty of his followers, he becomes one more obstacle to be manipulated and deceived. Under reasonable conditions the followers will retaliate in kind, forming their own group and their own authority, but if their cupidity or their fear is played upon too insistently to make this possible, they may very well end up by hating one another with the peculiar hatred we have for competitors who remind us of our own weakness.

From now on, each forms his own society and each is forced to carry the burden of being his own leader. Each is his own tiny city state, at war with one and all. For where there are no superiors there are no equals. And that is no more than Freud said in the beginning.

NOTES

1 In a well-known summary of the data on leadership, for instance, that of C.A. Gibb in 'Handbook of Social Psychology', vol. 2 (ed. Lindzey), there is scarcely any reference to this factor at all.
2 Presumably students (this study was reported as part of an unpublished doctor's thesis by Beatrice Shriver). See Launor F. Carter, Leadership and small group Behaviour in 'Group Relations at the Cross Roads', ed. M. Sherif and M.O. Wilson, Harper Bros, New York, 1953, pp. 278-81.
3 Beatrice Shriver in Launor F. Carter, op. cit., pp. 280-1.
4 C.A. Gibb's article on Leadership in 'Handbook of Social Psychology', vol. 2 (ed. Lindzey), p. 904.
5 Tavistock, London, 1956.
6 On this, see Sidney Willhelm and Gideon Sjoberg, The Social Characteristics of Entertainers, 'Social Forces', 1958. See also S. Kirson Weinberg and Henry Arond, The Occupational Status of the Boxer, 'American Journal of Sociology', March 1952.
7 To return to the ruler for a moment, it is possible that usurpers so frequently launch into a career of foreign aggression, not just because they wish to consolidate their position at home by directing the attention of their subordinates to a common enemy, but also because they hope to bolster their position by making plain the only real claim they have - their demonstrable competence.
8 Routledge & Kegan Paul, London, 1960.
9 Op. cit., p. 99.
10 Op. cit., pp. 98-9.
11 On this see Morris S. Viteles, 'Motivation and Morale', Staples Press, London, 1954, ch. 8 and 17, and see Leadership Practices in Relation to Productivity and Morale, by R.L. Kahn and D. Katz in D. Cartwright and A. Zander (eds), 'Group Dynamics, Research and Theory', Row, Peterson & Company, 1960, pp. 554-70.

12 For this, see Viteles, op. cit., ch. 9.

13 Chester I. Barnard, 'The Functions of the Executive', Harvard University Press, Cambridge, Mass., pp. 168-9.

14 On the importance of this see two articles by D.C. Pelz, Leadership within a Hierarchical Organization, 'Journal of Social Issues', 1951, 7, 3, 49-55 and Influence: a key to effective leadership in the first-line supervisor, 'Personnel', 1952, 3, 209-17.

15 L.G. Wispé and K.E. Lloyd, Some situational and psychological determinants for the desire for structured inter-personal relations, 'Journal of Abnormal and Social Psychology', 1955, 51, 57-60.

Chapter 3

THE OWNERSHIP OF WORK: A PSYCHOLOGICAL APPROACH

In a paper entitled The Stimulation and Sharing of Gains in Productivity, Shultz and McKersie, in discussing the 'buy-out' approach to productivity bargaining, refer to 'compensation for property rights which are being relinquished'. This 'compensation', in the form of a lump sum, would only go to those who are being asked to abandon their 'traditional but now out-dated practices'. Those who joined the firm after the 'buy-out' would not get such benefits - 'since he had never worked by the old rules he had nothing to "sell" to management'. Nothing to 'sell' since he would have 'owned' no 'property rights'.

This paper is concerned with the problem of 'felt' - as opposed to 'legal' - ownership rights. When do we 'feel' we own - whether we do in the eyes of the law or not? When are the claims of others to extra legal 'rights' accepted or resented? When, to take Shultz and McKersie's example will the unions assert and the management acceed?

The psychological assumptions on which this paper is based are of the most elementary. These will be, first, that human beings try to maximize their satisfactions - satisfactions that very largely spring from a sense of mastery and power over the environment - and, second, that the single-minded pursuit of these satisfactions will be inhibited by fears that may well be phantasy fears, and sated by rewards that may well be phantasy rewards. Humans, in other words, will be treated as self-maximizing entities that are oppressed by unreal fears and seduced by unreal hopes.

Somewhat brutally and contentiously, perhaps, I shall here dub 'unreal' anything that is not 'real' - in the most mundane sense of 'real'. Thus all ideals will be considered 'unreal', even all statements of what 'ought' to be. Indeed any statement that implies an other-wordly and morally preemptive criterion - i.e. the 'right' or the 'good' - or owes its force to an association with such highly charged and mythical entities as 'God', 'the Law', 'our Ancestors', etc. - will here be thought of as 'unreal'. In nature there is but inevitability, there is neither good nor bad, trivial nor significant. This paper will largely deal with the illusory consolations of a 'sense of justification' and, hence, of 'ownership'.

It is in childhood that we learn the language of justification. Odd as it may sound, a brief look at the vicissitudes of our sense of self-righteousness is necessary for the thesis of this paper. Our self-righteousness for us is Paradise enow, and somewhat fancifully I shall call the stages of our emotional development Paradise, Paradise Lost, Paradise Regained and Awakening. (1) The Awakening is, alas, an Awakening to reality, doubt, and an awareness of our human limitations. Fanciful these titles may be but they do attempt to bring out one fact clearly - that in human development, the ideal precedes and is more primitive than the real. It is only later, and then in piecemeal form, that we attain an Awakening.

This launches us on our study of the emotional development of the individual. It is a wild paradox in human affairs that the less we know, the less we realize what we cannot do. There are none so convinced of their powers as those who are ignorant, and at the very beginning of our days we are wholly ignorant. When on top of this, we consider that the child before birth is almost totally, and the child immediately thereafter is very largely, shielded from all noxious realities, we can see how the ground base of a sense of personal omnipotence can be formed - an omnipotence based not so much on the control over others as their irrelevance. That which is outside can be ignored.

This is the earliest stage of Paradise, the source of our illusions and our ideals. The illusions and the ideals indeed are one, for it is a wholly illusory sense of mastery that we deem ideal. But this sense of mastery cannot last. Willy-nilly the outside world presses upon us. We realize that the other cannot be ignored and so, at about the age of five months, we attain that qualitative discontinuity of outlook that I have here called Paradise Lost.

The growth of knowledge in the very small child is the cruellest fruit that the tree could offer, for it teaches us - who were erstwhile omnipotent and alone - of our dependence on others. Torn from our solitude we realize that our very existence depends upon those that appear arbitrary and incomprehensible. We could have no greater fall - we lose the sunlight garden of our warm self-sufficiency and are made open to sorrow.

But Paradise is not Lost for long. For the very agents of our fall allow us an opportunity to return. God who evicted us from Eden may yet let us back. For the parents are now invested with the awe we grant those whose behaviour we cannot control or understand. They are the heirs of our ideals, and it is through our relationship to them that we reattain our earlier self-sufficiency. This 'return', here called Paradise Regained, is known as the 'identification of the child with the parent'. It comes but slowly but is usually complete by the age of five.

This process is critical to our development as social beings. As 'myself' I am no one, but as 'my father's son', I am of consequence. This pattern is repeated in later life - 'as a solitary individual' I do not count, but 'as a member of an esteemed regiment, profession, or nation', I rate. In later life, as in early childhood, we invest ourselves in others and see those others in us. We live through our profession, our nation, or - and this is what I am coming to in this paper - 'work'. It becomes 'our profession, our nation, our work'. The work will be ours because we will have put ourselves into it.

This transaction of the self with the non-self involves loss as well as gain. The loss is the loss of our autonomy. The child takes into himself a will other than his own (his parents or those around that control) and so gains a conscience - an alien voice within that, alas, he may come to love. But there is not only loss there is also gain. Gain that is complex and unexpected.

We are granted two victories - the victory of defeat and the victory of forgetting. The first of these allows us to identify with a power that triumphs over others and so will hereafter be called the 'victory of triumph', the second and greater victory allows us to relegate into the unconsidered that very power. This victory will be referred to as the 'victory of solitude'.

The 'victory of triumph' is fairly straightforward: through our identification with St George, we can see his victory over the dragon as a victory of our own - just as in later life, we will be able to see the victory of that other heavily idealized social entity, England's football team, as something for which we can modestly take part of the credit. Vast vistas of splendour in later life are thus opened up - the standing of our nation, the university or car - all these and an infinite amount of other paraphernalia will allow us the illusion of an inner triumph. By an identification with that which we revere, we can relegate into insignificance those entities that are beyond the orbit of our concern. Rival authorities, rival gods, nations, football teams will not 'count', they will not count because, safe in our loyalty we can afford to ignore.

This gives us a glimpse of our second victory - the 'victory of solitude', and the irrelevance of the other. The child, in identifying with the parent, may not just relegate into insignificance that which is beyond the parents concern - in a queer and yet important way, he may relegate that source of authority, the parent himself, into the limbo of the unconsidered. For if the parents' demands upon the child can be, through identification, internalized as the child's own demands upon himself, then can that very parent - oh! subtle triumph - be anticipated and so reduced. The anticipated can be subsumed under current assumptions, and so ignored. This second victory - the 'victory of solitude' over the ideal itself where the ideal is rendered irrelevant since it has no further hope to surprise - is also seen in later life. It is, in my view, the basis of ritual. For through the ritual of solemn ceremony we can recreate our gods anew and, through our performance of the demanded obedience, deny to them once again the right to demur. (2)

So much for the infrastructure of our childhood. Most of us do not escape it for very long and, at least in my view, we have now all the apparatus that is necessary for a discussion of an adult's guiltless claim. However, for the sake of completeness, it may be worth briefly mentioning the last stage of development -

the stage I have called the Awakening. This stage witnesses the loss of justification and the growth of doubt. (3)

From about four or so, children come to play more and more together in groups. They come to associate, in other words, with those who are in the same position as themselves. This has never happened before - for so far the child has either been alone and indifferent to reality or has been preoccupied with the parent whose actions are incomprehensible and so revered. This is now changed. The child can consort with those fellow children who manifestly live in the same world as himself. As a result the child can 'take the role of the other', 'see his point of view' and - what he could never do with the parent - observe the operation of external pressures. Child A can 'understand Child B's position' because Child A can see the difficulties that beset Child B. In other words, can see how another child is acted upon - how, in psychological terms, he is a 'dependent variable'; how, in human terms, he is vulnerable, weak, in need of support. Presented with the comprehensible we can afford to be charitable.

The birth of understanding is frequently the birth of compassion. The lessons learned from the child's play can have an effect far beyond what might be thought plausible. To 'understand' is to understand the antecedents thereof; where we know more about delinquency (i.e. become aware of its psychological, social, physiological, etc. antecedents) so do we become more compassionate and tolerant, less punitive and absolute in our animistic assumptions. We have Awakened (to use the name I gave this stage of development) to the existence of a blind external causality that cannot be changed by anger; we are wiser, sadder - and nicer - men.

However, this should not concern us too much - at least here. In this paper we need not consider the wise and the tolerant, we are concerned with the assertive and the self-justifying. For a person to feel he is 'right' in any absolute sense, or that he has 'rights', we have to go back to a more primitive apprehension of reality. We are concerned with Paradise, not with any Awakening.

All stages are present in us simultaneously - we are all part anarchic, part weak, triumphant and compassionate. But of these qualities the third is the most important. For it is in our relationship to our idealized authority that we find justification - assertion without guilt and acceptance without resentment. In particular, the third stage is important for it is the basis in early life of 'group sentiment'. A 'group' in the terms of this paper is an assemblage of men that use each other's presence to facilitate their return to Paradise. Fellow group members worship the same authorities and so allow each other the illusion of an extended control. Where others around us revere the same gods and shun the same enemies, there can we be reaffirmed in our belief that our gods are potent and our enemies of no concern. The idealized victory of Paradise Regained can be spread wide and triumphant on the social scene. A 'group' in other words, allows us the 'victory of triumph' and defeat of the other.

But a 'group' can do more than that. In the obedience of our fellow group members to the dictates of the group we can attain a 'victory of solitude' and so come to ignore those very group members. For in the obedience of others (just as we could in the consistency of our parents' demands) we can reattain that yet earlier state of primitive Paradise where none existed except ourselves. All that is needed is that the other obey. Both our 'victories' are dependent upon obedience. Odd as it sounds, of paramount importance for any willing accession to group demands is that these demands be enforced.

Groups are important in real life for they are the basis of morality and felt due; before proceeding with some of the other implications of group membership though, two further points must be made - points that bring home the relevance of what we have so far discussed.

In the first place it should be evident that the entire programme from Paradise to the Awakening, can be seen in terms of the fluctuating status of morality and 'reality' in the face of varying 'power' situations. The earliest situation gave us the illusion of power, the second the loss of power, the third the sense of power regained at one remove. Where power is regained there do we consider 'good' and 'real' the source of such a power. The last stage, that of the Awakening, can also be seen in power terms - but negatively. It is the one in which we acknowledge the powerlessness, not just of the self (that occurred at the second stage) but of the idealized other to boot. There are now no backs on which to climb, our heroes are as lonely, frightened and in need of support as we. Hence our escape from a morality of power. Where we have lost all hope, there are we no longer envious. There can we afford to comfort.

In the second place - and of course crucially for this paper - both morality and power can be looked upon in terms of property. Psychologically, 'property' can be seen as that which is an extension of the self. That with which we have identified is 'ours'. This identification need not just be with material wealth. As Iago explains to Othello, one may well value most that which is most abstract. Iago disdains money, or says he does, because it can also be owned by others:

> Who steals my purse steals trash; 'tis something, nothing;
> 'Twas mine, 'tis his, and has been slave to thousands.

and so prefers that which can only be his and his alone:

> But he that filches from me my good name
> Robs me of that which ... makes me poor indeed.
>
> (Act III, Scene 3)

The 'best' and 'highest' forms of ownership are, by this argument, those that reflect the most inalienable bonds - and are seen to do so. The parent whom we have internalized is 'our' parent, the country whose commands we obey is 'our' country - the only country that really 'counts'. But whether transactional, like money, or unique to itself, like one's good name, the notion of 'property' implies a preoccupation with the self and an indifference to the claims of others that is implicit in the whole notion of power that has been here expounded. Where an object is 'ours', there do we control guiltlessly - and deem such control 'good'. And when do we feel we own? This brings us to the central point of the entire paper - we feel we own when we feel we control. 'Ours' implies 'my' and 'my' implies an extension of the self. Legally it maybe that the notion of property is held to rest upon certain anterior rights, psychologically, there is a strong case for inverting this. Property precedes morality - we consider 'ethically ours' what we feel to be 'practically ours'.

Hence, to come back to them, the importance of groups. Groups are important socially since they are the determinants of consensus. A 'consensus' can be defined as the 'willing' accession to controls on the part of those that use that particular set of controls for their own inner psychic needs. A 'group' indeed can be seen as a collection of men who use each other's public behaviour for their private ends. Where there is a consensus, there will there be peace, where not, there all too often, will there be war. Fellow members are at peace with one another since they recognize the validity of each other's rights and claims. This again highlights the difference between the legal and psychological approaches, for, whereas legally ownership would appear - at least to the layman - to be of its very nature mutually exclusive ('mine' means 'not yours'), psychologically, the reverse is true - possession (in any adult group at least) is corporate. 'Mine' implies 'ours'. This is not to say that group members may not have their individual possessions, but that this individuality is not resented since the basis or justification of these possessions is considered corporate. Thus I will not resent your owning a house that is not mine provided you paid for it - that is, justified your possession in terms of a morality - payment - that I accept. Your possession meets the demands of 'my' morality. Where this is not so, had you not bought your house, for instance, but inherited it, then, when inheritance is not part of 'my' morality, would I claim your possession invalid. Then would we have war.

'War' implies coercion, not consensus. It can be seen as the arbitration of naked (as opposed to idealized) power amongst those who do not share the same gods. Some, indeed, may prefer 'war' - at least out of the matrix of relational comparisons there is greater hope for change. Nothing, by definition, is more permanent than value. However that may be, a discussion of the nature of a 'group' is useful in that it shows us how consensus is based on power - how agreed 'rights' and 'ownership' are acceded to by an individual to the extent that they accord him the illusion of an extended control and a heightened 'significance'. Groups vary enormously in size and composition (nations, professions, religions, drinking clubs, sewing clubs, bridge clubs - all can classify as 'groups'), group membership is always a question of degree (we all belong to innumerable groups) but, to the extent that there are consistent demands, that are enforced and obeyed, there can there be group life, there can we reinforce our sense of 'ownership'.

We have now discussed the psychological background to the sense of ownership in sufficient detail. The kernel of the argument so far can be simply stated as 'we feel we own where we feel we control'. Not where we really control but where we feel we control - such a feeling either coming from a real mastery or from the purely illusory sense that there is no barrier to our will, no occasion to Awaken into doubt. At the beginning of this paper I said that the psychological assumptions that would be made were that man was a self-maximizing animal inhibited by unreal fears and seduced by unreal victories - it should now be clear that one of such victories is the sense of having a 'right' to 'ownership'.

So much for the psychological background, now for the work situation. This will be taken in two parts. First I shall deal with the worker alone with his work, then I shall deal with him as a member of a group.

There are two conditions under which a person may well come to feel that he owns his work. These two conditions reflect the two victories already mentioned - those of triumph and solitude. The first of these is that he makes decisions about his work, the second, that he is left alone.

Where we make a decision, there do we 'put ourselves into that which we do' and so feel an identification and a sense of ownership. Here a sense of ownership springs straight from a sense of control. Locke expressed something of the same sentiment when he said that 'property' should be considered as 'that with which a man hath mixed his labour'. Where decisions are made there are the stakes raised - for not only do people work harder for their pride is engaged, they are by the same token more resentful of criticism and the more reluctant to change. The importance of decision-making has of course been stressed on innumerable occasions. It underlies the emphasis put upon 'consultation' and 'democratic leadership', it is taught in most human relationship training courses and written about in most chapters on leadership and man management. The opposite of 'identification with' something can be seen as 'dissociation from'. A man 'dissociated from' his work will be indifferent to it, will see it purely as a means to an end - the pay he gets at the end of the week - will take no pleasure in it and cannot be given offence. Frequently enough this feeling occurs when the work is felt to 'belong' to another' - 'my victory will be his'. A graphic account of this state of mind comes at the end of the 'Loneliness of the Long Distance Runner' by Alan Sillitoe:

> I only want a bit of my own back on the In-laws and Potbellies by letting them sit up there on their big posh seats and watch me lose this race.... When I hit him [the governor] in the only place he knows he'll be sure to get his own back on me for not collaring that cup when his heart's been set for ages on seeing himself standing up at the end of the afternoon to clap me on the back as I take the cup from Lord Earwig or some such chinless wonder with a name like that.

Elliott Jaques has argued that the degree of discretion permitted in any particular job is of such overriding importance that it determines what is felt to be equitable in terms of pay. (4) Whether we accept this estimate or not there can be no doubt that the pattern of decision-making in any particular organization has a profound effect upon the quality of relationships within that organization.

Here we find ownership and identification springing from a sense of triumph and mastery. There is an external environment and that environment is overcome. The second determinant of a sense of ownership can be said to be in a sense the opposite of the first. It is still dependent upon power, for power is of the essence here, but it is the sense of power that follows an undisturbed peace rather than the sense of power that comes from conquest. Here we find something resembling the 'victory of solitude'. Time in and of itself will legitimate. Those left alone will feel they own. This is the common law of 'custom and practice' and squatters' rights. Nor need we be in any way superior over the attempt of the dispossessed to stake a quasi-legal claim: we all of us need a continuing ground to our existence and a sense of ownership here is the grateful sense of certainty of those that have overcome their fears of interruption and so can return to a world where none others 'count'.

I should now like to discuss the complications caused to a sense of ownership by membership of a group, for it is in a group that the most extreme examples of our psychological 'victories' can be found. Before discussing worker groups, though, I shall first describe a more extreme case of occupational ownership - namely that which occurs with the professions. Professional groups have more power than worker groups but are otherwise much the same. They therefore behave like others would like to if they could. As a result they give us a pretty good 'ideal type' for purposes of exposition.

Clearly they are a 'group' - at least as defined here ('an assemblage of men that use each other for their return to Paradise'); they feel that the idealized dignity and status that comes from their membership grants them certain unquestioned 'rights' and so allows them to remould their psychological ambience closer to the heart's desire. To say that they 'own' their work (i.e. that doctors 'own' the practice of medicine) is virtually redundant since 'ownership' implies at least the possibility of dispute.

The professions are pressure groups that have arrogated certain areas of work to themselves. Three questions are of interest here - how have they gained control? how have they justified such control to themselves? how do they gain acceptance from others?

Professions have gained control by power. They have emerged where an alliance of those that share the same interests has been able to form. Hughes (5) has shown in the case of Real Estate Operators of Cook County, Illinois how, over time, and through increased wealth, the 'respectable' elements united and forced out those who would not conform. In this case study we see gradually emerging the development of reciprocal sanctions and control that is characteristic of all such bodies. The sanctions are all too often those that impose a united front on the outside world and so deprive the public of the leverage of choice - advertising is frowned upon, entry is restricted and, in some cases, through the provision of advanced examinations, promotion is determined from within. The power position of the older professions was even more fortunate for they were able to supplement these features of internal control by the advantageous position they occupied in the community. Thus doctors and lawyers were 'fee-paying' and so were independent - at least from anyone large enough to threaten them. The clergy and the universities (if they can be said to count) were dependent - but only on there own kind. All these professions were favourably situated and could establish themselves. Teachers were never so fortunate - all too frequently they were dependent upon some alien body for support - with the financial results that we all know so well.

Nothing succeeds like success. Once a profession is established, then will further factors conspire to reinforce the sense of ownership. Only professional men will now make decisions, for only professional men will be allowed to make decisions; further, professional men, once secure in their acceptance by the general public, will become ever more confident and justified in the practice of their occupational 'rights'. Thus will corporate membership reinforce the two conditions that, I argued, would give an individual alone in his work a sense of possession.

Corporate membership can give us more than this though. It can also provide a leadership and a hierarchy (though this clearly applies more to some professions than to others) and so can give us our idealized leadership in corporeal form. Where our leaders are distant, there may we revere. Distant, moreover, we shall ensure that they will be, for as one of Shaw's Maxims for Revolutionists from 'Man and Superman' declares:

> No age or condition is without its heroes. The least incapable general in a nation is its Caesar, the least imbecile statesman its Solon, the least confused thinker its Socrates, the least commonplace poet its Shakespeare.

In creating our gods, we create the conditions that allow us to return to an earlier Paradise. In this, group membership helps - creating gods is helped by help.

This question of leadership brings us to the second problem raised by the existence of the professions as a body. How can they justify to themselves the rights they have assumed? How can they be a state within the state - with their own laws and systems of enforcement - and not feel guilt for what one might think were the near treasonable rights they assume over their fellow citizens? This should be a problem - if the law of the land came first, like it says it does. But of course it does not - for justice, justification, a sense of 'rights', along with an individual's sense of identity and the ideals he pursues - are group based. In the beginning was the group. It is all we can do to love our neighbours and it is quite impossible to love our enemies. Most of us will only grant 'freely' our consent to the 'rights' of others where we can see the vindication of these rights as the implementation of a system that we have taken as our own. 'Rights', 'duties', penalties and demands, provided they are enforced - and consistently enforced - can then justify and make us armoured to external attack.

Hence the importance of a professional hierarchy - they are the agents of control and the repository of corporate idealism. Someone must police and be seen to be justified in doing so. This brings us to our third problem. Why, if this be so, should anyone else - anyone outside the group - put up with such pretensions? Why does the public tolerate in its midst groups that feel so exclusive that even going in politics - surely a reputable vocation for any democratic citizen - is frowned upon since it might compromise their 'independence of judgment' (6) (and presumably imply that other values have value)? The answer to this question is of great interest and provides the most ironic of all the consequences of the approach I have taken.

To some extent such bodies are accepted because they cannot be helped. Since they are there we may as well take the sting out of our impotence by claiming they have 'rights'. Anyway, who knows, we may belong to a group ourselves and so have a vested interest in the very notion of corporate autonomy. This is true, but there may be a more interesting reason besides, namely that, in becoming organized, in the very arrogation of power cloaked in the guise of unexceptionable 'rights' and 'duties', they may well provide the general public with a condition under which they may be discounted. This sounds absurd but follows from what has been said, for the public, although - goodness knows - they will gain no 'victory of triumph', will none the less gain a 'victory of solitude'. Where the professional man can be relied upon - and 'trust' is of the very essence of a professional man's capital in the eyes of others - there can their code of behaviour be anticipated and so ignored. As we have seen members of a profession can in some sense ignore each other - at least where they are confident that the rules are enforced - how much more readily then can those outside the group ignore! Professions will attain the status of that which is 'there' - taken for granted, a body of men whose very assertiveness is necessary for our sense of continuity.

Squatters' rights - the legitimating powers of continuity - is more than something that occurs with difficult unions on a shop floor. It can be seen to be (or at least has been argued to be) (7) the very bones of society, the prime determinant (more important than any idea of abstract justice) of larger social cohesion. Further, all three problems set by the existence of a profession - how they gain their position of strength in the community, how they justify such an arrogation of power in their own eyes, how they justify such power in the eyes of others - depend for their resolution upon the existence of an internal code internally enforced.

Thus do we return to Paradise - through the essential conservatism of our loyalties and codes. Groups - all groups - are at heart conservative and reactionary. A 'group' is a self-determining system or it is nothing. To dare, to innovate, is not just to risk failure, it is also to risk being considered trivial.

So much for the professions. Now the point of talking about them at such length is simply that, being unencumbered by external restrictions, they show us how others would behave if they could. The only remarkable thing about the professions is their spectacular success. William Gomberg (8) is in my view misleading when he states that the unions have evolved the notion of 'work rules' as a protection against the demands of management. He is misleading because, at least by the thesis advanced here, all groups would have behaved like that - conservative and assertive - anyway. Indeed it is quite possible to argue that, were it not for the strength of management, worker groups would have been very much more like the professions - more conservative, assertive, successful - and acceptable - than they are.

Workers are no nastier than doctors, nor, for that matter, are they any nicer. Workers, organized or unorganized, are just people. Everything that has been said in this paper so far is therefore relevant to them: workers who are allowed to make decisions at their work will come to feel more possessive of that work, workers who are left alone and so have come to take their work for granted will also when threatened resent such interference. To the extent that they can organize themselves successfully - that is become a 'group' and so impose their corporate will upon each other and upon the outside world - so will they gain an enormous accession of self-righteousness and acceptability.

But it is here that all too often we can fault them. It is this that we cannot forgive - worker groups may not be powerful enough to appear inevitable nor old enough to appear venerable. As a result we may resent and consider illegitimate their claims to autonomy. 'What right', we ask, 'have they, to make claims as they do?' - claims for the ownership of work, claims to enforce a closed shop and to resist innovation. We resent these pretensions - pretensions we should expect from all groupings and which, in the case of the professions, we have come to accept - simply because we have not as yet resigned ourselves to their inevitability. Their conservatism and internal discipline is as yet haphazard and, the worst of all crimes, too recently acquired. Victory and defeat would both lead to acceptance, it is the issue being in the balance that disturbs our rest. Were the unions strong enough to control themselves, there would we accept the 'triumph of solitude' they could afford.

It may be that the worker battle may never be wholly won and that total legitimacy may never be finally attained, for, despite their very great potential strength, there are certain flaws in the workers' position that may always lead to an underlying weakness in their composition, a weakness that will lead to doubts in the minds of others. No doubt several reasons for this could be adduced but only two will be mentioned here. In the first place, and crucially, workers cannot give each other as much support as can the members of professions. Those in the professions who are employed in organizations (such as those in the church, the universities and the army) promote each other. Even the teachers do to some extent (many local education subcommittees being 'lay' in more than one sense of the term) but workers are usually employed by alien organizations where promotion means removal from friends and colleagues, removal from the union itself.

A small minority may make a career in the unions, but for the greater part, worker groupings have few powers of patronage. Life in such groupings can hardly become a 'way of life' - not unless one fails, that is. Thus worker groups, official and otherwise, are always in danger of losing their most energetic and successful members. Thus are they simultaneously shorn of much of their professional hierarchy - a hierarchy vitally necessary for their internal cohesion - and left with those whose allegiance is tainted by the awareness of failure. Those who are left will feel the defiance of those who know that others have won. It may be that trade unionists had more dignity in the past when there was less hope and so were forced to look amongst their own to find someone to idealize.

The first weakness of the worker groupings - their inability to grant their more capable members sufficient support to warrant their continued loyalty - is cast with the sharper relief by their second and complementary weakness - their exposure to demanding, unsatisfactory, and transient work. Workers quite frequently are given, since there may be great division of labour, but part of a technically evolving process. This simultaneously destroys their interest in the work (since the work is so simplified that all decision-making is obviated), weakens their bargaining position (since they will have lost what all groups seek, the dignity of permanence) and yet renders their efforts to deal with the situation the more captious in the public's eyes. For technical change is not only unsettling, all too often it pits union against union. There is nothing that excites our sympathy less than the internescine squabblings of an alien faith and the public, bewildered by these upstart claims, will react in dismay at the self-centredness of the rival unionists' demands; forgetting, in the process, the self-centredness of their own.

The professions are more innocuous and have less to lose. They are more innocuous because their demarcation disputes were settled years ago and, although quaint, are now almost venerable; they have less to lose because their membership - short of a radical unfrocking ceremony (and not even then in the case of Catholic priests) - grants them certain inalienable rights. Once doctor, always a doctor, however long ago he qualified. The unions have the bad luck to inhabit less of a backwater. Confronted by technical change - change that can be painful in its own right - their squabbles are repeatedly encouraged to break out anew. Their claims are perforce new and so will appear illegitimate. This is unfair for their lot is harder than that of a professional man. A worker is granted no inalienable rights - not at least in practice: once rendered redundant, he may lose his livelihood altogether, just one more victim of economic change. No wonder they are so repeatedly hostile to innovation: those that are weak are more in need of support and by the same token, they will be the less likely to get it.

Morality - at least for those that have not Awakened - is the luxury of those that have attained power. In our discussion of the 'rights' and 'wrongs' of worker ownership we may very well be doing little else than refine the implications of a set of moral postulates that our own background - as conservative as anyone else's - will not allow us to question. As individuals we may to some extent escape from the closed circle of the self-evident, but society as a whole - that largest of self-compensating systems - will probably never lightly forego the pleasures of moral continuity. For those who are successful will, through their control of those legitimating agencies of parliament and the law courts, be able to elevate their point of view to the status of an absolute. There it will reign, above the fray and inviolate, a moral lever in the hands of the pure, the timid and the assertive, until the fullness of time grants us another set of self-evident truths.

Of such truths, the sense of ownership - who should possess what - is one. What today is taken as an outrageous demand may tomorrow be granted a respected position in our system of property rights. It has been the object of this paper to show some of the psychological and social mechanisms that would underlie such a change of heart.

Before stopping altogether, I should like to point out one moral that may have a wider application. What I have attempted to do is to show how a criterion may evolve, how the standards used for making judgments come into being. This surely has a lesson for science in general - not just for the social sciences where discussion of such value-laden matters as 'is conflict a good thing' is constantly vitiated by the fact that the standards we use to make our assessments are themselves the product of the society we are trying to judge, but also elsewhere. Is not the criterion always more important than the evidence, the measure than the measurement? Where there is no agreement on the measure how can there be agreement on what is measured? The prime question in science, then, must always be what determines our choice of criterion - the conditions under which we consider data permissible, our notions of a 'fact'. In psychology we have had the disputes of the Behaviourists and the Gestaltists on this issue and such a conflict of orientation is basic to the continuing division between Psychoanalysts and Experimentalists - those that sense and those that divide. Whether a resolution of this problem is possible I do not know. Perhaps science - the pursuit of the inevitable - will remain a matter of choice. All we can say is that in the study of the ownership of work we can get some insight into the conditions under which men will feel that they do or do not have the right to decide.

NOTES

1 It would be difficult to give any one reference for the approach given here, since my account is somewhat abstracted and eclectic. However the ideas on Paradise are based on those of the psychoanalytic school. See, for instance, the chapter on the Projection of the Super Ego, in J.C. Flugel, 'Man, Morals and Society', Penguin, Harmondsworth, 1959. The part on Awakening, though, has been derived from a different source - that of Jean Piaget (see note 3).

2 That 'ritual', the ultimate social act, is for all that a lonely act, is one of the points I make in my paper The University Seminar and the Primal Horde, 'British Journal of Sociology' June, 1967 (chapter 4 in this volume).

3 This section directly stems from Piaget; see 'The Moral Judgment of the Child', Routledge & Kegan Paul, London, 1960, especially the end of the first chapter and the end of the last chapter.

4 Elliott Jaques, 'The Measurement of Responsibility', Tavistock, London, 1956.

5 Everett, Charrington, Hughes, 'Men and Their Work', Free Press, Chicago, 1958.

6 That sociologists and economists might want to go into politics, that social workers might want to engage in social action, that university scientists might be asked to do secret work for the government, that an architect might be on the board of a building firm - all these have been considered as involving the professional man in a 'dilemma' of divided loyalties. See Timothy Raison, In Defence of the Professions, 'New Society', 18 August 1966.

7 By me. Freud and Social Class, 'British Journal of Sociology', March, 1965; Freud, Piaget and Democratic Leadership, 'British Journal of Sociology', June, 1965 (chapters 1 and 2 in this volume).

8 William Gomberg, The Work Rule Problem and Property Rights in the Job, 'Monthly Labour Review', June, 1961; reprinted in 'Labour: Readings on a Major Issue', edited by Richard A. Lester, Random House, New York, 1965.

Chapter 4

THE UNIVERSITY SEMINAR AND THE PRIMAL HORDE
A study of formal behaviour

In this paper I hope to show that the myth of the Primal Horde is of use in that it:

1. helps to account for behaviour that is observable at formal meetings,
2. sheds some light on the earlier socialization process (and by this I do not just mean that the oedipal situation is a repetition in miniature of an earlier social event), and
3. can give us some insight into the operation of wider social groupings.

This obviously is a formidable task, beyond the scope of any one paper. All I can really do here is to show some of the implications of the approach I am suggesting.

I shall spend most of this paper dealing with the first and I do hope the most illuminating of the problems I have set myself - a discussion of what occurs in small-scale ritualized meetings. I shall here discuss the university seminar of the formal kind where there is a chairman and sometimes a vote of thanks. I shall hope to show that the myth of the Primal Horde not merely explains what goes on but can even be said to describe to some extent behaviour at such meetings. Later in the paper I shall extend the implications of this approach to the second and third headings mentioned above: I shall also attempt to show how the ideas first used in the context of the university seminar can be (arguably) applied to formal settings that are apparently very different - namely those of the military parade and the religious service. But first, the myth.

Freud postulated the 'scientific myth' of the Primal Horde to account for the birth of society - and a good deal else besides. Reduced to its essentials this myth assumes that there existed a pre-social era when living in groups was wholly dominated by a virile and aggressive male. This male, usually called by Freud 'the father', kept all the women - or all the women he wanted - to himself, and forced out all competing males to the fringes of the encampment. This male would eventually weaken and die; he would then be replaced by a younger man whose outstanding physical strength - and presumably sexual desires - encouraged him to usurp the now vacant seat of power.

This state of affairs, wherein the only relief from gloom was provided by the camaraderie of those who concurred in their hatred of the father, continued until an occasion arose when there was no clear successor to the now ailing leader. The old father was on the wane and was in due course killed but none of his potential successors was powerful enough to impose his will upon the rest. A stalemate was reached. It was out of this stalemate, Freud contends, that society was born. The sons, willy-nilly, came to an accommodation amongst themselves. They agreed on what might be called a 'social contract' - that each would renounce his (in any event untenable) claim to succession and would in return receive the renunciation of others. This 'social contract' in Freud's view was the beginning of 'law', 'morality', 'justice' and much else besides.

The surviving sons were bound together by the memory of a common triumph and a common guilt. Their complex attitude to the father - one of simultaneous triumph and remorse - was symbolized in the commemorative totem meal. In the totem meal the death of the father, represented by some sacrificial animal, was re-enacted and the father was slain anew. But if the triumph was repeated so was the expiation, for the ceremony was ostensibly an atonement. The animal that was slain was held in honour and his venerable body, once eaten, not only enhanced those who participated in the feast, but also bound them together in deed. They became in Freud's term, 'commensables': in partaking of the same flesh, they became one substance and one kin. A common reverence for an object of common hatred, a common atonement for an act of common guilt lie with Freud at the very basis of the social contract that is social living.

The 'scientific myth' of the Primal Horde does not end there. At a later stage, Freud argues, the 'longing for the father' led to the transformation of the totem animal into a human god - a god that was held to preside over his own totem feast. This god marked a development over the original totem animal in two senses. He was seen to be benevolent - for the anger once felt towards the power of the father had now abated - and, second, he was seen as himself responsible for the totem meal. This latter is a development of some importance - god, who, it will be remembered, in his earlier form as the 'father' was seen as the victim, was now believed to himself exact the totem sacrifice. The responsibility for killing the animal/god and erstwhile father was his. The sons could now claim that in expressing their aversion and in killing the father/god anew, they were but doing what the father/god himself demanded. The ultimate act of aggression became an act of homage.

So much for the 'scientific myth' of the Primal Horde. Now I am not arguing here that such a Horde ever existed. Whether or not such a Horde ever did exist (or does now in monkey or other societies) is, for my purposes, quite irrelevant. What I am claiming is that this myth has two explanatory features of enormous potency, of sufficient potency, indeed, to account in some measure for that civilized antithesis of primitive relationships - ritual and protocol.

The first of these explanatory features implicit in the story of the Primal Horde is the assumption that power is anterior to and indeed the begetter of morality. The earlier state of society was a non-moral state in which society was ruled by force and force alone. Further, it was out of a force stalemate that morality arose - for each accepted the 'rights' of the others only because he was unable to replace the father. As Freud somewhat drily put it in a footnote (p. 143 (1)), 'Failure is far more propitious for a moral reaction than satisfaction.' The myth of the Primal Horde asserts very clearly that jealousy is at the root of our desire for justice.

The second useful explanatory feature of the myth is that the 'primitive' state of man is one in which society (if it can be called that) is polarized around a 'leader' or father. Man, as Freud stressed, is a horde, not a herd animal. In the beginning was the father. But even when the father was destroyed, he could not be escaped - he returned, first as the totem animal and later as a god. He returned, because, despite the hatred of the sons, he was still needed by them. Indeed, it was out of the collusion of those who hoped to regain their lost father and who relied upon one another for the atonement of a guilt they could not disavow, that a 'group' was born. Thus was the pattern set. With Freud, indeed, there is an imbalance at the basis of all groups, for all groups need - for the maintenance of any 'group' life - the perpetuation of an authority that each one, as an individual, secretly resents.

This basic imbalance is, actually, greater even than might be inferred from what has been said so far, for in a later work, 'Group Psychology and the Analysis of the Ego', Freud argued that it is not sufficient for the leader, around which the group must be polarized, to be dead, a totem animal, or even a god - he must be human and alive. But if he is alive, how then can he be tolerated? Without such a leader, the group - any group - would break apart; with such a leader, flaunting his power and privilege, life is surely intolerable.

I have discussed this point, which in my view has not been adequately explicated, elsewhere (2) and I will not go into any great detail here. However something must be said since I will use the argument later on. Suffice it to say that I accept the instability of the Freudian position and that it seems to me that the leader must, in order to meet these quite contrary demands made upon him, namely simultaneous existence and non-existence, be the same and yet different from those he leads. He must be the same or his existence cannot be tolerated ('Why should you be superior to me?'), he must be different or his preferment cannot be justified ('Why should you - if you are the same as me - be preferred to me?').

But how can this Janus-like stance come about? It could only do so, at least by my argument, if a third party - I have called it the 'Authority' - be invoked, that is at once superior to the leader (and so forces him down into the position of a fellow group member) and yet has a special relationship to the leader - and thus raises him above the ruck of his common followers. This 'Authority' is, in my view, some sort of moral criterion that validates the pretensions of a chosen individual - that endows with 'rights' he who is essentially 'no better than' those over whom he must lead. Thus the moral 'Authority' of divinely sanctioned primogeniture, for instance, will legitimate the preferment of individual A and validate the inferiority of individual B - individuals who, before the 'Authority' has been invoked are equal. A king must be a fellow mortal (i.e. the equal of others) somehow preferred by that Authority God (and so rendered superior to others). The leader is tolerated provided he is raised by an outside source, provided he meets an external yardstick.

For this to work, of course, the Authority must be 'believed in' by those concerned. God may legitimate the relative positions of king and subject - but only to those who believe in God. This third party is an article of faith - and whence the faith? Whence the belief that unites? This I hope to deal with later in the paper.

So much for the apparatus of Freudian theory - pure and what might be called (in the case of my additions) applied. I must now attempt to show how such a myth can be of use.

I will begin with the university seminar. The university seminar (and the reader should remember I am concerned with the formal seminar where there is a chairman and sometimes a vote of thanks) can usefully be seen as a Primal Horde. The leader is the speaker, the followers are the audience. As in the Primal Horde, every member of the audience wishes to dispossess the speaker and become the speaker himself. In this wish he is of course restrained by twin fears - fears of retaliation from the speaker if he attacks the speaker and of the revenge of his fellow members in the audience if he shows any likelihood of succeeding. For they, too, it must be remembered, would like to succeed - they too would like the power and the women that are the fruits of ascendancy. I shall try to illustrate this contention by discussing one of the few areas in which there is any measure of choice left to the audience - that of where people sit.

Of course the language of power and the fruits of victory have changed. It is in belief not force that power resides; derision has replaced muscle as the agent of humiliation ('You are not taken in by that nonsense, are you?', 'You are surely not so naïve as to assume ...?') and, further, I need not remind the reader that the rewards of success are not sexual - not, at least, at any meetings at which I have ever spoken - but exhibitionistic. An intellectual rather than a sexual potency is flaunted before the multitude.

Still a similarity remains - in each case, each is the enemy of all. It is because each is frightened both of the leader and of his fellows that no one will sit in front. No one will sit in front since each is afraid that his hatred and envy of the speaker will take possession of him and that he will literally lose his self control and attack the leader - this will, in turn, leave him open to retaliation by any secret powers the leader may have. Whether or not the leader indeed has any such powers the follower is not quite sure. There must be something to him - even if it is only the knack of being invited to speak at formal meetings. Indeed the follower is enormously ambivalent to the speaker. He cannot tolerate (and of course the closer to the follower's particular expertise the speaker approaches, the more will this apply) the thought that the speaker has been rightly called on to talk - for this but underlines the follower's own inferiority. But, at the same time, he is frightened that if he press his derision too far, he will miss something that a fellow - and now rival - may pick up. This would not do at all - better the leader you know than a replacement from amongst those who were erstwhile no better than yourself. Indeed one of the major reasons why the leader, when all is said and done, is usually allowed to remain in the seat of his pretensions is that he is so useful to each follower in the threat he imposes on everyone else. If the speaker really can speak with authority, this at least acts as a check on those fellow members of the audience who might, in a free for all, get ahead. Better not start a race if one is not sure of winning.

Let us then take the speaker seriously. Let us see what he has to say and incorporate it into ourselves that we may gain from our attendance and indeed become so learned that we may one day supplant a leader who now has no further intellectual treasures to despoil. Alas, here too there are difficulties. For, if we take the speaker too seriously, there is the further danger that this too will lead to derision and attack from another quarter - from our fellow followers. After all, the leader of the seminar, unlike that of the Primal Horde, is very much a temporary leader and very much on sufferance. How can we be so weak that our reserves of doubt are so easily overcome? This is the dilemma that every member of the audience must face - should he or should he not take the speaker seriously? Putting it in the bluntest possible terms - will giving credence to the speaker increase or decrease his own chances of being asked to speak on a subsequent occasion? It is a measure of the difficulty of his position that he may find positively rewarding the approval of the speaker by others! At least it would assure him that there was something there to capture for himself and to deny to others; at least, then, he would be saved from the tawdry resort of standing alert before mangers hoping that the desires of other dogs would reassure him that he had something to lose.

This further source of concern - the fellow members of the audience - gives us another good reason for not sitting in front. For the way out of our dilemma is the classic expediency of scapegoating. If we wish to believe and yet are afraid our credulity will but underline our naïvety then what we must do is clearly - attack the naïvety of others. We must cut the Gordian knot and pour scorn on what others may attain. We must stand aside and deride both speaker and listener alike. There are no flies on the intellectual wide boy, he enjoys the boredom of those who have achieved cynicism. There is nothing new in what he hears - it can all be subsumed under second-hand, shop-worn categories. Since each member of the audience has these feelings to some extent, each fears - rightly - that the others have as well. Consensus is a luxury of civilization, those who return to the jungle of derision must expect attack on all sides. All the more reason then for not sitting in front - for not risking reataliation from the speaker and derision from one's fellows. How much better to join the Doubting Thomases, who - once they have turned up - take up their defensive/aggressive positions along the back, round the sides, and, best of all, near an exit. From there, of course, they can pour scorn upon the speaker and gullible alike, and, by the barbed tones of their ostensibly polite questions reveal their superiority to those to whom alas! they cannot remain indifferent.

So much for sitting and (to some extent) questions - one of the few areas where animosity and hope can still be observed. Most of the speaker's - and the follower's - behaviour has been so encroached upon by ritual that it does not readily lend itself to interpretation in terms of a pre-moral power conflict. However, this development need not delay us too much, for as Freud stressed, ritual itself can be seen as the result of ambivalence - it both enhances and restricts. The leader of the ceremonial group - the queen at the coronation, for instance, or the priest at mass - are clearly surrounded by some quasi-magical aura and yet they are simultaneously wholly emasculated, in that their behaviour is rendered totally predictable. What I shall do now is to take the forms of behaviour that are required of a speaker at a seminar and show how the assumption of an underlying Primal Horde can account for the development of ritual in this particular instance. I shall begin by simply describing the behaviour required of the speaker: later I shall discuss to some extent this behaviour in terms of the Primal Horde.

The speaker must read his paper and the speaker must quote his sources. Surely, it might be thought, these are perfectly reasonable demands. And yet, reasonable or not, what is the effect? The effect of the first is the elimination of the speaker as a human being and the effect of the second is his intellectual castration.

Nothing, in my view, is more likely to reduce one to anonymity than the recital of a predetermined text; those who do things by numbers cannot do things by impulse and by this expedient of reading a prepared script, the discourse is deprived of any of the dangers associated with spontaneity. This, of course, is the very essence of ritual - ritual allows us to see it coming. Again, what could be more reasonable than that the speaker be required to state his sources and evidence? But, reasonable or not, what could more effectively render him neutral as an intellectual force? The speaker is reduced to the level of saying, 'Look, it's not me saying this, it is someone else - it's the data, Pavlov, Freud on the Primal Horde.' In a very real sense, the speaker - who is listened to for what he has to say - is only tolerated because his words are not his own, because - ultimate absurdity - it has been said before.

But this is just the beginning of the ritual demands - demands that in the end result in outright humiliation. The speaker must go further than this. Not only must he consent to the abrogation of his individual assertion and spontaneity, he must roundly declare his delight at the role he is enjoined to take.

This surely is humiliation and no less, for it is difficult to see what greater coercion anyone can exercise upon another than the coercion of required gratification - 'You will do it and like it.' And yet this and more is demanded of a speaker. The speaker is expected to grovel. He must stress what an 'honour' it is for one so 'unworthy' as he to be called upon to speak; how really it is not for him to address this distinguished audience where there are so many on all sides so much better informed, so much more intelligent and downright deserving than he is. For a speaker frankly to declare his dislike of the occasion and the audience is to commit a social outrage not unlike that of taking his trousers down.

Can propitiation be taken further? The answer is 'Yes' - for this is not the end of the road and by a final twist of the knife, and by what one would really have thought a gratuitous and redundant cruelty, the speaker is then not allowed to address the meeting at all - he is expected to address all remarks to the chair. Eminent and distinguished though the speaker may be, yet he is reduced to nothing before the infinitely greater distinction and eminence of the chairman. At one blow the speaker is forced into equality with the members of his audience. He is ground down, he ceases to 'figure' as the Gestaltists say.

The speaker, then, to some extent, may be permitted to speak - but only provided he does not surprise, provided he does not speak for himself, provided he becomes qualitatively indistinguishable from those he addresses and provided he rejoices in his reduction to anonymity.

Now it seems to me that these very onerous restrictions upon the speaker imply considerable underlying jealousy and resentment. 'Yes we will have you, but on our terms,' the audience says. It is the pre-moral competition of all against all - that substratum to social living that the myth of the Primal Horde describes - that in my view accounts for this jealousy and resentment. But I have only been able to do this - to reconcile ordered ritual with an underlying battle of power - by introducing the notion of the chairman. This introduction of the role of the chairman into the discussion introduces a factor that is different in kind from anything that has been said so far. For the chairman does not just restrain and restrict the speaker, he transmutes him. He renders him into a different form of clay - a clay that is indistinguishable from those he addresses. No device could conceivably do more to reduce the speaker to the same level - ontological and moral - as his audience. At the heart of the meeting lies the chairman, dumb and blind though he may be. The remainder of this paper will be largely taken up with explicating this phenomenon.

For phenomenon it certainly is - the office of chairman is a mass of contradictions. He is the source of ontological validity and moral good, he is omnipresent and all pervasive - and yet in a sense he is impotent and, indeed, does not exist at all. The chairman is the only one who counts, his is the only approval that has any real validity. We all speak by permission of the chairman ('Mr Chairman, if you will permit me to remark ...'), and it is because the chairman has smiled that the speaker, feeling 'honoured', must recite his sycophantic formulae ('You can have no idea, Mr Chairman, what a pleasure it is to address this distinguished gathering'). In a very real sense, he is the only one who is really 'there'. All remarks must be addressed to the chair, he is the sole recipient of communication - leader and follower alike are but propitiators before this fount of moral good.

And yet the chairman is impotent. His role is so prescribed that the role of the speaker, is, by comparison, the very acme of unlicensed spontaneity. Further, that ultimate honour we all seek - approval in the eyes of this august source - is the most freely available commodity on the social market. What else can the chairman do - except smile and smile and be enchanted? But there is worse to come - he does not really exist - at least as a man. He is not a chairman, he is just a 'chair' ('All remarks must be addressed to the chair.'). Ideally he is not only seen and not heard - he is not seen at all. He may be incarnate but he is a kind of incarnation of the disincarnate. He is a totem figure - he would be better up a pole.

Can these contradictions - omnipotence and impotence, ultimate reality and non-existence - be reconciled? I believe they can and I shall now attempt to do so. Before doing so, though, I can hardly forebear to point out that the role of the chairman is a beautiful example of the 'Authority' or third force that I posited as necessary (provided the initial Freudian presuppositions were accepted of course) for the maintenance of stable group life. The 'Authority', I argued, resolves the dilemma that we need a leader for the existence of anyone favoured above us by the introduction of a third force above both leader and follower alike. And so it turns out here for the Authority of the chairman elevates the speaker above the others whilst stressing the essential similarity to the others. Before the chairman, the speaker is but a fellow participant - by his accolade does the speaker gain licence to speak. But what is this phenomenon, the 'Authority'? I must now try to explicate this oddity - an oddity which lies at the heart, in my view, not just of formal meetings but of all formal social occasions.

What is at once omnipotent and impotent? The answer is, of course, a foot rule. A foot rule is wholly passive but, once invoked, provides us with an answer of total finality. The same goes for any measure, criterion, law, or system of morality. All these owe their very existence - i.e. their non-circularity in any specific context - to their independence of that which they are called upon to judge. Indeed a measure that did not have this total omnipotence within its restricted area, that is, that was itself influenced by what it measured, would be discarded - or, to say the least of it, be deemed unsatisfactory.

So much for the first antinomy, what of the second - simultaneous existence and non-existence, can this be reconciled? The answer, of course, is an immediate 'Yes'. The answer is a projection. We all of us live in a world of illusions and see reality where it is not. We invest women, music, the tenure of university positions - and chairmen, with illusory qualities. Indeed, what is a group but a collusive delusion - an agreement to accept the 'same' self-created fictions, a form of holding hands in the dark?

Such a fiction is a chairman. He is the incarnation of a common illusion, an illusion that unites because it is held by leader and follower alike. But if this illusion is but an impotent yardstick - how then can it unite? It can unite because the initiative for its use is given to one and all - there are none so humble that cannot appeal to morality, there are none so feeble that cannot point (in hope if not in expectation) to the rightness of an external fiat.

It is because 'being moral' is a luxury that can be afforded by all that the therapy of the 'chairman-authority' can work. This third force will allow us to tolerate the existence of those 'better than ourselves' simply because it permits each of us the illusion of himself being the chairman. Each of us can live through him, each can see the obedience of the others as an obedience to the self - the very passivity of the phenomenon allows each to gain his solitary victory. For solitary the victory must be - in a formal meeting no one exists but the chairman, each is alone in the presence of that which exalts those that revere. The explication of these points will, as I have said, take up the remainder of this paper. However, to do justice to them, I shall first have to make something of a detour. A detour that will take us back to the Primal Horde.

The reader will remember that after a while, the anger at the dead father abated and remorse for the deed and longing for the father returned. This longing for the father found expression in the totem meal - a corporate act of atonement that simultaneously reflected the reverence for and the hatred of the father. The father was killed anew, each became part of the father through eating him and yet each could celebrate the ceremony as an act of contrition. Indeed, as I have said, when the human God later developed out of the totem animal, the follower then claimed that the sacrifice was instigated at the God's demands. Thus was the guilt of the follower appeased and thus did, to use Freud's words, 'The scene of the father's vanquishment, of his greatest defeat ... become the stuff for the representation of his supreme triumph.' (3)

But who has really triumphed out of this transformation? Is it God, as Freud claims? or is it, as I shall assert, the worshipper? God may indeed rise again in triumph on the third day, but does not the worshipper gain as much if not more? What indeed has happened - to us who were oppressed and now believe? We have exchanged the arbitrary rule of an omnipotent bully - a bully that deprived us of all satisfactions - for an idealized, benevolent figure that cares for us in his infinite mercy, that allows us to participate in his holy substance (literally) and that will even - if we allow him to - absolve us of any guilt we may feel. He will take upon himself the burden of his own sacrifice. What more indeed can the most sadistic of worshippers demand?

What I am trying to do, the reader will remember, is to account for the importance of the chairman - the position that I hold to be the pivot of group life. This is the position, I have claimed, that allows each to acquiesce in the presence of more potent others, and it does this because it gives to each the illusion of control over those others. Being moral, as I said, is a luxury that can be afforded by all. Now I believe that we can account for the importance of the central concept of the 'Authority' that the chairman exemplifies, if we return to the myth of the Primal Horde and see it not as a paradigm of public atonement, but rather as a model of private triumph. I have already tried to show that the subordinate may be triumphant, I must now try to show that the totem meal can be seen as a private rather than a public enactment.

This may sound perverse for Freud stressed the social rather than the private consequences of the totem meal. The totem meal was indeed the beginning of society ('The sacrificial feast was an occasion on which the individuals rose joyously above their own interests and stressed the mutual dependence existing between one another and their god'). (4) It was out of this common enactment that they became kin - those that had eaten of the same body became one kind. I would not want to deny this, and yet it seems to be that in a very real sense we remain throughout the ceremony of the totem meal - or, indeed, any other, as men apart, each imprisoned in his solitary world of personal omnipotence.

In ritual we are alone. In order to explicate this point I shall have to return once more to the myth of the Primal Horde, only this time to deal with it as an element in the psychological development of the individual, not of the race. Freud did something of the same thing when he used the myth as the original example of the oedipus complex, but I hope to use it in a slightly different way.

In some ways the myth of the Primal Horde fits better into our private unconsciouses than it does into social prehistory. For there is an essential absurdity in the idea of the sons fearing the return of the father they have killed. Why atone when there can be no fear of revenge? But this absurdity on the reality level is, of course, perfectly in order at the phantasy level, and it is as such that I shall treat it here. It seems to me that we have all killed the king - that which inspired awe through the mystery it evoked - within ourselves - and we all, as a result, feel guilt. What indeed is guilt, in this instance, but the dread of a returning avenger? How then, can this guilt be evaded? how can the forces of internal revenge be palliated? Freud's answer is clear on this point - through the totem meal as a corporate act of atonement. With Freud the totem meal is a public penance for a private act, for it is only in this way that the loneliness of the original guilt can be overcome. Freud quoted Robertson Smith here in saying that the re-enactment of deed, 'Can only be justified when the whole clan bears responsibility for the deed'. (5) (Shades of our law courts!) Now it seems to me that this is perfectly unexceptionable. In particular the implication (which I do not know if Freud himself followed up or not) that we are guilty because we are lonely and not that we are lonely because we are guilty, sheds a whole new light on our perception of man as a social being. Having said this, though, it still seems to me that there is no real social behaviour there, that we remain imprisoned within ourselves and act out our lives in the solitude of triumph.

Why should ritual be therapeutic? Why should automatic behaviour that is more reminiscent of the antheap than of any intelligent purposeful behaviour of which a human being is capable allow us to atone; to be reunited with that which is deemed 'significant' - and as a result gain a moral and an ontological respectability? How can such an enactment come to be deemed 'good' and 'real', a reflection of a less transitory existence beyond the cave? This seems to me to be a quite astonishing thing about human beings - almost as astonishing as the fact that no one seems to be astonished by it. The force of ritual, of course, must lie in its predictability - but why should the predictable be so potent? Why, to put it at its most brutal, should time 'honour'? The answer I am giving to this question - and this is the central point of the entire paper - is that where the other is predictable, there can he be discounted. It is only the unanticipated that must be anticipated and where there is no need for such an anticipation we can withdraw once more into the private worlds from which we first emerged. In ritual, the acts of all - the leader and of the fellow followers - can be seen as acts of our own. And what is the drama in which we enact all parts? Who are the characters in whom we variously project ourselves? By this time the reader will have easily guessed that it is the re-enactment of the Primal Horde.

The primal drama - a drama enacted within the solitude of our inner selves - is a drama in which, alone as we are, we must play all parts. This drama is one of power - in ritual we live through the leader and attain the power, and, simultaneously we live through the sons and suffer the indignity of defeat - a defeat that allows us to atone and propitiate the very god we have replaced. Thus can triumph be married to guilt - for, although the obedience of others can be seen as obedience to the self, it can simultaneously be seen as obedience of the self.

This is the ultimate victory we all seek and it is this victory over ourselves that endows ritual transactions in our eyes with their aura of 'significance' and 'morality'. These qualities are the imprimatur of our approval upon circumstance - we deem 'significant' and 'good' that which allows us to be truly ourselves - brutal, callous and alone. For there is nothing pleasant about this morality. I am referring to what might be called the 'morality of conformity' that we adopt as absolutes from our parents: the morality that is based upon an adherence to an external standard. I am not referring to a morality (let us call it the 'morality of concern') that troubles itself with the feelings of others. There is nothing in the least pleasant about this 'morality of conformity' - 'bad' is 'unlike us', the acknowledgment of 'the other' on his terms, not ours. We deem 'moral' in this sense where we can delude ourselves into believing we can control - and we can delude ourselves thus where one condition is met - where we can predict. This, to put it crudely, is why time 'honours'. All we demand of others is that they too conform and so allow us to perpetuate the illusion of our solitary triumph. A great deal of the outrage we feel against he who does not obey - the deviant - is but the petulance with which we attack those that call our unreal pretensions into doubt.

And what are these pretensions but those of the brutal narcissism of a primal leader we all aspire to be? In a sense the more horrifying the brutalities we can predict, the greater the satisfaction we can feel, for it allows us an even greater vicarious triumph. To those to whom this assertion may sound somewhat implausible I would like to point out that the locus classicus of moral respectability - I mean, of course, God - was for long held to have (and may still be by some for all I know) as the main weapon in his war against evil, the institution of hell. Hell - whose brutalities are eternal and wholly self-justifying - was regarded as a moral institution. To say that, by comparison to the orthodox view of Hell, Auschwitz was a convalescent home, is to make the understatement of the year.

I think that part of the confusion here lies in the confusion underlying the word 'power' - a confusion that has led, in my view, to endless difficulty. A man may be powerful in two ways - he may have the fate of others in his hands, he can condemn to death or to imprisonment, or - and this is quite different - he may be above the law. The latter is he who in my view has real power - he is the inheritor of the wilful and capricious primal father, it is he we would all like to be. But this leader is rejected - for he does not give his followers the illusion of control. Those that are beneath the law, however odious the may be, can provide the comfort of this illusion to others. After all, the judge that condemns to death, the warder that flogs the prisoner, are, provided the legal niceties are observed, but carrying out the behest of those others that in anticipation of such a use of force have identified themselves with it before the event. What indeed is the law, when all is said and done, but an apparatus that allows us to predict?

Predictability is all - for it is the predictable that allows us the illusion of control. We deem an act moral because others conform to it. Ritual, the subject of this paper, is but an extreme example of this phenomenon and so more highly charged with 'significance' and 'moral' worth, than more 'mundane' - because less precise - predictabilities, than more 'trivial' - because more adventitious - eventualities.

Thus, to return to our example, provided the speaker conforms to the requirements - reads his paper, quotes his sources, keeps his t's tested and his chi's squared, does not mention people like Freud - or does according to the audience - so will he be accepted. He will be accepted because he will spring no surprises and will allow each member of the audience the illusion that he himself is the speaker - and that the actual speaker is somehow just his spokesman. The audience upon this will set the seal of its approval and feel that the cause of science has been vindicated anew.

So far I have dealt with relationship of leader to follower, what I have not yet done is to discuss the relationship (at least in any adequate detail) of leader or follower to the all-embracing 'Authority'. The problem is an important one for it is only within the framework of a predictable set of categories that the follower can use the public leader to win his private battles anew.

The follower will believe the chairman because the speaker does. In accepting the validity of a code of those we fear and revere, we strike an immediate moral equality with them. This seems to me to be one of the main agencies of socialization - the child accepts not just the parent, but the parent's super-ego. In so doing he gains control over the parent, for he is identified with that which the parent fears. Those that accept the notion of God from their parents can invoke his wrath in return. Morality, to repeat, is a luxury that can be afforded by all. As stated right at the beginning of the paper (the second heading of the first paragraph), the myth of the Primal Horde, as well as telling us about formal meetings can give us an insight into earlier socialization. So much for the follower, or child. In believing in the chairman (or parent's super-ego) he becomes not just the equal of the speaker (or parent) but his superior.

But what of the speaker or leader - why should he conform? This is a much more difficult question, and an answer to it would begin to take us away from such small scale events as the university seminar and lead us to the fringes of wider social rituals. The leader will conform for he too is frightened. He too must propitiate his internal primal father. The result is an ascending spiral that allows in due course an entire society to be absorbed into ritual and predictability. I shall very briefly comment on this extension as my last task - an extension that will justify to some extent the claim I made in the third heading of the first paragraph, and give us a brief glimpse at what I hope are some of the wider implications of the thesis I have advanced here.

The ascending nature of the legitimating nature of the hierarchy is beautifully seen in a military parade - here the same features of ritual and significance can be noted and here we can see tier after tier, level after level, each in turn subordinated. Even the Queen at the Trooping of the Colour is seen saluting. Saluting what? The flag, presumably, or some abstraction that embodies an infinite regress. And oddly enough, in the military parade we can see the essentially moral egalitarianism and the enhancement of the meek that springs from participation in the hierarchical. For the meanest private can also identify himself with the flag and so in a profound sense become 'as good as' the Queen - as good as the god he has consumed. We must first lose our souls that we may gain them.

But is this in itself enough to explain the infinite regress into the evermore 'significant'? Must leaders all feel guilt and so build justificatory authority around them? Surely certain situations must be more propitious for the development of the hierarchical than others and surely it must be those situations that raise simultaneously the greatest doubts in the minds of the leaders and the greatest needs and resentments in the hearts of the subordinates. The most 'significant' will, in the last resort, be the most punitive.

The army is an authoritarian organization - each level is attacked by those above. Thus each level needs at once the consolations of a yet higher level in order to curb those immediately above who persecute them and, simultaneously, they will feel the need to justify, in their own eyes, their own persecutions of those below. The sergeant will need to believe in the 'spirit of the regiment' to act simultaneously as a moral protection against his officers (who must not 'let the side down') and to give him the strength to be punitive in turn to the recruits (who also must not 'let the side down').

All these points come out clearly in the last example I shall take - that of a religious ceremony. A religious ceremony strikingly confirms all I have said about formal seminars - conformity is all, a communication is judged by its source rather than by its content, all is predictable, all is significant. In particular the religious service brings out the essential loneliness of the formal act. For although a religious ceremony is of its essence a social event ('Where two or three are gathered together ...') yet is each alone wrapped in sole communion with his god.

And God? God is the chairman of the religious ceremony. All remarks, as the reader well knows, are addressed to the altar. The leader is the priest, but he is frequently so predictable as to be often enough easily discounted. And God himself, cannot he be discounted? After all God is even more impotent at a religious service than the chairman at a university seminar - God has never lifted a finger at any religious ceremony that I have ever heard of. Should He not then wane in his power through sheer attrition? The chances are, it seems to me, that He will - unless He can re-recruit through an occasional random and arbitrary - that is unpredictable - plague or holocaust.

Formal behaviour, according to the view expressed here, owes its 'significance' to the triumph it celebrates. It must therefore be essentially unstable - for where the triumph is too complete there will the need for defensive morality be dissipated. Where the speaker at a seminar, for instance, is so platidudinous that there is in our eyes no danger that others are impressed, there may we well cease to deem 'significant' that social enactment that has accorded us no victory.

However, it is unlikely that there will be any early end to formal behaviour - and this for two complementary reasons. In the first place formality and ritual is a matter of predictability and predictability must always be a question of degree: the logic argued here should be relevant to some extent to almost all social behaviour. In the second place we all, in varying degrees, carry with us the burden of our primal past; we all in some measure retain the phantasy hopes and phantasy fears of our childhood. As a result we all remain in the loneliness of our identifications and earlier preoccupations and we continue in need of the exaltation and atonement of ordered social behaviour.

NOTES

1 References to 'Totem and Taboo' are from the James Strachey translation published in London by Routledge & Kegan Paul, in 1950.
2 Freud and Social Class, 'British Journal of Sociology', vol. 16, no. 1 (March 1965), pp. 48-67; Freud, Piaget and Democratic Leadership, 'British Journal of Sociology', vol. 16, no. 2 (June 1965), pp. 123-39 (chapters 1 and 2 in this volume).
3 Op. cit., p. 150.
4 Op. cit., p. 134.
5 Op. cit., p. 136.

Chapter 5

THE NATURE OF MORALE

> The term Morale refers to a condition of physical and emotional well-being in the individual that makes it possible for him to work and live hopefully and effectively, feeling that he shares the basic purposes of the groups of which he is a member: and that makes it possible for him to perform his task with energy, enthusiasm and self-discipline, sustained by the conviction that, in spite of obstacles and conflict, his personal and social ideas are worth pursuing.

In this paper I am concerned with the nature of 'Morale' - perhaps the most frequently invoked of all motivational concepts in occupational social psychology. But what is Morale? The frequency of its use would sometimes seem to be only rivalled by the number of different meanings that the term is given. What I shall try to do here is to give some of the kinds of uses to which the word is put and then to show the ways in which these uses can be seen to be interrelated. In the course of such an analysis I shall argue, in the context of a very much wider discussion of group relationships, that the kinds of uses I shall have outlined are, indeed, interrelated and that the confusion surrounding the term is due to the fact that one kind of 'Morale' can lead to another.

But what are these various meanings? The above quotation (which shall remain anonymous) seems to include within its span most of the various ways in which the word is used. I shall therefore use it as an anchor point in this discussion. At least three meanings are implied, and I shall take these three meanings one at a time.

In the first place it refers to what I shall call 'identification with the group goal'. This is brought in when the quotation speaks of an individual 'feeling he shares the basic purposes of the groups of which he is a member'. Later it comes up again when it speaks of a man having 'high morale' being 'sustained by the conviction that his personal and [more to the point here] social ideas are worth pursuing.'

In the second place, and somewhat differently, the quotation implies fairly strongly that the man with high morale is somehow euphoric, or at least is generally hopeful and enthusiastic. 'Morale' is spoken of as 'a condition of physical and emotional well-being in the individual', an emotional well-being that allows him to perform 'his task with energy, enthusiasm and self-discipline'.

Last, the quotation implies that the individual with high morale is not just identified with the group goal and satisfied with his identification, he is also effective. The implication in the passage above that those with high morale work better than those without is fairly clear.

I shall now take these definitions and give them labels. Later I hope to show their interrelationship. First, then, some definitions.

(1) Aims Morale. This is the name I am giving to the first meaning I distinguished in the above quotation - that of identification with the group goal. 'Morale' is frequently used in this sense. It is, for instance, the definition that Viteles (1954) used in his 'Motivation and Morale in Industry'. 'Morale', he quoted, was a state of 'satisfaction with, desire to continue in and willingness to strive for the goals of a group or organisation'. The meaning of this kind of Morale - if it mean anything at all - lies in the fact that the individual renounces his direct, personal, advantage for the sake of the common good. It describes, in other words, a form of altruism. The individual with high Aims Morale is concerned to 'give' and not to 'get', to support the group cause, not to maximize his individual return. Put like this it sounds somewhat extreme - but this is the implication none the less. Indeed if we examine the consequences of this particular state of mind, it is hard to resist the assumption (and I shall not attempt to do so) that the 'group cause' or the 'common good', or the 'group' itself, for that matter, is not only reified, in that it is seen somehow to exist 'out there' in its own right, but also to some extent idealized. The larger whole with which the individual is identified - be it the regiment, the school, the country, etc. - is considered to have a status of ontological 'significance', is venerated and treated with awe. There is a discontinuity between an individual and the qualitatively superior entity, that he is 'proud to serve'. Most of this paper will be taken up with explication of this phenomenon - a phenomenon that, on inspection, turns out to have a very wide application indeed. But this is to come; at the moment I shall give what seems to me to be another common usage of the term 'Morale'.

(2) Progress Morale. This is the name I am giving to the second meaning I extracted from the quotation I began with. This refers to the state of feeling that allows the individual (to quote again) 'to work and live hopefully', performing his task with 'enthusiasm'. This refers to the commonly noted feeling of exhilaration that can come to those who are adequately pursuing a task that is within their powers. Hence the title I have given it, Progress Morale. A sense of failure or inadequacy - defeat in battle, failure in one's examination, can put a very severe strain on Morale in this sense - for it is, after all, basically a state of optimism and hope.

This form of Morale seems to me to be different in one important respect from Aims Morale - Aims Morale, at least as described here, is of necessity a group phenomenon - one must revere something outside oneself - one's God, king, discipline, profession, or institution. Progress Morale, on the other hand, can be either an individual or a group phenomenon - one can get the corporate sense of progress that is known as 'team spirit', but one can get equally well an individual sense of progress or despair. We can talk of a student having 'high morale' or 'low morale' all on his own. He may get up early in the morning, whistling as he greets each day, confident of his First, or he can slump ever further into the Slough of Despond, growing for evermore certain that his present bafflement with his subject-matter will later on be translated into an official verdict.

These are the only two terms I shall deal with, and before rejecting the third distinctions I drew from the original quotation - the effectiveness of those who are committed - I should like to return to Aims Morale for a moment and make a further distinction.

I shall distinguish between what I shall call Vocational Aims Morale and Organizational Aims Morale. In the former case one joins an institution because one already believes; in the latter case, belief is an emergent property, one believes because one belongs.

If one joins a particular school because one wants to 'educate the masses', if one volunteers in war-time because one wants to 'do one's bit', if one enters a religious order because one wants to 'spread the word of God', then, clearly, one's identification with the cause comes first, and one's membership of the institution is an expression of that identification. This I shall call Vocational Aims Morale - the Aims Morale of those who have a sense of 'vocation' or dedication before the event. Such 'prior dedication' may be totally pre-emptive, but, on the other hand, it may be almost totally lacking. Particularly it would seem amongst those who enter a hum-drum concern for the sake of private gain. Who, for instance, would enter a firm because he wanted to 'make biscuits'? Or even (although perhaps this may be treading on more dangerous ground) to 'advance the cause of psychology'? But must we therefore assume that there can be no Aims Morale outside the heady preserves of the remote and the ideal?

I do not think so, and this on two counts. In the first place Vocational Aims Morale must always be a question of degree and so applicable to some extent. If we join an organization we are bound to see that organization as some sort of reflection, however pale, of our earlier authorities to which we may still in some measure be in thrall. Organizations, then, may be respected just because they are there at all. A measure of 'loyalty' may be natural rather than the reverse.

Important as such a diffuse loyalty can be, I shall not be concerned with it in this paper. I shall concern myself here not with the legacy of a moral past, but with the emergence of a morale present. I shall concern myself with the second way that an Aims Morale that is different from any clear-cut Vocational Aims Morale may be of interest to us - I shall concern myself with the development of loyalty to a superordinate cause that is the result of working towards that cause. This form of loyalty, the loyalty that springs out of activity rather than itself determining it, I shall call Organizational Aims Morale. Organizational Aims Morale, unlike Vocational Aims Morale, presents us with a difficulty - how is it possible to become loyal to a superordinate group goal? to abjure one's autonomy and to acknowledge the existence of that which is greater than the self? This, as already noted, is the main problem to which I shall address myself in this paper.

Indeed, the main assumption that I will attempt to spell out may as well be stated here - I shall argue (to put it very briefly) that Organizational Aims Morale arises out of successful group Progress Morale - that dedication to a group cause will arise out of a common striving for that cause. The reader will note that this hypothesis - if it can be made in any way plausible - has the advantage of reconciling within itself the various uses of the term 'Morale'. Indeed, the very confusion surrounding the term will in some measure have been explained - confusion is not surprising when the different meanings of a term can be shown to be causally related.

Before discussing this assumption in any detail though, I should like first to make clear what I shall not be concerned with. This is the third usage of 'Morale' derived from the quotation I began with - that concerning the euphoria and effectiveness of those who enjoy 'high morale'.

Morale is sometimes loosely used to cover a state in which those involved are simultaneously happy and hardworking. This indeed was implied in the quotation I began with where the individual with high morale was said to be working both 'hopefully and effectively'. This type of usage has been particularly common where the 'objective indices' of Morale have been used - lateness, voluntary absence, labour turnover figures, for instance, for 'satisfaction' and output per man hour for 'satisfactoriness'.

I shall not discuss Morale in this sense at all - here I shall be solely concerned with Aims Morale and Progress Morale as I have defined them. There are already two acceptable terms, 'satisfaction' and 'satisfactoriness' and I see no reason why the confusion caused by giving the term Morale indiscriminate meanings should be compounded by me. (The reason it has come about is fairly clear - we can only measure what our measures let us measure and in our dissatisfaction after the event, we are all too prone to deny ourselves this fact: since Morale is 'there' - after all people talk about it - we must somehow have measured it.) It is quite true, in my view, that 'satisfactoriness' and 'satisfaction' can be closely linked (indeed this is implied in the single hypothesis I am advancing in this paper, namely that group Progress Morale can lead to Organizational Aims Morale) but they need not be so and the use of any term which suggests that they somehow must coincide is but leading us into wishful thinking. One can be perfectly happy and not work hard and one can be perfectly miserable and work like mad. One may work like mad seeking an anodyne for a private sorrow or from sheer stark necessity. To claim, further, that this dubious fusion of 'satisfaction and 'satisfactoriness' must coincide in 'loyalty to the group cause' seems to me just silly.

Not only is it silly, because, as has already been suggested, one may work for all sorts of reasons, but also because there is no good reason for assuming very much that a 'loyal' employee - as defined in my terms in Aims Morale - is a better worker than one who is more mobile, more pragmatic and more critical in his approach. Leaders may wish to have 'loyal' supporters for they wish to receive the unearned adulation of those that 'believe' in what their superiors ask them to do, but they may, for all that, be putting greater stress on their own psychological rewards than on the objective needs of the situation. There is no necessary relationship between committal and either satisfactoriness or satisfaction - committal refers only to why you do something, not how much you do or how happy you feel about it. Committal can certainly lead to constancy in the face of adversity (a 'loyal' employee may not leave the firm so soon), but against that it may equally well lead to parochialism, conservatism and a general ossification of the pragmatic spirit. Further - and this may sound odd - it can very well lead to outright insubordination. There are few more dangerous subordinates than those who are more identified with the group cause than are their masters. Such a subordinate, where he feels that his 'betters' are wanting in dedication and application will attack the 'betters' not with a secret guilt but with the relish of those who see the presumptuous exposed. From the point of view of the Pope, Luther took Christianity too seriously.

'Morale' here, will then refer to Aims Morale and Progress Morale. Indeed I am only really concerned with one problem in this paper - Organizational Aims Morale, the nature and derivation of emergent group committal.

So much for the various uses of the word Morale. Before proceeding to the main point of my argument - the explication of my hypothesis that group Progress Morale leads to Organizational Aims Morale - I shall have to analyse the notion of Aims Morale in some greater detail.

If Aims Morale is in any way relevant it is worth taking seriously since it would seem flatly to contradict the notion (particularly dear it would appear to certain of the tough-minded) that man is a self-centred being who indulges in intelligent (as far as he is able), instrumental, 'problem-solving' behaviour in order to maximize his individual returns. To the extent that my description of Aims Morale holds, and to the extent that Aims Morale actually does exist, then man is, by that measure at least, not acting like this. An individual that wishes to 'serve the group goal' in the way I have described fails on both counts. In the first place he does not wish to maximize his direct personal returns, he wishes to 'give' and not 'get' - to 'serve' not to 'make use of'; in the second place, he does not behave in an instrumental, 'problem-solving' way. He wishes to 'give', not 'get' because he regards the group goal - idealized and reified as it is - with awe. For him the apperception of the group goal is abstracted from those relational comparisons that are the basis of intelligence. To treat such a group goal in a rational, instrumental way - i.e. to be loyal out of calculation - is to treat such a group goal with less reverence than it deserves.

What are we then to make of Aims Morale? Are we to consider it but an instance of aberrant behaviour only to be found amongst idealists, largely irrelevant to the general run of men? We might be tempted to answer 'yes' - but before doing so we should pause a little because the state of mind that I have attempted to describe turns out, on inspection, to be very widespread indeed.

If we look a little closer, it turns out to be co-terminous with the concept 'group'; not a 'group' that is a group by geography or ascription (thus an experimenter will put four people round a table and claim he has a 'group', presumably on grounds of propinquity, or again one can define a group in industry in terms of the interlocking roles that one has prescribed), but a 'psychological' group that resides in the loyalties and in the sense of identity of its members. This form of 'group' can be of any size, but however large or small it may be, it can be shown to possess the lineaments of Aims Morale.

Thus to take an obvious example, we have a national 'group'. Certain people feel very strongly that they belong (psychologically) to a certain nation state. This state is reified and idealized in their eyes, they regard it as somehow 'existing' in its own right and they regard it with awe. The state is an entity they are 'proud to serve'. Anyone that tries to maximize his returns in an instrumental way - i.e. goes over to the enemy when he is persuaded that the enemy has a better chance of winning - gets very short shrift. There are few more emotive words than 'treason', 'traitor' and 'betrayal'.

That the same orientation exists towards God as towards the nation hardly needs saying. (God is the most absolute of absolutes, you do not question His existence, nor do you praise Him for something - not if you are regenerate, that is - you 'give praise' and 'serve' Him simply because God is God and it is no more than His 'due'.) What may not be so immediately obvious is that our attitudes are the same in time when we consider such disparate groupings as the profession and the face-to-face 'primary group'. In the professions, too, one is expected to be loyal, and to 'serve'. This 'service', a reflection of a loyalty that may profoundly affect someone's sense of identity, involves again an idealization and a reification ('the standing of the medical profession'), and a suspension of any problem-solving behaviour that implies a preoccupation with direct, personal rewards. A professional man that did so - a doctor who used his standing in the eyes of his patients to maximize his sexual opportunities or a solicitor that did not charge the regulation fees in order to undercut his colleagues - would soon be hounded by those, more virtuous than themselves, who showed a 'proper respect' for the social demands put upon them. This even applies to the face-to-face group. What, when all is said and done, is a swot, a rate-buster, or a deserter but someone who is attempting to maximize, as best he is able, his individual rewards? A deserter very sensibly puts his own life first, a rate-buster, his own purse. What could be more rational - at least if one assumes a primal self-centredness - than that? With the face-to-face group, of course, the idealization and reification of a group as an entity as such is much less clearly seen than with the other example. Still even here the skeleton of such a reification can be perceived. Thus group members may talk about the 'group' as if it somehow existed over and above the members composing it. In the same way people may talk about 'letting the side down' as if 'the side' was an entity in its own right.

Thus there are similarities between states of Aims Morale and what might be called 'ordinary groups' - in both cases there is a 'psychological group', that is idealized and reified in the members' eyes, that evokes sentiments of loyalty and the need to 'give' and to 'serve'. All this can be opposed to the pragmatism of psychologically isolated individuals, who attempt to maximize their individual returns, who try to 'get' not to 'give', who regard the corporate entity, as such, to be an irrelevance. Are there, then, any differences? There are, and we must now look at the peculiar quality of Aims Morale in this respect.

The state of Aims Morale is essentially a 'dynamic' state. The 'group goal' - winning the battle, finishing the corporate task - is a problem that must be solved. Those with Aims Morale face the future - a future that is clouded in doubt. Where the battle is wholly assured, there would the characteristic element of 'striving' be somehow lost:

Onward, Christian soldiers,
Marching as to war.

When the war is won, where will the soldiers march? This is the question we must not ask, for then we would no longer feel the exhilaration of those that rejoice in the enemy being defeated. Aims Morale, in other words, as suggested in the hypothesis, is compounded of Progress Morale - a corporate sense of movement or purpose.

But there can still be committal where the battle is won - but it is a committal of a different order. It is the quiescent 'renewal' of those that have already 'arrived'. This is best exemplified in ritual. Ritual is surely the opposite of Aims Morale. In ritual, one is not facing the future, one is facing the past - a past that holds the moment of our acceptance and decrees how our behaviour should be enacted. There is no 'problem' facing us in the same sense - instead of doubt we find certainty, instead of the clear-cut criterion of success, there is the conformity implicit in cleaving to precedent. The exhilaration of achievement is replaced by the reaffirmation of those who testify their faith anew.

Thus there are two dimensions not one of individual activity. There is the 'commitment - self-sufficiency' dimension that distinguishes all forms of 'group behaviour' from non-group behaviour, and there is also a 'static - dynamic' continuum, that distinguishes between an orientation to the past and an orientation to the future. These two dimensions can be set out as shown in Figure 5.1.

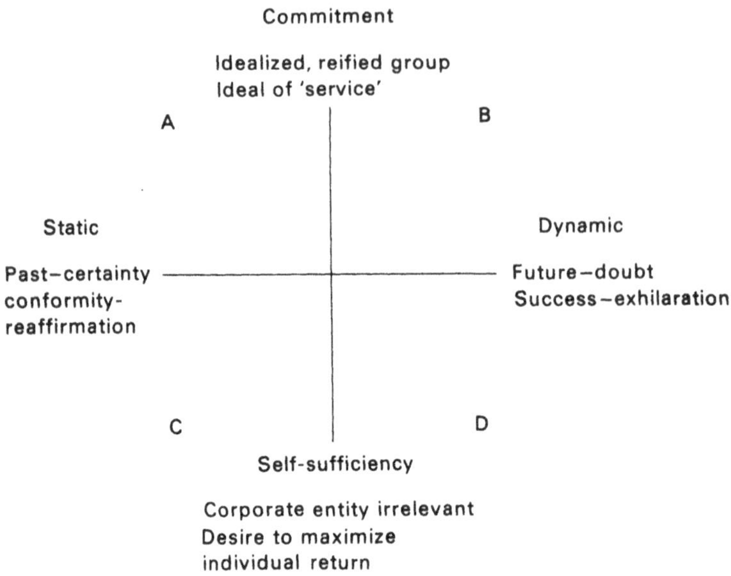

FIGURE 5.1 Two dimensions of individual orientation

Point A reflects pure ritual, point B, pure Aims Morale. Point C gives us an individual indulging in solitary, compulsive behaviour, point D, the pragmatic individual facing the future alone.

Before discussing the problems posed by the existence of these two dimensions, two further observations must be made.

In the first place, a 'group' can find itself, not just in one of the four corners of Figure 5.1, but anywhere on the space described by the two axes - thus none of the four 'ordinary groups' I described would find themselves all the time at point A. A group may find itself on different points at different times. Thus at times of corporate reaffirmation - such as religious services and military parades - groups may well be at position A, but the same group in times of challenge and doubt - the church 'militant', the army 'in war' - will move to position B. Having said this, though, the compound of conviction and pragmatism that probably characterizes all groups may be differently constituted in different cases. All groups (national, religious, professional, and face-to-face, for instance) have their problems and their rituals. However, certain groups seem to be of their nature more 'problem-centred', others, more 'ritual-centred'. Thus it may not be altogether fanciful to regard the Fascist (for all his supermanic pretensions) as one who is nostalgic for a pure and primitive past, while a Communist looks forward to the dawn of a new era. But what happens if the Communist succeeds? 'Doubt' may not last for ever and with 'certainty' a reaction may set in - the successful Communist runs the risk of becoming indistinguishable from the Fascist, defending the status quo for its own sake. Either that or he may resort to such hysterical re-evocation of 'battles-yet-to-be-won' as currently seen in the behaviour of the Red Guards in China.

'Red Guards' are fortunately rare, and most organizations, on achieving success, relapse into the quiescence of ritual. The movement is usually not from B to an evermore hysterical B, but from B to A. In the literature of organization theory, this movement from B to A has been clearly expounded by Merton (1940). In discussing the 'pathology of bureaucracy' he shows how the most 'rational' and pragmatic of all organizational systems (Weber's 'legal-rational' bureaucracy) becomes ritualized through sheer success. Where the problems can be anticipated, so will 'means' become 'ends in themselves'. Bureaucracies are not geared for challenge - there is no challenge left where the work has been adequately codified - they are geared to continuity. Where the future cannot surprise, there can we grow our roots into the past. Torn from the sanction of failure, actions derive their legitimacy from precedent. Filling up the form correctly becomes more important than getting the job done; as a result we can get the total triumph of ritual - every act can become normative, valued in and of itself.

The import of all this for our paper is clearly this - Aims Morale may be something of a sensitive, and even a self-defeating plant: what could be more self-defeating than to be frozen by one's very success? This brings me to the second observation I said I would make. Norms - all norms - are essentially conservative. A norm implies an equilibrium, that is a state of affairs that is psychologically valued in and of itself, and in which there are resident forces that will reassert this balance when the balance is disturbed. Thus, in the 'ordinary groups' I cited - the national, religious, professional, and face-to-face groups - one is not supposed to give 'aid and comfort' to the enemy, blaspheme, advertise, or 'grass'. If one does, sanctions, designed to re-establish the status quo will follow - one will be shot, sent to hell, struck off the register or ostracized. Now the oddity lies in this - a state of Aims Morale, although facing the future and not the past, is none the less heavily normative. One is expected to 'muck in' and 'pull one's weight'. There is a clear code of 'what must be done' despite the fact that 'what must be done', since it is conditioned by an evolving situation, may be constantly changing.

This is odd enough, but there is a similar contradiction in the static situation. Aims Morale is characterized by 'purpose' and 'purpose' implies a future state of affairs that it is intended to reach. (An act is said to be 'purposive' if it is better described by its end point than by any of the specific measures used to attain that end.) Since 'purpose' is forward-looking, ritual cannot be said to have a 'purpose' in the same sense that instrumental, problem-centred behaviour can. And yet - and this is the oddity - ritual is said to have a 'purpose'. Ritual, which in strict learning theory terms can be explained in terms of pure reflex chains, is sometimes said to possess the qualities of more forward-looking complex behaviour.

So much for a description of the problem. It is now high time I turned to explanation. However, I have set myself several further problems since I first explicated the hypothesis I put forward, and the total range of the issues raised is now something like the following:

1 In the first place, and this is where this discussion began, I must attempt to account for the growth of Aims Morale - movement from D to B on Figure 5.1. I must further justify my assumption that this movement comes about through group Progress Morale.
2 But this is but part of movement up the 'self-sufficiency - commitment' dimension. I should also, therefore, simultaneously account for the development of ritual - movement from C to A.
3 Next, I have mentioned a further problem when speaking of the self-defeating nature of Aims Morale - movement from B to A.
4 Next, there are the two oddities I have just outlined - that of B being 'normative' and A being 'purposive'.
5 Finally, for reasons of parsimony (and perhaps cynicism) it would be pleasant to explain the growth of commitment through a 'self-centred' non-commitment assumption. Commitment cannot in any event be explained in terms of itself.

I shall attempt to deal with these problems in two stages. First, I shall be concerned with the vertical axis of Figure 5.1 - the problem of the growth of commitment. Next I shall turn to the horizontal axis, the peculiar nature of Aims Morale and its distinction from ritual. I shall try to explain the growth of commitment in the simplest possible way. I will make the overall working assumption ('hypothesis' is too grand a term) that we are all anarchic and self-centred in our preoccupations, that we are at root indifferent to any higher order law and morality and are primarily concerned to control our environment and maximize our individual returns. (The reader will note that this comes very close to the tough-minded assumption I said was held by certain observers.) Such a narcissism is our ideal - but it is an ideal that, alas, can never be realized. It cannot be so, for we must live in the company of others - others as narcissistic and as self-centred as ourselves. How then can we gain our solitary victory - a victory that we will not be denied? We can do so by forming an alliance with those whom we cannot ignore. With their co-operation we erect a code that is revered by one and all. This code is then identified with and each group member can see such a code as 'his own', as an extension of himself. Each is then granted the illusion that compliance to this code is compliance to himself. Each can gain a vicarious victory and thus can we all reattain, in the bosom of our group, our earlier lost self-sufficiency.

We are reduced to morality. Where we cannot gain our victories alone, there will we erect a common code that prescribes the behaviour, not only of ourselves but of others as well. This code is idealized, for it is seen as an extension of that which we hold most dear - our narcissistic selves. We are then prepared to 'give' and to 'serve' this code for we are but 'giving' to that which is our own. The conflict between primitive narcissism and corporate 'service' can be reconciled if we talk in terms of an extended rather than a bounded self.

A 'group' in these terms will be a collection of people that use each other for the creation of a corporate self-justifying myth. By this argument, 'groups' should arise under certain circumstances rather than others - namely when there is a large enough (or at any rate a powerful enough) number of those present that have an interest in the creation of such a myth. This should occur where people are dependent upon each other but have common interests. Thus we would expect, for instance, a code of restriction of output in a face-to-face group to arise where there are a sufficient number of those present that would fear a genuine state of free enterprise. The fastest worker will not be in favour of such a code, since he would lose money, but the 'average' worker would - he would run the risk of being 'shown up' by those who are better than himself.

This principle has a very wide application. Thus it could not only explain the growth of a 'professional ethic' by exactly the same logic, but it could also account, for instance, for laws against murder and adultery. These laws can be seen as the result of a coalition of the weak - those of problematic physical and sexual prowess - against the strong. After all, what the weak man has to forego is very much less than he gains. He foregoes a problematic right to take the law into his own hands, he gains security from such unilateral behaviour on the part of others.

This code is the inheritor of our primitive narcissism and so it attains that state we all seek - indifference to others. There are none so heartless as those that believe. To each other, group members may well feel a warm sympathy, but this is not surprising for each group member can see the compliance of the other as a compliance to himself; it is in their attitude to those 'who do not belong' that this heartlessness becomes manifest. Our code has the arrogance of an absolute - 'our' law is above all. Those who do not obey - the heretic, the deviant or the alien - must be proscribed (or at best despised) because they call our unreal pretensions into doubt. In a very real sense they challenge our power. Hence the most tragic and common of our failings - our intolerance of those who do not share our convictions

If what I have said is given credence - if there really is a war of all against all, personally self-centred as we are - then suspicion of the other must be endemic. It will only be when we are able to see for ourselves that the other is equally obedient that we will be able to form a relationship with him, and accept him as 'one of us'. This is easy in the face-to-face group - and hence, in my view, its psychological importance, but how will we form such a relationship in the large group, in the national group, the religious group, the group of those who have foresworn murder?

This brings us to the position of the leader, a position of central importance in any account of 'group life'. The leader must 'serve' the code - for an exhibition of unlicensed narcis-sisism is something that we could never willingly accept - indeed he must give so much 'service' that he must become, in a strict sense, its outright 'servant'. The leader is expected before all else to enforce the dictates of the group. Only thus can we have an extended group: we must rely on others - the government, the police force, public opinion - to do our enforcement for us. We rely on the traitor being caught and the heretic being arraigned - by those that we have granted power to do our will. Were it not for this consolation, a larger 'group' could not form at all.

But what of the strongest men of the tribe, the fastest workers - why should they accept a code that can but hinder them in their pursuit of their goal? They will accede because, provided the code is enforced, they may well have no alternative. They may choose to be a rebel against the code of their fellows, but then they must risk the persecution reserved for those who do not obey. Why not join the big battalions if one has no hope of winning? Why not identify oneself with a morality that can in any event not be evaded and see its power, not as an alien force that constrains, but as an extension of one's own will, providing opportunities for a wider glory upon the social scene?

Those that are confronted by an ongoing morality, then, are grievously tempted to join. Those that are forced to go to church will come to believe in God, those that are made to form fours will become identified with the army. A law that is enforced will probably always find its willing adherents. We can even, by this argument, account for the development of morality in the young child. When the parent enjoins, the child will identify - not with the parent but with the code that the parent invokes. (In Freudian terms, not with the parent's ego, but with his super-ego.) In this way the child can repair the disadvantage of his own weakness. By identifying with that which the parent reveres, he can strike an immediate equality with that parent. Where the parent now errs, there can that code be invoked in turn. The mother that comes to table with dirty hands can be greeted with, 'Oh but mummy, you told us we should always wash our hands before meals.' We saw the same point when, discussing Vocational Aims Morale, we spoke there of the difficulties a superior could have when he had a subordinate that was more identified with the group code than he was himself.

In this short account I cannot hope to follow the implications of this account at all adequately. Still certain features of the 'commitment' end of our vertical dimension have been to some extent catered for - we will have a 'group' where we find a collusion in a joint phantasy of power. We will 'give', for we will be but giving to that to which we are intimately dependent upon for the maintenance of our illusions; we will idealize for we will have found, in corporate means, a return to a primitive narcissisism. All the points have been touched on except for reification. Why should we reify the object of our reverence? But surely there is no problem here, what could be more self-centred than to assume that our phantasies really exist as discrete objects in the world of a higher reality? What could conceivably be more narcissistic than to make the jump from 'I like' to 'it is good', from 'I think' to 'it is so'? Reification is but part and parcel of reading the outside world as an extension of the self.

So much for the first problem I set myself, the movement to commitment from self-sufficiency, described as best I could in terms of the explanatory predeliction I avowed - that of an explanation that did not imply an anterior commitment for its force. I must now turn to the horizontal axis and deal with the distinction between Aims Morale and ritual, and the relationship between them. In this account I must also be concerned with the 'oddities' I mentioned - that the two states may have more in common than we have any right to expect - that Aims Morale can be normative, and ritual purposive. I shall first deal with Aims Morale in isolation, later I shall turn to its relationship with ritual.

The development of norms under 'dynamic' conditions - conditions that present one with a problem and where the future is in doubt - must be an exceedingly precarious affair. And this on two counts. In the first place those confronted by a problem must use their brains, they must be resourceful in anticipating the future, they must be prepared to be flexible and to adapt their actions to moving necessities. Behaviour must, as I have already said, be 'problem centred' and, in terms of the end point, rational. Now the difficulty in this state of affairs - where what is 'right' cannot easily be laid down before the event and where conduct must be judged by its results rather than by conformity to procedure - lies in the perennial problem of stilling suspicion. This does not apply to ritual or to acts which are 'good or bad in themselves', such as murder. Where there is ritual there can compliance be immediately noted. The same applies to murder - and murder can be very difficult to hide. But this does not apply to instrumental behaviour. Here one must wait and see the outcome before behaviour can be judged. Shorn of our knowledge that certain behaviour has already been legitimated, our problem of ensuring to ourselves the compliance of others is very considerably increased. It is perhaps for this reason that conditions of Aims Morale - unlike those of ritual - will probably always be found at its most intense, in small, face-to-face groups. Those that know each other intimately and are able to see for themselves - as no one outside the group can ever see (even perhaps with the very best of leadership, although that can help) - the dedication of the other to the common good.

This difficulty is rendered the more acute by the very nature of a 'norm' at all. This is the second point I said I would make. As we have seen, a 'norm' is essentially static, an equilibrium, to which there are ever pressures to revert. Norms, all norms, are at bottom reactionary and conservative. How then, can there be a norm at all in an ongoing changing situation? The answer is that there cannot - not in any ordinary sense. What one is enjoined to do is to enter into a higher order commital with a wider application. One is expected to 'enter into the spirit' of it, one is expected to give 'willing co-operation and not count the cost'.

These are pretty vague prescriptions, difficult to define and so difficult to enforce. It seems to me that the precarious nature of any 'dynamic' situation is that which accounts for its peculiarly exhilarating qualities while it lasts, and accounts also for its ossification into ritual when the pressure is released.

The exhilaration will be that of a perilous victory. Where compliance is the more difficult to exact, there will that compliance be the more valuable to us; where we are reduced to relying on 'good will', there will that 'good will' be greeted with the greater gratitude. Hence the camaraderie of those that fight together and do not defect. But such a camaraderie must be precarious while it lasts and of necessity short-lived.

It will depend, for its very existence, on the continued success of the joint enterprise. Only with continued success can this unstable fusion of volitions be preserved. Organizational Aims Morale (to come to the hypothesis I outlined at the beginning of this paper) must be based on group Progress Morale: while group progress is being maintained, doubts may be stilled in the light of the overwhelming evidence of objective achievement. But only so long. Failure will put a very severe strain on the relationship for it can well imply that some other has been disloyal. Particularly incensed will be those with Vocational Aims Morale who arrive armoured in their committal, whose loyalty has a stronger wind and is not so dependent upon outside success. These may all too easily convince themselves of the weakness and turpitude of others.

But failure is not the only predator upon the spirit of corporate venture, success itself can pose an equally dangerous, although different, challenge. The corporate goal must be constantly renewed. A new challenge must replace the battle that has been won, for once the problem is solved, and 'what needs to be done' becomes more and more explicitly known, so will we no longer need to resort to the discretion of others. We may thankfully withdraw to a safer, if less exhilarating, set of relationships where prescriptions can be more explicitly laid down and compliance more readily enforced.

This movement from the 'dynamic' to the 'static', conditions, is the re-establishment of the equilibrium to which all groups will return once the pressure of the environment is removed. This development, provided it is not taken too far, is by no means all sheer loss. Some measure of 'ritualization' allows of a wider identification with the firm itself. Organizational Aims Morale, I have argued, will probably always find its most natural home in the small primary, face-to-face group. This now no longer applies. A measure of continuity can become the very bones of the wider society, it can provide us with a conceptual framework to which we can relate our corporate existence. It is difficult to see how, without such continuity, the individual could come to have any feelings about the larger organization at all. (Indeed some such certainty of ground, coupled with a residual Vocational Aims Morale, or at least a predisposition to venerate authority, may serve well enough for most individuals. They may even come to evince feelings of diffused 'loyalty' to the firm at large.)

However, the outcome may not be so fortunate - not, at any rate, where this process is taken too far. Where the adventitiousness of the environment is wholly removed, we may, through our insatiable appetite for power, reattain that equilibrium to which all groups will tend. We may demand greater and greater dominion over the minds of others and thus attain the total, satisfying 'pathology' of bureaucratization that we in our hearts desire. Everything - but everything - can become symbolic of our obeisance to that which exhalts us. We will become timid, reverential - and exhalted - men. But such a 'consummation devoutly to be wished' is as a rule attained only in high ceremony. Only there can we gain our final, solitary victory. But even then we may have doubts, and it is for this reason, in my view (and to come to our second 'oddity') that those engaged in ritual may yet talk in terms of 'purpose'. The 'purpose' of a ritual is that of winning our battles anew, of reassuring ourselves of the continued dedication of others. Indeed were this not so, were the behaviour of the other to be totally predictable, there might we very well ignore that compliance that can offer us no triumph. No sect, as far as I know, has ever prescribed that its members should sometimes sleep.

This discussion of ritual throws into relief a problem of Aims Morale that I have not yet tackled head on. The problem is that of the nature of the 'cause' around which the group is polarized. Certain causes are attractive and will readily appeal, but others are less so. How can we be inspired by the humdrum? How, I asked somewhat superciliously, can one be dedicated to the cause of 'making biscuits'? The answer is now clear - an injunction or a cause derives its power to inspire us, not because of its nature or the objective purpose of that required behaviour, but because of the relationship with others that that behaviour implies. This is particularly clear in the case of ritual, for there we see wholly automatic behaviour, surely reminiscent of ant societies, invoking in us the profoundest feelings of significance and reality. Such an effect upon us is not due to the acts themselves - these acts could be of any kind - but to the total victory of each over all that is symbolized in our enactment. The same argument can be said to hold for 'dynamic' conditions - (only slightly less clearly because of the greater prominence of the 'objective' task) - it is not 'making biscuits' that is revered, it is the compliance of others in the making of biscuits that we value.

So much for my approach to the problem of morale. I have considered it but a special case of the wider problem of commitment, the underlying need of us all to gain a victory over all others. Aims Morale is but an perilous and exhilarating example that requires, for its maintenance, continued success - or 'progress'. Once the pressure of circumstance is removed though, we shall return to that quietus in which all shall obey. That such a quietus has on the whole been so little reached in our own western civilization, is, in my view, due to one of the two desiderata of norm formation not being met. Although we are interdependent, we do not have common interests. Competition, itself dependent on continued technical change, is the saviour of the Open Society. Even war, for all its brutalities, may well have had a part in reorienting us to external realities, in posing us problems for which there is no wishful solution.

However the elaboration of these ideas would require a further paper, a paper that I have anyway already in some way written (Holmes, 1965) and so they will not be pursued here.

In conclusion, though, we can revert to our original quotation and show how the argument given here would invert the sequence there suggested. The members of the organization do not 'work and live hopefully and effectively' because, as the quotation suggests, each one 'shares the basic purposes of the groups of which he is a member', but rather does each one share the basic purposes of his group because he (and what the quotation missed out, others as well) works hopefully and effectively; again each one is not 'sustained' in performing 'his task with energy, enthusiasm and self-discipline' by the 'conviction that, despite all obstacles and conflict, his personal and social ideas are worth pursuing', rather are such ideas worth pursuing because each (again with others) performs his task with energy and enthusiasm and (above all) self-discipline.

The approach I have taken here has been jaundiced and partial. It has been partial because this paper is incomplete and much more could be said: it is jaundiced, because in what I have not said I have consistently left out anything that might relieve the gloom. The warmth of camaraderie, the possibility of a heartfelt generosity and a love for, rather than a mere use of, the group cause has not been taken into account. This is true. Still, this approach, incomplete as it is, none the less allows us to relate together a fairly wide area of somewhat disparate material. More to the point, it gives us a possible set of relationships for the various meanings of the word 'morale'.

REFERENCES

Holmes, R. (1965), Freud and Social Class, British Journal of Sociology, March (chapter 1 in this volume).

Holmes, R. (1965), Freud, Piaget and Democratic Leadership, 'British Journal of Sociology', June (chapter 2 in this volume).

Merton, R.K. (1940), Bureaucratic Structure and Personality, 'Social Forces', May.

Viteles, M.S. (1954), 'Motivation and Morale in Industry', Staples Press, London.

Chapter 6

MARXISM AND THE NATURE OF GROUPS

This paper is concerned with an analysis of some of the meanings that can be given the word 'group'. By an analysis of this concept I hope to outline the form of association that can be expected to lead to Marxist-type formulations. I shall also hope to show that the form of association concerned - frequently known as the 'Primary Group' - is fragile and has within it, through its internal contradictions, the seeds of its own decay.

In elaborating this thesis I shall first analyse certain forms of association, and only later relate such an analysis to Marxism direct. Any discussion of such an issue is open to bias. My own will be found in the next sentence.

The problem raised by living in groups is that of having to put up with the proximity of our fellows. The fear of being observed keeps us apart. How we cope with 'shame' - the sense of being seen by those that remain mysterious - is largely the concern of this paper. To argue that relations amongst humans may have at their core a primitive distaste of the other, not unlike that revealed to us by animal studies of 'territoriality', may seem unduly pessimistic. However, I hope that, on expansion, my argument - really no more than that coherent, peaceable relationships have to be accounted for, and cannot be taken for granted - may appear less implausible.

I shall argue that there are three ways in which such relationships can be attained and perhaps somewhat dramatically, I shall call them 'Fascism and the Acceptance of Authority', 'Communism and the Rejection of Authority', and 'Science and the Irrelevance of Authority'. This division into three must be taken, of course, as reifying what is really a matter or degree.

FASCISM AND THE ACCEPTANCE OF AUTHORITY

We talk of 'double standards' as if they were wrong ('women should not be treated as second-class citizens', 'if you are going to be tolerant of the Communists you should be tolerant of the Fascists' etc.), and conceive of the best morality having a universal application. Thus the Decalogue tells us that we shouldn't kill anyone (even women) and we come to think that this is the model of what morality should be. Whether we think it or not, it is clearly not what the model happens to be about nine-tenths of the time. Indeed, society in large measure depends upon the very idiosyncrasy of the morally required. Only it is not called 'morality', it is called 'rights' and 'duties'. By 'morality' here I mean that mandatory behaviour that induces guilt in its infraction and self-righteousness in its defence. ('I feel morally justified in stopping someone kill someone else.') Such a morality of principle is, in society, infinitely fragmented amongst the various categories that such a society acknowledges. Different categories will have different demands made upon them and will be granted different privileges in turn. Such a categorization need not be 'official' (i.e. articulated by a self-conscious authority) but whether official or not, it tends to be hierarchical and acknowledged, a Fascist ordering of power. I shall first show the scope of the categorization and then its hierarchic disposition.

I shall take three types of such a categorization and call them the 'formal legal', 'formal local' and 'formal informal'. Throughout, the word 'formal' is used to stress the central feature of this kind of relationship - the self-conscious assertion and acceptance of the rights and duties inherent in a certain categorization.

By 'formal legal' I am referring to categorization approved by Parliament. Thus it may dispose that 'as someone who earns an income' you have the 'duty' to pay taxes, and 'as someone who is over 18' you have the 'right' to vote. Note that such a morality owes its validity to a privileged source (i.e. Parliament) that to the extent that it is believed in, will occasion guilt in its infraction (not paying taxes) and righteous indignation in its denial (those who don't get their rights); further - and this is very important - such allocation of 'rights' and 'duties' may in no way be egalitarian. Thus, to take an extreme example, those that are under 18 don't get the vote. Again, society grants certain categories privileges over others - put in a jury they have the 'right' to pass judgment on their fellow men, etc. The whole can be exceedingly hierarchical - after all we still have the monarchy - but may well lead to a perfectly viable form of relationship of a certain type.

All this is cast into sharp relief if we move on to the second type of formality - the 'formal local'. This refers to local legalities - the authority systems of regiments, firms and universities. Again we have our division of labour - foremen, managers - again there is a delineation of 'rights' and 'duties' often very precisely laid down in a job description; again we note the hierarchical nature of such an ordering of relationships. Again, acceptance can lead to a viability of relationships. Finally, the 'formal informal'. Categorization of this kind is not just due to evil men exacting power in organizations, it can also be seen scattered informally in society at large. Thus it is currently held in some countries that 'as an older man' I am more worthy of respect than you are 'as a younger man'. Again, some people believe that 'men' have the 'right' to boss 'women' around, or that 'white men' have the 'right' to boss 'blacks'. Certainly, in many firms it is felt that 'as someone who has been around longer' one has the edge on those with less seniority. As before, if it works, it works. The black/white relationship is 'working' less and less, with the results we know; but if it does work, it will lead to certain social consequences.

And what are these consequences? Unfairly and contentiously I shall call it 'Fascism'. By 'Fascism' I mean a form of relationship in which each identifies with an over-riding 'authority' and so accepts as legitimate the demands made upon himself and others. Such relationships are authority dominated, hierarchic and cold. They will be cold for each is using the authority for his personal ends. The fear of all for all is attenuated by the sight of the subservience of those around to the same invisible mandate as oneself - a mandate we have made our own. We are all cock of the walk where a morality of principle rules. Morality, as nothing else, is a luxury that can be afforded by all - for Fascists are the 'father' of the Primal Horde.

Freud has often been berated for his use of the myth of the Primal Horde. Such a fanciful account of men's origins cannot but be unscientific and must surely be a hindrance to clear thought. Unscientific or not, I myself find it helpful to put social relationships in its terms. The myth speaks of a pre-social era when society was dominated by a potent male called 'the father' or 'the king'. This 'father' excluded all competing males and kept all the women - or all those he wanted - to himself. Thus he ruled in an arbitrary, narcissistic, pre-moral, pre-legal way, until advancing years took their toll and he was killed by a more vigorous 'son'. So it went on, for uncounted years, until one day no 'son' was strong enough to win through on his own. Willy-nilly a social contract was drawn up, each rival 'brother' agreeing to foreswear his claim to total dominion and receiving in turn the assurance of others. This was the beginning of the law, religion, and morality - and a good deal else besides. Just how important it was for religion, one may get some idea if I say that the father was thereupon eaten by his now grieving sons and that this feast was none other than our Communion Service.

Now, leaving aside the religious aspect (the later parts of the myth are even more hair-raising, the father turning into an animal and ending up on a pole) it is still useful to see social relationships in terms of 'fathers' and 'sons'. The 'Fascists' we have been talking about would all like to be 'fathers'. They identify with authority, against the rabble of those around. They are exclusive and will need someone to despise. However humble he be, he of the Fascist mentality will see himself writ large in the laws, institutions and powers of the 'categories' that are given moral life and existence in his community. In fantasy he lives alone - omnipotent over hirelings at home and lesser breeds abroad.

COMMUNISTS AND THE REJECTION OF AUTHORITY

The trouble with the Fascist superman is that he must have an unending supply of 'inferiors' to be superior to. When Hitler had finished off his Jews he would have had to find someone else to flex his muscles on. The same does not go for the Communist. The Communist is a 'brother' that allies himself with his fellow 'brothers' against the 'father'. This is the alliance of the dispossessed, the informal, personal, intimate relationship of those that stand in opposition to formal power. The Fascist wins his make-believe battles by jumping into uniform, adopting a 'role', a mask, in short a 'category' of what 'ought' to be. They are naturals for organizations, they are super 'organization men' revelling in the power that the legal framework can give them. Not so the Communists. They see the formal structure as the latter day example of the hated 'father', the hated alien superior force. The Fascist is cynical about human nature and sees the need for strong government. Everyone, he assumes, is as power drunk as he is. The Communist is optimistic and would do away with government altogether.

The Communist is inclusive and not exclusive, internationalist not nationalist, in favour of co-operation, not competition. 'Alle Menschen', he tells us, 'werden Brüder.' This is the egalitarianism and compassion of the earlier Christian church as well as that of Schiller and Beethoven. There is a dawn that we can recapture. How? By doing away with government, power, the formal, the impersonal - the 'category'.

The savage, Rousseau tells us, was 'noble'. Man has been corrupted by an alien, outside, monstrous force. This force, in the case of Rousseau, is science, letters and, for some reason, the cultivation of grain; for Marx it is property and the profit motive - but the argument is the same - man is perfectable and is corrupted by authority.

In my view this is the mirror of the Fascist. The Fascist yearns to be the father, the Communist yearns to kill the father. Both see the father in the formal, hierarchical structure, a structure that is loved or hated, but always idealized. The Communist hates: it is the system that is at fault. Change the system and all will be well. The very idealism of the perfectability of man masks a torrent of aggression against the stronger, alien 'power' - i.e. the ruling, formal 'authority', the system that we must all endure.

Although basically muddle-headed in that it posits an outside source of evil - the profit motive, etc. - which is itself not explained and so acts somewhat as an explanatory deus ex machina ('Anything wrong? Blame the profit motive'), it may yet have a form of validity in that it describes the way men act. In other words, men may behave quite well to each other if there is a ready-made structure that can take the social strain. It is in these terms some of the warmth of the face-to-face primary group may be regarded.

The big thing about primary groups is their setting. Quite frequently they are put in opposition to the secondary group as if they were alternatives - 'let us do away with structure and get down to intimacy, then we will all be free'. This, in my view, is misleading - it is quite artificial to take such a group out of its setting - to talk about schoolboys without reference to the framework of classes, teachers or exams; to talk of workers, without reference to payment systems, promotion policies or training schemes; even to talk of street-corner groups without reference to such extra-personal matters as the unemployment situation, the behaviour of the police, or the hospitality of the local bars.

Schoolboys, workers, street-corner groups - classical 'primary groups' - are weak and placed in a setting they revile. They practise - a hatred of authority - what the Communist preaches. Yet they are less than fair, for it is upon this very authority that their camaraderie must rest.

For it is the authority - alien, hated and reviled - that makes an undiluted love possible. Authority is like the social sewer man who performs a necessary function and gets scorned for his returns. It is because the law is enforced - and everyone knows it is enforced - that suspicion can be lifted. Nothing would break up such a primary group faster than the suspicion of another being favoured by the local power. The Fascist acts as his own policeman, his dealings with others are therefore distant, the Communist delegates that ungrateful task to a convenient source of evil - the management, the school system, the urban ecology - and relieves each member of the need to control. No one can harm his neighbour, for they are all weak. I shall call this relationship the 'intimacy of the impotent', for impotent they must remain. If they eat the fruit of the tree of power, they will lose the innocence of irresponsibility. Someone must enforce the law and be seen to be doing so.

The terms 'Fascist', 'Communist' are dramatic, loaded, and perhaps misleading. What I am talking about is not just the theories of a minority that mask their hatred in idealism, or even the blameless behaviour of those that are not in a position to hurt each other - what I am talking about is the bones of social cohesion. As such, Fascism and Communism are a matter of degree. Any 'group' will have its Fascist and Communist elements in this sense - the acceptance and rejection of a status quo with consequent effects on relationships. The same group may be simultaneously both intimate in their opposition to a higher power and yet coercive within themselves in the implementation of their own moralities. The same person may simultaneously accept and reject authority. The same person may have to. Nothing so bespeaks the complexity of such relationships than the position of the leader. I shall end this section on the wider moral frame by illustrating that most ambiguous of social phenomena, the leader.

The Fascist leader is one of 'them', the Communist leader is one of 'us'. The Fascist leader is cold and controlling, the Communist leader, warm and supporting. The Fascist will persecute his men in the name of 'duty', the Communist will sacrifice himself for the 'greater good', lead his troops in battle, be in the forefront of the fray. What could be more different? Different they may be analytically, but the same they are too often in reality. The same man may punish and yet protect, be simultaneously concerned with standards of achievement and effort of achievers. One of the dilemmas facing organizations - all organizations - is that of resolving this dual role of leader. Does he represent authority to the men, or the men to authority? Whether or not such a split 'should' or 'should not' exist, it nearly always does, since, short of any wholly welded sequence, such as occurs in mass ceremony, different sections of the population will find themselves in different situations, and different situations have different interests and so a different sense of guilt. The development of the trade union system is in a sense an eloquent testimony to the failure to combine these conflicting roles - let the foreman look after the interests of the management and the shop steward the interests of the men. And yet this is sometimes felt as a second-best solution since it institutionalizes conflict and implies a rend in the seamless garment of consensual whole-cloth for which we seem to hanker. The Christian solution to this problem, in the notion of the Trinity, is one of the most radical and perhaps one of the most successful - though it too depends on a 'mystical' (i.e. unquestioning) acceptance in the last resort.

In Christian terms, Christ is the Communist leader - the leader of his people against the tyranny of an alien authority. Christ is 'one of us', he is the Son of Man, who died on the cross that we may be forgiven. And who then is the Fascist that unites? It is God the Father, distant and severe, that demands the sacrifice. And yet - and here the mystical part comes in - the two are fused into one where, together with the Holy Ghost - they form the Trinity. (In terms of an earlier paper (Roger Holmes, The University Seminar and the Primal Horde, 'British Journal of Sociology', vol. 17, no. 2 (June 1967) 135-50 - chapter 4 in this volume), God the Father may be seen as an assertive speaker, God the Son as the spokesman for the audience and the Holy Ghost as a kind of infinitely 'regressive' - in the logical sense - chairman.)

Such a fusion I think is satisfying, since it is an echo of an earlier and more impressionable fusion - that which, in the eyes of the child, lay in the parent. The child saw the parent as warm and yet controlling, close and yet distant, sympathetic and yet abstracted, intimately known and yet strangely mysterious, weak and in need of 'service' and yet strong and to be deemed 'responsible'. He is weak and needs our help, yet he is strong and to be feared. Most of us, I would suspect, sense this ambivalent echo, not just because in childhood we were incapable of fully understanding the parental role and saw it confused, but also because it was in reality confused - the parent being in truth both protector and controller. This ambiguity is imposed by the situation. Even the members of the Trinity themselves - the purest case of an abstracted aspect - bear witness to this split. God the Father is the punitive authority that demands the sacrifice of his son - but, when we meet the even more alien figure of the Devil, he becomes our shield and protector; similarly, Christ is our interceder before the punitive father but it is fairly clear from many of his pronouncements, that, given the chance, his pre-eminence would express itself in a fairly stringent exaction of the morally required.

The assumption that Christ, given the chance, would have become a second God the Father may have been unduly pessimistic, but certainly we must see social situations - all social situations - as shot through with that particular ambivalence to authority that finds its most explicit expression in the great political and religious articulations. Even in a director's dining-room can there be found a Communism of the oppressed of those that suffer at the hands of a Labour Government. They too will have their leader-martyrs who defy authority and fail to get their knighthood! Per contra, even amongst the poor and the dispossessed, will be found the petty tyrant who imposes vindictive punishment in the name of some absolute. There will never be a shortage of those that will tyrannize for an ideal, just as, I suppose, there will never be a shortage of those that are prepared to die for an ideal.

SCIENCE AND THE IRRELEVANCE OF AUTHORITY

Any discussion of 'authority' is a discussion of the invisible powerful. The authority of principle is the pivot that allows of organized internal restraints and of the acceptance of the legality of the status quo. Even where rejected, as with our 'Communists', authority could still be 'used' as a framework that allows society to survive within. Such an 'authority' is crucial to our understanding of social behaviour. Crucial, but not sufficient.

Two other forms of association are also possible. There is, as already mentioned, the primal relationship of 'shame' between those that have found no common committal to take up the slack of their suspicion. This form of association, I have suggested, can be seen in animal studies of territoriality. A more latter-day example is perhaps the behaviour of nation states, at least to the extent that any supra-national authority (the Papacy in the Middle Ages, the UN today) is weak or non-existent. It is also the basis, I would suggest, of our preoccupation with those visible forms of assertion - fame, status and dress.

This pre-social relationship is really but a set of conflicting narcissisms. The second form of additional relationship possible is, in a sense, the opposite. It is post-social rather than pre-social. It is a form of relationship that springs from the relation of older children - the causal, empathetic, egalitarian relationship of those that are aware of the context of the other's acts.

From about the age of five, peer groups of children can gain some insight into the mind of the other. They can come to know of others 'like them' in a world they both share. Now, for the first time, they can 'understand' the other, for they can see the other as acted upon, not acting. Thus it is we come to think and understand. Piaget argues that in the last resort children can only learn from children, since it is in the elaboration of a shared framework that we come to the higher orders of abstraction. This could be called a 'cognitively pure' effect. We can also talk of a 'socially pure' and finally a 'cognitively social' effect.

First, the 'socially pure': being more aware of causes, we are more tolerant of the short-comings of others. Retribution ('an eye for an eye') depends for its attractiveness on the assumption that the other's behaviour is 'inexcusable' - pointless, wanton and avoidable. Where there is a shared framework, and hence insight into the circumstances of others, this may collapse. We will accept the other for he is not free. He too is impelled by forces he cannot control, forces we recognize in ourselves. Deprived of this mystery, we cease to fear. Hence the greatest of all consequences, the 'cognitively social'. The whole superstructure of the corporately asserted, morally pre-emptive - the 'law', in other words - collapses. Gone are others that 'exist' but as formal categories, organized in a legitimating authority that allows the loyality and so the enhancement of those that accept the validity of its claims.

There is no 'group' left amongst those that empathize. No self-conscious awareness of a corporate existence - they are only 'people in situations'. Each person, vulnerable, acted upon and in need. Lost is the 'identification' with the idealized, an 'identification' that transforms. In its stead is the 'identity' of those that accept their essential loneliness and do not use their loyalties to forget.

Forget, of course, we do. We never become so tolerant that all means are alike. It is all we can do to love our neighbour and quite impossible not to covet his wife. In any case, the insight of awareness must follow, not precede existence. And existence in itself must always remain blind, pushing, irrational. No one can say it is 'rational' to be alive or, in the last resort, to prefer one path to the other. But certain immediate paths and goals are lost - and the greatest casualty, there can be no doubt, is the authority of principle. Such an authority is the quintessence of the a priori, a power that has no past. A power that single-handedly and mysteriously lays the world in tribute at its feet. The decline of such an authority is reflected in the position of the leader, for he has lost the shelter of his inevitability. Of all those that 'suffer' in the egalitarian relationship, there can be no doubt that the leader suffers most. Here is no Isaiah prophesying doom from on high, no Prometheus, throwing immortal challenge to the gods, here is the diffusion of authority, the primacy of those who know. Any 'leader' such as there might be, is but he that knows most and teaches what he knows; and, like all educators, he will be in danger of working his way out of a job.

THE THREE TYPES CONSIDERED

So much for my three forms of 'group', of which the last is not really a group at all. They can be schematized as shown in Figure 6.1. First, though, comes the pre-social 'shame' relationship. In A each views the other as mysterious, fearful

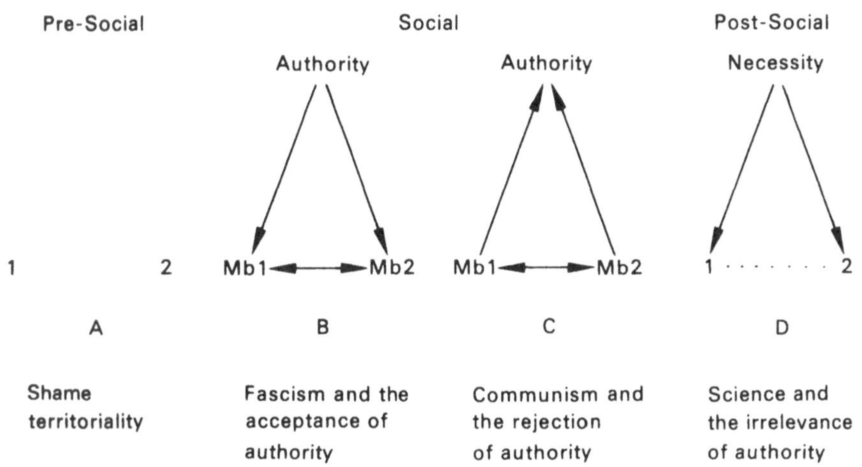

FIGURE 6.1

and alive. This is the basic fear of each for the other seen in territoriality. In B this fear is overcome by a cross-identification (seen on the horizontal arrow) based on the acceptance of a common 'law' or authority: 1 and 2, now 'members', are described as Mb1 and Mb2. In C the mutual suspicion is overcome on the basis of a common hatred and rejection of authority, and in D, each accepts the other (an acceptance described by a dotted line) because the animistic root of A - the assumption that the other is 'free', and so mysterious - is dissolved. Each has now shed his 'membership' again.

So much for the forms of relationship. Before proceeding to a discussion of some of the epistemological consequences of this classification, a very brief elaboration of its social import may not be out of place.

In the first place, any 'social' situation is likely to be an amalgam of all four: common fears (C), common assertion (B), forgiveness (D) and a remaining personal pride (A) are almost always present. In the case of the 'social' relationship of common fear (C) and common assertion (B) we come into the world of reified, idealized categories, of legitimate authority and the formal role. Despite the idealization, though, existence, here as elsewhere, remains a matter of degree. The law did not spring from a rock on Mount Sinai but form the hopes, fears and fantasies of men. 'Informal' situations are ever hardening into formality, even as formality can drop into desuetude, a forgotten word in the vocabulary of power.

The 'primary' group, that stamping ground for the group-bound ideologue, too can be subsumed. It is but a somewhat dramatic example of characteristics C and D. Because they are weak, they have a common enemy, C; because they are physically close, they can have a common empathy, D. Thus can they understand and love somewhat more readily than others can and so we can forget that such groups also have their little tyrannies, B, and that here too we find the anarchist beneath the skin, A.

MARXISM AND THE DERIVATION OF CRITERIA

So much for 'groups'. What now of Marxism? Well in the first place, such an analysis asserts that the Marxist/Communist ideal must of necessity be transitory. Marxism depends on hatred of the authority that is being killed. Once the Communist awakens to the reality of power, he too must, as Freud foresaw, create his own 'categories', derive his laws and his civilizing restraints that, as restraints, restrain.

But Marxism has greater resilience as a system of knowing than is implied in the fragility of the primary group. Were it no more, it would have died long ago. At the very least it would not have gained the intellectual respectability in certain quarters it so manifestly has. For the Marxist approach as given here is one of the twin poles of any scientific approach to the accretion of knowledge. The other pole is the Fascist. Between them, the social relationship seen in B and C of Figure 6.1, make Science or the pursuit of necessity, D, possible.

Science is a dialectic of spontaneity and restraint, of creativity and discipline. Such a distinction depends on the introduction of an alien party whose social analogue has, in this paper, been called 'authority'. For it is authority that influences but is not influenced, that judges but is not itself open to judgment. Such an authority appears in science as measurement or non-circularity. A measure, in science, must, to be a measure at all, be usable across instances and so independent of them. Just so must any definition of a word, to avoid circularity, be anchored in a context separate from that in which it is used. Such a detachment of the measure from the measured is essential for evidence, logic, and, in short, justice. It is also essential for the existence of a hypothesis - for the very notion of a hypothesis separates the locus of the derivation of an idea from that of its possible refutation or confirmation.

All this, in a way, is analogous to what I have called 'Fascism'. It is cold, it is detached - it is 'alienated', in current parlance. It prides itself on exactitude, a pride that frequently leads to specialization and the division of labour. As such it occasions revulsion for those that hope, in their grasping of the nature of reality, to attain the warmth, the synthesis, the involvement - in short, the participation and the love - that they feel is possible in the primary group.

It was part of Marx's great contribution to show that there were no final Platonic absolutes, but the values and codes of a society were themselves dependent on that society. Put in terms of the discussion immediately above, that the measure was itself dependent upon the very matrix that it was called upon to judge. Since then, the notion of 'objective truth' has taken several further knocks, particularly from Freud with his stress on the emotional roots of much apperception of the external, and Piaget, with his feed-back model of learning, a model that fits well with Marx's notion that understanding comes from doing, not remaining apart.

This development stresses the subjectivity, not the objectivity of the known. This may be seen as a loss. But it also stresses what is valuable - the creativity and possible originality of science. It is not enough to verify one's hypotheses, one must think them up in the first place. Ideas are first subjective before they can ever be objective. Perhaps as good a definition of 'originality' as any, is behaviour that determines the standard by which it is judged, behaviour that forces us to re-evaluate our ideas of the relevant, the emergent property that cannot be arrived at by logical exhaustion of the known.

Such an originality, Marx claims, must crystallize out of a 'dialectic', that, circular though it be (since thesis and antithesis are mutually defining), yet allows the emergence of that which is genuinely new. It is out of fusion and committal - a committal reminiscent of the camaraderie and self-sufficiency of the ideal face-to-face relationship - that we will attain our more evolved perspective.

Science must be both creative and evaluative. Without the one it will decline into the sterile elaboration of received dogma, a ritual island in time in which the known is accepted through its very repetition. And without the other? ... It will not be, as the Marxists hope, the happy hunting ground of a people united and freely acknowledging the final synthetic truth. Much more likely, where the law, alienation, refutation has been overthrown, is the tyranny of those that use their new-found spontaneity to assert what they feel to be the privileged rightness of their own position. A Marxist group may be based on love - but what is love but the sunlit side of hate?

For Marxists can be hoist with their own petard. If they stress the social origins of beliefs, they must acknowledge the social origins of their own. Now, in a sense, they do this, but in a way that, ironically, renders them more vulnerable - not less - to attack. For they pride themselves on their cohesiveness and unanimity - satisfying qualities in any relationship. They look upon conflict and alienation - absolutely vital for any independence of observer from observer, or observer from observed - as a sign of primitive weakness, soon to be outgrown, springing from our class-bound capitalist system, rent as it is by the profit motive and the division of labour.

But this, to come back to where we started, is the utopian hope of those that are still trapped in a hatred of an oppressing authority. Kill the king and all will be well. Marxists have not yet awoken to the existence of another possible third party, every bit as ineluctable as the most tyrannical of masters - necessity. They have not attained D in Figure 6.1. Trapped in their narcissistic, impotent dreams, they look forward to a day where none shall disagree - this being but another way of saying that none shall say them nay.

Chapter 7

THE POLITICS OF THE KNOWABLE The relationship between intellectual and social factors in student dissent

This paper will discuss current student discontent in terms of the 'politics of the knowable', the possible social effects of a view of reality. I shall argue that the current revolt - itself but part of an age-old revolt - is bolstered by an ideology that is by no means so weak that it can be wholly disregarded - particularly in the social, as opposed to the natural, sciences. I shall throughout assume that student extremists mean what they say and, further, that in doing this they are but expressing in articulate language what a far greater number of inarticulate moderates happen to feel.

I shall begin with a brief review of some of the intellectual and social features of the protest, point out what I hope is a feature common to both of them, and then discuss the political consequences of this orientation (here to be called the 'new look'). First, the intellectual protest.

This, too, can be seen to have two aspects - dislike of what the students see to be the implicit aims of university education, and dislike of the means. Beginning with the aims, it is fairly clear that there is considerable resentment of what they feel to be the hidden and virtually explicit purpose underlying much modern further education - the 'processing' of human endeavour for the needs of a materialist, competitive society. Some students feel that a university career but renders them fit for capitalist consumption, tailors them to dummydom, seduces them with an appeal to cupidity, thus endowing them with the status of a kind of organization courtesan - a rich, kept amenity of the status quo.

So much for the purpose. Education, in these terms, is not seen as a liberating force that allows each to develop his potential and grow. Rather than e-ducation in the original sense (e-ducere, to draw from), it is seen as in-ducation (from inducere, to lead into). They feel they are being 'induced' into the mould of the currently desired. Society will need so many doctors, dentists and administrators, and these doctors, dentists and administrators will have to be of a certain type. The universities will provide.

The present system is felt to be excessively vocational.

Individuals are turned out to meet pre-determined ends - not to expand. These ends are resented. They are felt - to put it kindly - to be beside the point. They are felt to be 'irrelevant', of use neither to society as seen by them nor to the individual.

Modern, professionally trained academics - trained to standards which, with all their self-conscious rectitude and tiresome elaborations, are finally based on a pragmatic ground - must consider this charge to be grossly unjust. Are we not these days almost excessively concerned with results so that departments that pay (such as the natural sciences) get paid and departments that do not (such as the classics) get starved? Not, according to the students. Moreover, the very machinery of pragmatism - the establishment of standards, the painstaking clearing of the problem from its accretions - this too comes under fire. Syllabuses are accused of being too detailed, studies are accused of being too rule-bound - both are held to be symbols, not of professional rectitude, rather of social decadence. It is clear that students do not mean by 'relevance' what we might have thought they would.

This brings us fair and square into the student dislike of 'means' - the way in which their education is conducted. There has been a complete turn-about. Rather than being concerned with the analysis of facts, they are concerned with the synthesis of facts, rather than treating data in isolation - held in a non-social suspense - they are interested in data being held and determined in a social context. And how is this synthesis to be achieved? Not just by the abandonment of specialization and the cross fertilization of subject matters - important as these demands may be - but by the involvement of the investigator himself. Rather than standing apart, he must immerse himself in his matter. The word 'academic' has moved from being one of the cleanest to being one of the dirtiest words in the language. The word 'involvement' has taken its place.

The ideal of analysis, dissection and detachment - the biologist, a God apart, observing through his microscope the animate forms he can choose and then control - has been replaced by the counter-ideal of integration, synthesis and involvement of the participant observer, the active politician. Detail for its own sake is seen as decadent elaboration, an individually harmless but socially noxious waste of intellectual effort.

To the alienation of the nineteenth-century factory worker has succeeded the alienation of the student today. And for what are argued to be very similar reasons. It is not for nothing, it would appear, that they complain of being 'processed' by production techniques. Just as the worker in the nineteenth century was alienated from his work both in the sense that it was taken from him for profit by another, and also in the sense that it was so subdivided by the division of labour that he could gain therein no satisfaction in the completion of a meaningful whole, so too does the student of today complain of his work being used by another (a capitalist system) and of being deprived, through excessive specialization and attention to detail, of any sense of final 'meaning'.

At this point we must take a grip on ourselves. Surely the

comparison between the nineteenth-century factory worker, escaping from long hours of deadening work to the foetid squalor of the slums, surely such a comparison with the subsidized, hostelled, health-serviced, appointments-committee-d, students of today is so grotesque as to be almost obscene? Rather than seeing his children die preventable deaths whilst awaiting the inevitable destitution of old-age, he is courted - final insult - by the very big businesses that have the means at hand to seduce.

Yet despite the offensiveness of the contrast, it is worth taking this analogy of the alienating academic conveyor belt seriously for the light it sheds on the problem of revolt. In particular, it gives us an insight into the social as well as the intellectual aspects of student revolt. And this brings me to the second aspect of this initial statement.

The nature of the social revolt surely needs far less exposition. Put in a nutshell, it is a demand for control. No longer do the students want to be determined from outside - like a factory hand who has no rights - they want to have a say. They want to have a say in syllabuses, in teaching methods, in how - assuming they are - examined. No longer is the university administrator seen as some distant inscrutable power it is but empty gesture to decry. On the contrary, he may well be seen as a superannuated and almost pathetic old fogey to be placed somewhere between nought and a hundred on a scale of possible malignancy.

Students want 'participation', and a certain amount of it they have certainly achieved. Indeed, they have achieved it at the intellectual level as well as at the social level. It is not just that they are invited to sit on innumerable committees that are concerned with the actual administration of many universities, it is also that they have had an influence on methods of examination, methods of teaching (it has even been suggested in a public document that staff should be graded by students) and, to a lesser extent, in the construction of syllabuses. Yet despite these successes - and this is the important point - they are still not satisfied. Nor - and thereby hangs a moral - can they be.

That they are not satisfied is perfectly clear. Places on committees are not taken up - not at least in my experience. The same discontents are as alive as ever. When trouble is avoided - as it was last year at the LSE - it is virtually avoided on the students' terms - that is, the staff not reacting to what might well be considered student provocation.

Part of the enduring student disenchantment is with the hollowness of their victory. They claim, and rightly, that despite concessions, the administration remains in control. That this is an inevitable consequence (as in my view it is) of the very existence of a specialized, professional staff is perhaps sensed in the more extreme demands of the more far-out students - the demand for a General Assembly.

The demand for a General Assembly, staff, of students and workers, is the demand for a classless, divisionless concord of free men. Instead of decisions being filtered down from on high, they should unanimously be asserted by the acclamation of those involved. Instead of being given to those with the specialized competence to decide (that is, very often in academic affairs, the academic staff), it should be given - and this is very typical - to those who, rather, are going themselves to be affected by the results. Free men should join in a free assembly - join as equals, undivided by rank or specialization, there to make decisions whose sole consideration would be the general good.

Extremist views must be taken seriously for the diagnostic insights they provide. Nowhere is this more true than with the notion of the General Assembly. Rather than expressing the irrelevant phantasies of a crackpot minority, it gives us the whole guts - the strengths, weaknesses and aspirations - of the current student movement, a movement in which all of us - young and old - are, willy-nilly, whether we like it or not, a part.

The desire for a General Assembly reflects a rejection of the past in relationships. This is crucial: for it is on this pivot - the rejection of the past as a determinant - that the social and the intellectual protests merge. The rejection of the past is a rejection of formalism, and formalism with all its strengths and weaknesses is what the protest is all about. The current cry of 'alienation' is but an aspect of this malaise - it reflects a dislike of the self-consciousness, the distance, the excessive specialization, the heartlessness and the ultimate sense of hierarchy implicit in that notion of the imported past that is the formal.

Much of the rest of the paper will be taken up with the nature and status of this imported past or 'third party' as it will be called. (A third party that has been deemed necessary for science and society alike.) I shall now discuss the nature of the assumptions implicit in this third party. This will be done in the social and the intellectual field, beginning with the intellectual.

These assumptions will here be called the 'old look'. They have been prevalent in science for the last three hundred years or so - if not a great deal longer. The 'old look' assumes that there is not just the possibility, but also the necessity for there to be three 'parties' to any statement of fact, 'parties' that are in some final sense 'independent' of each other. The 'first party' is the 'knower', the 'second party' is the 'known', the object of the knower's concern, the 'third party' is, as already mentioned, the past's imported formalism - in short all definitions, measures and categorizations that are derived elsewhere.

The 'independence' of the various parties is necessary lest the mortal sin of this system of thought be committed - the sin of circularity. In part, non-circularity is just assumed, in part it is bolstered by an appeal to this 'third party'. It is taken for granted that the 'knower' (first party) can stand apart from the 'known' (second party), that statements applying to the one (such as 'subjectivity' and 'value statements') are different in kind from statements applying to the other (such as 'objectivity' or 'factual statements'). It is indeed enjoined that the 'first party' be internally independent and 'free', for where an observer's motivations are involved, there will his conclusions be suspect.

This assumption of independence, strongly though it is held in its own right, is even more strongly bolstered, as noted, by the invocation of the 'third party'. The 'third party' is involved when we move from a pre-articulate to an articulate level of an awareness. To define, to categorize and to measure - features of the 'third party' already mentioned - all imply the importation of a standard or criterion that must - the whole system depends on it - be defined elsewhere. This 'criterion' can be as small as the solitary independent definition, but can also be as vast and as expanded as the entirety of previously achieved knowledge that is brought to bear. The 'theory' by which the newly known is assimilated into the previously achieved, is itself part of the 'third party'. The more varied the material that can be so absorbed, the more successful does such an aspect of the 'third party' become. We would be lost without our 'third parties'; they not only allow us to measure, categorize and define, they also allow us to generalize, to interpret and predict.

This 'third party' is also assumed to be independent - of both earlier parties. Again this assumption must be maintained in order to preserve non-circularity. 'Necessary' or not, this assumption runs into hopeless difficulty, as the students - articulate students with an expanded personal 'third party' - are all too willing to point out. This difficulty will be pointed out in a moment. First, I must mention its social analogue.

It can be argued that the 'social' differs from the 'intellectual' in that, in the former case, the 'second party', as well as being a 'known', is also another 'knower'. Society can be seen as a relation of 'knower' to 'knower', not just, as with science, of 'knower' to 'known'.

Again there is the initial assumption of independence, again there is the bolstering of that assumption by the importation of the past. That each 'knower' exists in his 'own right' and is 'free' is taken for granted - isn't he 'there', damn it! Would society be possible if we did not make these assumptions? Whether society would or would not be possible, there can be no doubt that it (society) very heavily depends on the integrity of its 'third party' for its maintenance.

This 'third party' is the system of imported expectations that regulate relationships between men. It is, as noted, the 'formal' in its widest sense. Customs, habits, norms, formal roles - specialized and general requirements of all kinds - constitute this 'third party'. Society even as science can be seen to have its problems of prediction and its problems of generalization. How could we organize large bodies of people if they started to do the unexpected in expected situations? How could we regulate even casual affairs without a body of 'rules' that such a regulation implies?

Such an independence of the social 'third party' is not just necessary, it is also desirable. How could there be such a thing as 'justice' if there were not an impartial criterion, impartially derived? If there were not, in other words, that external and independent arbiter known as 'authority'?

This brings us with a bump back to the students. They are

asserting - particularly as exemplified in the viewpoint that assumes the feasibility of a General Assembly - not just the redundancy, but the positive noxiousness of any such an 'authority' - of any 'laws', be they social or scientific. The measure, the imported categorization or theory, is held to 'alienate' and render 'irrelevant' - be it in interpersonal or impersonal relationships. It is government and the organized body of science that corrupts.

Students, in short, are attacking the 'old look'. This attack, too, goes further than rejecting the integrity of the 'third party' of lawful authority, it also rejects the independence of the first two parties on their own terms. The 'knower' they say is never 'independent' of the 'known' - any more than a 'knower' in society can be independent from his fellow 'knower'. Knowledge - 'relevant', meaningful knowledge - cannot come from such a divorce - it can only come from an immersion of the 'knower' with what he seeks. Hence the stress on synthesis, on emergent 'meaningful' truth that comes with committal to, rather than detachment from, the 'second party' in affairs. Hence the dislike of specialization, measurement, even past codified knowledge - anything that implies a break in the intimacy - the immediacy and the self-sufficiency - of the known.

These two positions - the 'old look' and the extremist student position - are graphically presented in Figures 7.1 and 7.2. It is tempting, as well as easy, to write off the student position, indifferent as it is to cause or consequence, as absurd, or worse than absurd, as driven by a self-interested rejection of 'authority' wherever it may be. Students, we can say, don't like being told to do things (social authority), nor do they like the implication that there is something they do not know already (intellectual authority), they therefore proclaim the noxiousness of the former and the 'irrelevance' of the latter. Such an ad hominem attack is telling - not less telling because, as we shall see, the students can reply in kind and point to the consolations that an established 'authority' (of whatever kind) can be to those who are mentally middle-aged - timid and unadventurous, with something to lose.

Still, we must desist for the students can be (unkindly) said to have a better case than they deserve. There always were clearly unsatisfactory features in the 'old look'. These features have now come home to roost.

They hinged on the assumption of the independence of the various parties - particularly on the independence of the 'third party' from the other two. To operate as the absolver of circularity - that which allowed us to be 'independent' in our statements - the 'third party' itself had to be independent - a measure that was corrupt, was as bad as a judge that took a bribe - but, and this is the point, how can such an independence be achieved? Short of intervention from heaven - the granting of 'authority', both social and intellectual to Saint Peter and his successors - the answer must be that it cannot. The 'third party', the imported past - is but the imported past, a past that holds no magic or intrinsic cogency. Theory - whether the scientific assumption or the social 'ought' - is finally based on

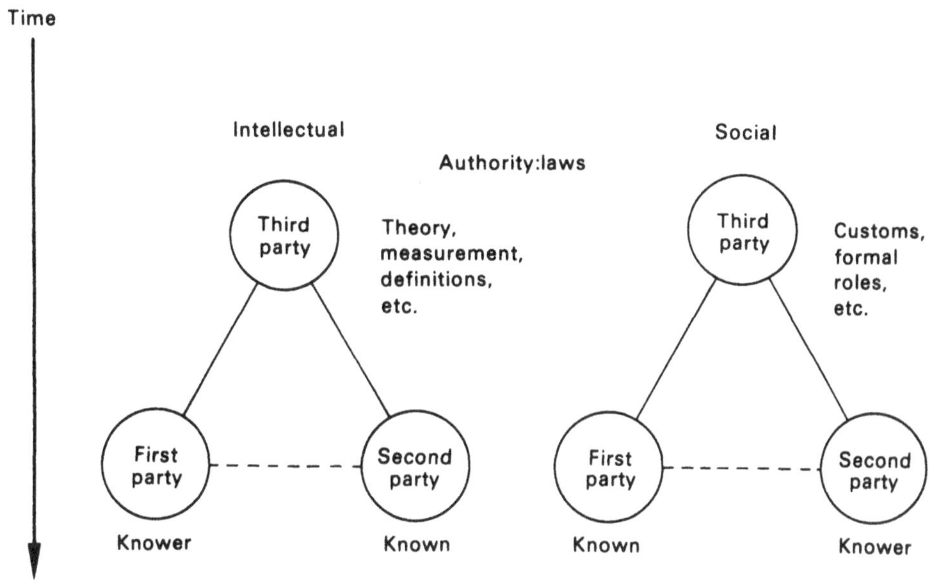

FIGURE 7.1 Old look
'Old look', now felt to be alienating. All three parties in both cases distinct (shown by firm circle), articulate relationship via 'third party' (unbroken line), pre-articulate relationship direct between first and second party (broken line). Third party antecedent in time, or 'imported' as a presupposition.

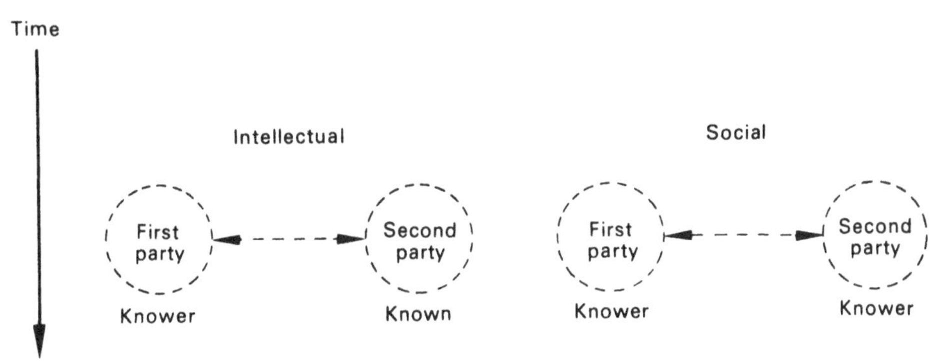

FIGURE 7.2 Extremist student position
Extremist student position. Pre-articulate first and second parties in constant pre-articulate interrelation, or 'dialectic' (double-headed arrow). No 'time' - i.e. pre-supposition or concern for consequence.

the very more humble parties over whom it once held sway. The old order committed its most cardinal sin - the sin of circularity.

This weakness of the assumption of the imported 'independent' authority, has received formidable support from a source that is at least as old as Hegel, but that for our purposes we can consider in terms of Marx and Piaget. Between them, these two have provided what is almost literally providential aid and comfort to the aspiring dissident. This can be found in what will here be called the 'new look'.

This 'new look' is dependent, not on the independence but on the interfusion of the first two parties - an interfusion that is often called a 'dialectic' - and can be considered - at least for purposes of this paper - as pre-articulate. 'Process' replaces 'entities' as the basis of the known. Out of the rhythm of process such independent entities as the 'knower', the 'known' and, a fortiori, the 'third party' of imported assumption, are derived. Independence is here an achievement, not a first cause - an independence that can never be finally maintained, however convincing its aesthetic force. (A force that, alas, Hegel himself came to believe in.) From this point of view, the extreme empirical position of granting a special status to the immediately visually presented (the 'second party') is a hopelessly naïve affair. It is naïve because the knower ('first party') is himself part of the flux, soaked in its texture - a texture that distorts at source.

Marx argued that the self-evident moral and political truths of a society were themselves the product of that society, more particularly of the economic infrastructure of that society. Thus, for instance, it may have been a 'sacred and undeniable truth' to Thomas Jefferson in AD 1776 that 'all men were created equal and independent', but it was neither sacred nor undeniable in 1776 BC, and the reason why it was neither sacred nor undeniable was simply that the different societies had different economic infrastructures.

A 'sacred and undeniable truth' is clearly an 'authority' - a 'third party' that all must heed. And here was Marx asserting that these mandatory claims of what could be called here the 'imported-inflexible' are not a reflection from heaven - or some other location where they could not be denied - but rather the product of lowly economic process. The economic infrastructure, with its stress on the trans-actional and the continuous, can be seen as the underlying interfusion of the first two parties from which the abstract and the undeniable third party can spring.

What Marx achieved in the social sphere, Piaget has done in the intellectual sphere. Piaget took the self-evident and discrete visual entities of the world around - our independent 'second parties' - and showed that they had a biological, rhythmical base. Here the integrity of the notion of a visual 'thing' - the germ of the idea of 'independence' is itself attacked. A perceived object looks like the same 'thing' from whatever angle it is approached - that is a 'conservation' - an object that is further away will preserve its apparent size relative to others objects - that is a 'constancy' - and both of these 'awarenesses' are but consequences of an underlying biological process of assimilation and accommodation - an adaptation of reality to the self through the success it achieves in that adaptation.

Piaget goes much further than this - he argues that not just visual but also the 'third party' logical and even hypothetical concepts have the same properties. This extension of the argument merely enhances, it does not modify its force. This force is that the conceptually self-evident, whether at the visual or the logical level - 'is this a dagger that I see before me?' for instance, or 'two plus two equals four' - is itself a product of an underlying process. Piaget's biological replaces Marx's economic, Piaget's 'tautology' replaces Marx's 'sacred and undeniable truth', but the logic is the same.

So much for the 'new look'. Clearly it has the most radical consequences for any view of the knowable. It is not just that the third party of theory or pre-supposition is undermined - that was always admitted, in any event, to have had its weaknesses - it is also - and this is much more serious - that the first two parties lose their 'independent' status. The term 'process' - even as the term 'events' in physics - is ambiguous in its distinction between, on the one hand, the 'entity' and on the other, that which occurs to it. There is now 'movement' rather than 'something that moves' - where the 'something' can be referred to independently of its behaviour.

This erosion of the status of the first two parties is catastrophic for the old order of settled reality, a reality in which identifiable happenings occurred to identifiable 'parties'. Where the first two parties do not exist independently of each other before the event, but rather crystallize out of their interaction, there are the crucial distinctions between the subjective and the objective, value and fact, all lost. No longer can we point at the world and call it 'there' - since the 'there' is a result of our knowing it - nor can we point to our own thoughts and claim a privacy or assert an irrelevance - since they too are the stuff of which the rest is formed.

Two widely different implications flow from this. The first is that there is no final subjectivity - people do not 'exist', in the way they think they do, whatever their gonads may tell them; the second, that the outside world does not 'exist' either in any stable, impersonal sense. It does not 'exist' in this sense, since there is but an outside world refracted through an observer's eye - an observer that is himself part of what he observes. From this point of view there can be no observed without an observer, an observer with an idiosyncratic past and an idiosyncratic derivation of his known.

This 'new look' is presented graphically in Figure 7.3 Here the pre-articulate relationship between the first pre-articulate two parties (broken line with double-headed arrow to show their interpenetration) results in the closed, independent third party of concept or moral assumption. This development has been described as 'formidable support' for the student position, and 'more than they deserve'. And clearly it is, for although the students - at least those described in Figure 7.2 - do not allow of the crystallization into 'third party' in any determinant sense, they stress, and rightly, its consequential, rather than causal status. For this reason they dismiss it, albeit somewhat hastily, altogether. Further, we can see that the student assumptions of integration, and 'involvement' in the moving present is no longer by any means so absurd. Certainly not more absurd, in the event, than the more orthodox assertion of detachment, measurement and control. Detachment is illusory, measurement in the long run is circular and presumption of control is laughable where the controller himself has no final independence.

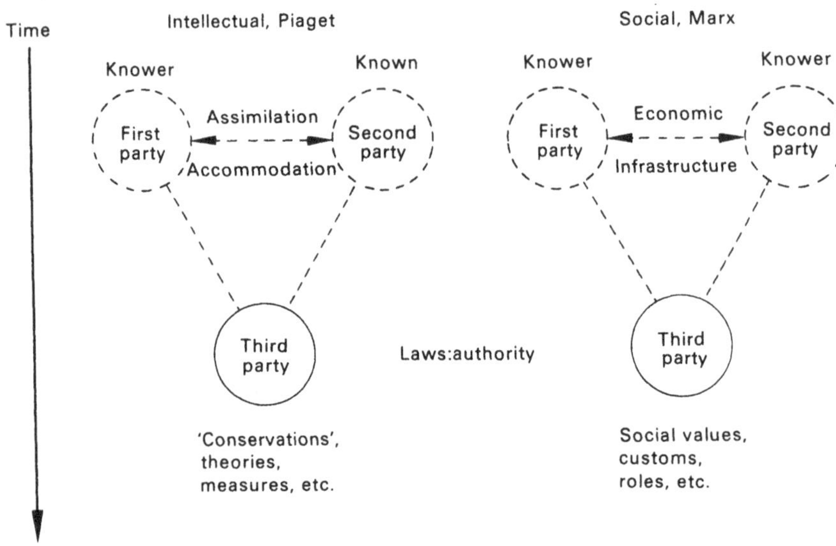

FIGURE 7.3 New look
New look: Intellectual, Piaget. Pre-articulate relationship of assimilation and accommodation between knower and known (broken circle), crystallizes into the articulate 'conservations' of intelligence (firm circles). Social, Marx. Pre-articulate economic relationships crystallize into social values.
As before, pre-articulate described by broken lines, articulate by firm lines.

So much for 'aid and comfort' for the student position. But does such aid and comfort, whatever its theoretical cogency, matter? After all, it would be absurd to maintain that, just because it had certain structural weaknesses, the 'old order' was therefore necessarily bankrupt. Whatever the students may say, the world has literally been transformed by science and the scientific ideal of detachment and specialization as exemplified in the 'old look'. And if this transformation be considered finally but 'illusion', the illusion of living longer in greater comfort is good enough for most people - including, I should hazard, the students themselves.

The short answer is - and this brings us back to a point made at the very first paragraph of this paper - that for the natural scientist it does not matter, but for the social scientist it does. Students are not just more active in departments of sociology and economics, they have every right to be.

The natural scientist is not worried by this progression. Indeed, he welcomes it. With the loss of the incubus of the assumption of the pre-existing 'independent' first and second (not to say third) parties, many of the logical problems are solved. The problem of originality - the emergent property - is solved, since there is no pre-existent, non-original to make such a development particularly noteworthy; the problem of induction and generalization is solved, for there is no independent third party that one must accept as necessary. There is now but the constant reconfirmation of the old assumptions; there is now but a third party constantly re-validated in time.

The resolution of the natural scientific approach is described in Figure 7.4. Out of the relationship of parties 1A and 2A - a relationship based on comparison and the rejection of the initial assumption - the third party is derived. This third party, we must remember, comprises the entire corpus of independent knowledge and assumption gained to date. It, in turn, makes an 'independent' definition of parties 1B and 2B possible, with all the detachment, specialization - and success - we know so well. Not 'independent' in any final sense, of course, but an independence that constantly gains in strength as yet more and more assumptions are shown to give each other an interlocking support. Orthodox science meets the Piagetian requirement of attaining a progressive independence from the here and now, a greater and greater 'conservation' or self-sufficiency. Initial bias - admittedly the final root of the knowable - is constantly pushed further back into the realms of the assumption that cannot command - and grant - a reciprocal support.

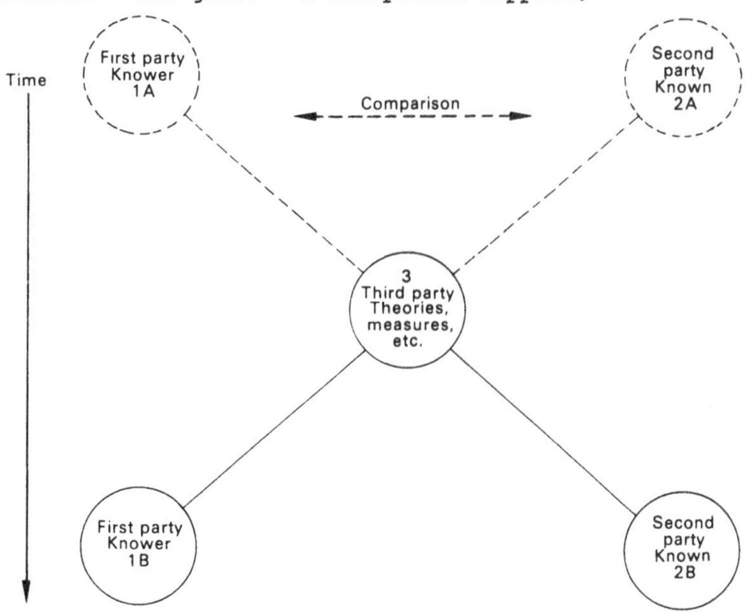

FIGURE 7.4 Scientific resolution
Scientific resolution. First and second pre-articulate parties (1A and 2A) by comparison derive independent third party (corpus of established science), that then adjudicates further relationships between first and second parties (1B and 2B).
As before, pre-articulate parties described by broken line, articulate by firm lines.

But if the natural scientist can look after himself, the social scientist all too often cannot. This is not to say that there cannot be general statements, reminiscent of the natural sciences in these areas, that would be a ludicrously pessimistic assertion, it is just that the subject matter has, in many respects, a difference in kind from the natural scientist's, a difference in kind that is far too seldom admitted. Natural sciences have gained such immense prestige that all - not least the Marxists by any means - must follow in their wake.

The kernel of the difference lies in the very 'first party' of all. For relationships between knower and knower are different in kind from relationships between knower and known. The latter is bleak and unaware. Natural science is about that which no one can help - water freezes under certain conditions at zero degrees centigrade and that is all there is to it: nothing could be more indifferent to our desires. The former, though, can give us hatred and love, support and derisory rejection. This former makes possible the existence of 'society' and the consensus and contention that such society can bring.

Most important here, for our immediate purpose, is the support that other people can provide - a support that can preserve the pre-articulate desires of our earliest dialectical interaction with the environment. Before the crystallization into the 'I' and the 'you' and the 'I' and the 'it', there is but formless 'desire', desire that confuses 'will' with the framework within which it must act. Such a desire can be considered omnipotent - for in this earliest interfusion of fact and value there is no awareness of an outside indifference that could refute. Gradually, though, we learn disappointment, and later still the inevitability - not the vindictiveness - of such a disillusion. So much is loss, but here society steps in. It rescues the relic of our earliest omnipotence, it gives us support for those desires that are yet unreduced. And so a new form of the public self-evident is born.

This is not based, as with the natural sciences, on comparison, it is based on agreement and support - the agreement and support of those who are just as anxious as we are to escape the doubt and guilt of loneliness. And so 'values' - for such are the unreduced, inarticulated presumptions for which we yearn - are given the blessing of those who have just as much to gain. They achieve a 'third party' status, and we proclaim them 'there', forgetting that they are but an extension of our hopes and fears.

And hence those 'social' phenomena of which we are all aware, phenomena that have the profoundest effects upon our inner lives. This does not just refer to that Marxist favourite 'property' - that formal legitimation that allows us to receive without shame and demand without guilt - but also to such elementary matters as 'leadership' or 'payment'. Both of these have a strong value basis in their first articulation - why, otherwise, do we make a distinction between 'leadership' and 'despotism' and 'payment' and 'blackmail'? Their logical, causal status of antecedent and consequent is, after all, the same. Whatever the final divisiveness of society, society - or at least stable society - is ultimately based on 'consensus', an agreement on value pre-supposition. And what if we have 'conflict', what then? (Conflict, indeed, has occasioned the writing of this paper.) Conflict is every bit as 'social' a phenomenon as consensus. One may, as Debussy, evoke an altercation between the wind and the waves, but no one today would seriously give such an animistic presupposition causal, or descriptive, status - at least outside the social sciences.

The full social resolution is given in Figure 7.5. It can be seen to have the same general form as that of the natural sciences. The difference lies, of course, in the nature of the relationship between the initial pre-articulate first and second parties (1A and 2A), and the nature of the resultant third party (3). The first, between 1A and 2A, is based on what will loosely be called 'consensus' rather than comparison - the second, the third party, has an inherent collusive animism, quite alien to those that deal in impersonal affairs.

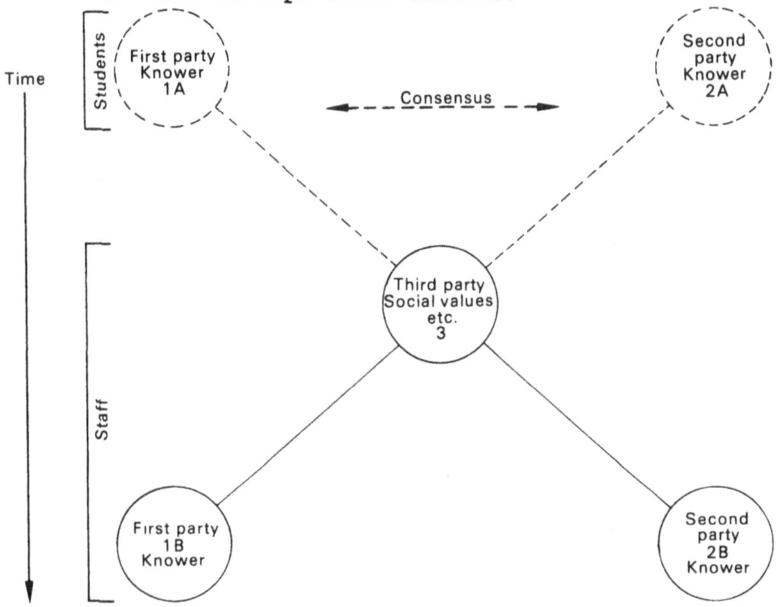

FIGURE 7.5 Social resolution
Social resolution. First and second pre-articulate parties derive values by 'consensus' so regulate 'articulate' and 'formal' relationships between people. Students assert the earlier basis (1A and 2A), staff the later consequence (third party 1B and 2B).

Now the full disagreement of students and their mentors can be outlined. Students stress the initial, pre-articulate relationship (1A and 2A), the interfusion of the primitive apperceptions. They are cynical or indifferent to its consequences - the formalization of definitions that occur with time (3) (a formalism so crucial, for our private peace of mind); the staff on the other hand (at least in the shorthand used here) stress this third party of 'authority' as a necessary (which it is) and inevitable (which perhaps it need not be as it stands) arbiter of latter-day regulated relationships (those between 1B and 2B).

Both sides overstate their case. The staff in their aspirations to scientific respectability all too frequently exhibit parochialism in their assumption of what 'must be'; the students with their dislike of 'authority' in any form, see such presumptions as but the intellectual rationalizstion of those that are attempting to maintain the inviolability of a political status quo.

And the students have, a priori, a formidable case indeed. On two counts. In the first place, the relationship between 1A and 2A in social affairs has a far greater immediacy and ongoing validity than any such earlier antecedent of the knowable in purely inanimate concerns. What, indeed, is a living 'relationship' between people (on which the students lay so much stress) but a mutual (i.e. circular) interdependence that never wholly crystallizes into impersonal, 'third party' status? This brings us to the second count. For what of any formalism we do achieve - a formalism crucial for any lasting stability? This, too, can have its mutability. Social 'laws' in the scientific sense no doubt there are - that has never been questioned in this paper - but social laws can, after all, be passed by Act of Parliament. To reject the power basis of much that is taken as 'there' can only lead to uncertainty about what can and cannot be helped.

The hope that it need not be 'there', of course, is what 'revolution' is all about. 'Revolution is the apocalyptic aspiration of the powerless 'will'. More and more we learn of the importance of 'the will' - not just in sociology and politics but also in psychology and medicine. And should not students, too, have a 'will'? It may be absurd to speak of the sea 'resenting' the 'exploitation' of the sun - the sun that demands a tribute to water vapour in evaporation - but it is not absurd to see individuals (i.e. members of the social, not scientific discourse) so resent. For the social scientist to overplay his hand these days - not to admit, for instance, the personal relevance and very ambiguous causal/descriptive status of a notion such as 'legitimacy' in a subject that claims to be on a par with the natural sciences - but renders the students the more prone to disbelief. To assert the 'inevitability' in any impersonal, scientific sense of much that is taught about society - as Marx himself, with his 'rein wissenschaftliche' aspirations, was all too ready to do - is but to incur the scorn and incredulity of those who, in their youth, feel all too easily that all is possible. Worse than this, it is seen as politically repressive, not just academically misguided. Students, then, feel 'processed' by a training that does not reflect their doubts. The social has absorbed the intellectual with a vengeance.

The young have probably always wanted to deride - to shake off, in their exploration of a yet pre-articulate second party, that which was felt to be the dead hand of pre-supposition and regulation. In the past, though, they had no refuge but acceptance. Latterly, because of wider social and economic changes it has not been the purview of this paper to discuss, they have achieved far greater independence. No longer is the teacher believed in for what he is, no longer have his words the sanction of inevitability. Indeed, the situation is reversed and those that assert the purity of their 'third party' creed unaware or indifferent to the weakness at its base, but encourage in the young an equal indifference to the other's cause.

Ideology is the opiate of the intelligentsia - of staff and students alike. The former too often take comfort in the pessimism and the inflexibility of those who pride themselves on the inevitability of their terms of discourse, the latter too often assert that the present synthesis is all. For them past articulation, the discipline of measurement and restraint, come to be seen but as arbitrary 'alienation' imposed upon their youthful will. Society, if anything, must be 'lived', lived in the inescapable present, not reduced to 'laws' that, disliked as they are in any event, may well be derived from a time that has now passed and has thus lost its 'relevance'.

And the students have half a case. Many of our 'laws' are not immutable. What may be the limits of human malleability - or the inherent strength of the formal social role - only time will tell. In the meanwhile we should see such challenge as useful antidote to our own complacencies - something that will allow us to escape the insidious certainties of our own creeping ideologies. We must accept the final ambiguities of the known, but defend what ordering we can see, aware of any internal consistencies we may achieve. Meanwhile, of course, we should not cease to hope - to hope the students have more of a case than we might at first suppose and that society - and even man - may change.

Chapter 8

THE TRANSIENT AND THE SUBSUMED: SOME EPISTEMOLOGICAL IMPLICATIONS OF CROSS-CULTURAL RESEARCH

In this paper I shall argue that cross-cultural data is weak, but that it is valuable. It is valuable, furthermore, because it is weak. Such data, I shall contend, presents us with problems of inference whose solution has a more general validity than might at first sight appear plausible.

At first sight it would appear implausible that a cross-cultural research worker should have much to teach his more rigorous brothers. For rigorous researchers are interested in 'science'. And what is 'science'?

> Information, no matter how reliable or extensive, which consists of a set of propositions is not science. A telephone book, a dictionary, a cook-book, or a well-ordered catalogue of goods sold in a general store may contain accurate knowledge, organised in some convenient order, but we do not regard these as works of science. (1)

All too often, we must admit, our data resembles more the catalogue than the 'logical system'. The knowledge we gather is but a record of the passing moment and so cannot readily translate itself into those generalizations that alone would allow us to predict. We know how many teachers are 'satisfied', whether American women teachers are more or less 'satisfied' than American men teachers, whether or not New Zealand teachers are more or less authoritarian than American teachers, and so on. Just what we do with this information is not clear. Much of it is surely, on the surface, 'transient', as given in the title of this piece, and does not lend itself into being 'subsumed' into the abstract and the timeless.

Reference to time is material here. For 'science' is surely timeless; we cannot but assume that the Creator is not changing the rules as he goes along. This is not to say that we cannot change our minds, but that we do assume that our data is in some way 'knowable ' - i.e. that some measure of confidence can be placed upon it. But what of our cross-cultural data? All too often the data we have gathered - about how satisfied, or authoritarian, etc. certain teachers are - is not 'knowable' in any abiding, scientific sense at all. Indeed, it may well be in some measure out-of-date before it is even published. And even if it were not, what would be the status of such data? Would it not be best looked at as raw material upon which an administrator should act, so that something can be 'done about it'? And does not the very idea that something could be 'done about it' at all prejudice its scientific status? For science, in a sense, is but the elaboration of that which cannot be helped.

This dilemma is always with the research worker. It is just that cross-cultural research - for reasons which will, I hope, become more clear as we go along - is more brutally confronted by it than anyone else. Is he to stress the transient - I shall call it 'news' - which may well get his name in the papers? Or is he to resist such temptation, and seek a more austere reward? If he does resist temptation he is not so likely to get money for research. But the chances are he will not. The chances are quite good that he will be seduced by the attractiveness of his material - for 'news' relies (successfully for the most part) on that most intriguing quality - idiosyncrasy. 'Dog bites man', as we know, is not news. Science is the pursuit of the predictable - and what could be duller than that?

All too often this distinction is masked by the ubiquity of the word 'research' - a word so holy that its use must be denied to none, presumably to avoid the charge of discrimination. If we begin to attempt to subsume, though, we soon become aware of how difficult, not just unglamourous, is the path of 'science'. For what do we find? We find that, in wide stretches of cross-cultural data, we cannot really even begin to 'subsume' - not at least by the standards of the currently reputable. It is not just that we cannot control our data, so that, however hard we try, our data is open in a very real, and not just a theoretical, sense to unknown contamination, it is also - and this is more serious still - that we cannot measure.

To engage in cross-cultural research is to hope - we presume - to make statements across cultures. But how can we do that if we are unsure that our measures will be equally applicable to all? Paradoxically, measures can only be used to make distinctions between materials that are in certain crucial (measurable) respects the same. Thus we can use a foot-rule to distinguish differences in 'length', but not between 'lengths', on the one hand and 'weights' on the other. And - and this is the point - what is 'the same' between cultures can, to put it mildly, itself be at issue. Hence the frequent stress on 'pattern coherence' and intra-cultural fit:

> The most convincing validation still remains one of pattern, of the testing of the hypothesis for intra-cultural and intra-psychic fit. Every piece of cultural behaviour is so over-determined in its systematic relationship to every other piece that any discrepancy within the material should immediately demand a revision of the delineation hypotheses established so far. (2)

But, at that rate, what price inter-cultural fit?

To a very large extent, then, the notion of culture does not even 'describe' let alone explain. It does not describe, for reputable description implies the existence of certain identifiable dimensions. All that the term 'culture' may do is to set a frame within which things may happen. As such, it should have its own name. Let us then call it a 'holding concept'.

A 'holding concept' can no more describe an area than a square mile of territory can 'describe' a battle that is fought upon it. And 'culture' is such a square mile, a stage where each society performs a play - a play that then defines the characters that enact it.

And so, unable to compare - certainly not explain - we reach the nadir of our cross-cultural fortunes. But nadirs have their uses. They can force re-evaluations, and re-evaluations can be hopeful. In this case for psychological as well as logical reasons.

'Psychologically', we can gain an insight into just how faulty our conviction that we understand something can be! It brings home very clearly the power of 'holding concepts' to deceive. It shows us how giving a name-invoking a source, quoting an authority - can be held to describe, or even explain. In the beginning, as we all know, was the Word.

For this is the attraction of 'news'. The Word is but the 'news' in holy script. 'News' like the 'Word' is but information that is held to have validity in its own right. And to assume that statements like American teachers are 'more satisfied' or 'less authoritarian' than English teachers, have somehow a form of validity, is not to be too simple-minded. An assumption of this order - that statements can be validated by their uniqueness rather than by their relation to other statements - is, after all, the basic assumption underlying Plato's theory of ideas. And if Plato leads, who shall blame those who follow?

Cross-cultural research, makes us more aware of our deficiencies - as observers and interpreters - than we would otherwise be. But it does more than this. It simultaneously forces us to re-evaluation of the 'knowable' itself.

It is for this reason that I said that cross-cultural data gave 'logical' as well as psychological grounds for hope. It is not only the cross-cultural research worker who is dubious of the status of his data, it is the professional philosopher as well. Philosophers have been occupied with such problems ever since they turned their backs on the 'good news' of the Holy Books and concerned themselves instead with what constitutes 'evidence' in the here and now. The result was greater, not less, doubt. Paradoxically, it might seem, the stress on empiricism in the eighteenth century led to greater, not less, diffidence - a diffidence which is still with us. Popper, unlike many of his admirers, has never held that simple refutation can be a passport to truth. It cannot do so for one has always more than one unknown; one can never before the event, for instance, say that it is the observation that is at fault and not the theory - let alone the observer or the measure or an infinite number of other possible factors. Indeed, Popper of late has cut the logical Gordian knot and laid stress upon 'growth', not refutability, as the yardstick of merit. (3)

But perhaps Popper has not been pessimistic enough, for 'growth' according to him, depends upon a theory producing more 'empirical content', and what, we might ask from our vantage point as soured cross-cultural research workers, is 'empirical content'? Indeed, the dilemma of the philosopher of science is that he must either resort to a logical or to a pragmatic filter for acceptability, but that he cannot appeal simultaneously to both. Thus a cast-iron procedure for refutation can be established - provided we take for granted the prior existence of data, theories, and measures that are held to be beyond question. Conversely, we can abandon such attempts at refinement and appeal to 'growth'. But then we leave in doubt what 'growth' - or indeed the whole distinction between what the 'empirical' and the 'theoretical' - could mean.

Now this problem as to what 'empirical' data 'is' and how, as such, it relates to what I have called the subsumed 'science', is the very problem that, I have argued, the cross-cultural research worker must face: cross-cultural research but presents us in an acute form with that which can be escaped by none.

And where the problems we face are of general interest, so too, we may hope will be our solutions. Let us see what can be done about it.

Cross-cultural research reduces us to conceptual childhood. Like new-born children we are confronted by a sea of data which we have no way of charting; it is one of the great merits of conducting cross-cultural research that it forces us to take seriously the psychology - not the logic - of the known. Despairing of the known, let us turn to the knower. Let us take seriously what we all should take into account, but too often ignore - the psychology of Jean Piaget.

For Piaget, concepts are derived from use. It is as the child develops that gradually distinctions are made between the measure and the measured, between the 'empirical' and the 'theoretical', between, for that matter, the 'I' and the 'you'. By tracing the growth of the known, we can learn the provenance of that which will later appear as 'axiomatic' or 'independent'. Piaget gives a historical root for the logically self-evident. He is concerned, to use his own words, with the 'dual' nature of intelligence as something both biological and 'logical'. (4) And of this duality, it is to the biological that we must look for the key. These logical relations are not irreducible. Formal logic, indeed, 'is simply the axiomatics of states of equilibrium of thought'. And how do we find out about these 'axiomatics'? We must study the 'psychology of thought'. (5)

Piaget is centrally concerned with how we come to see things as being the same. Crystallization of such similarities - the 'conservations' and 'constancies' of intelligence - is achieved by the development of 'equilibria'. These equilibria enable us to escape the distortion implicit in a perception that is anchored in the here and now - a distortion which, in our terms, has gained the self-sufficiency of 'news'.

This is achieved in time, by using our memory across instances. Even our ability to perceive a cup as stable on a table, for instance, involves abstraction based on experience (i.e. an articulated memory or a theory) and extrapolation. Piaget is concerned to show how the cup continues to appear the 'same' however much we move our head: how it can be that, from whatever fragmentary perspective we view it - and all perspectives are fragmentary - we appear to see the 'same', 'whole' cup.

This is the germ of Piaget. All else is but an elaboration of this ability to abstract and recombine. Even complex reasoning, measurement, and number are abstractions from past activities.

Piaget's approach is a feed-back approach. We act before we know, knowledge is but the transient relecting upon itself. This is of crucial importance, for as a result the problems of the independence of 'the measured' from 'the measure', which we have been wrestling with, are by-passed since the ultimate criterion is no longer adherence to an external standard, with all the problems of circularity which that raises, but resides, rather in the standards imposed upon his data by the observer himself. And that goes too for those uncalibrated standards we call 'definitions'.

We tend to think of definitions as arbitrary, self-evident and a priori. The formal proposition asserts the existence of a 'subject' and a 'predicate' and the 'predicate' tells us something about the 'subject' - a 'subject' that has been independently defined. But now we can see, not only that this 'independent' notion of a definition owes its force to its idiosyncratic 'news' status, but also, more importantly, that it is this forceful definition which gives rise to the philosophical problems mentioned above. For since, in a sense, all knowledge is interrelated, definitions themselves must be accounted for. Indeed, as with all feed-back formulations, all we can hope to do is to define - or rather to re-define. For there can be but the modification of an assumption. Feed-back knowledge is retroactive. With such knowledge, it is the unknown that defines the known, quite as much as the known the unknown. Where we do an experiment, for instance, consequence will illuminate what we thought was cause. For it is only by talking that we come to know what we mean.

Now this has very great implications for our studies, for we need no longer be ashamed of the circularity of our measures, of the 'holding' status of the areas we are concerned with. We need not be ashamed, for all definitions are in a sense but 'holding concepts', awaiting refinement and perhaps exorcism. Thus we are not alone. It is true that we cannot operate as the child does and as most scientists do and integrate across time, but we can do that which is logically analogous, we can integrate across space. Each separate culture is a venue in which the same casual laws surely must apply, and such laws and the measures implicit within them will be defined by the very consistencies that our data allows us to abstract. If the 'same effect' is found across cultures and we see that 'greater age' is associated, for instance, not just in England but also elsewhere with 'greater satisfaction', or that 'authoritarianism' is generally associated with 'disappointment in salary', then such associations can be deemed valid to the extent that the context in which they are embedded varies. There is no other form of confirmation possible for any of us: whatever we do, there can only be the flux defining itself. The great advantage of engaging in cross-cultural research is that it forces our attention to that which so many are able to ignore.

NOTES

1 Morris R. Cohen and Ernest Nagel, 'An Introduction to Logic and Scientific Method', Routledge & Kegan Paul, London, 1947, p. 21.
2 Margaret Mead, National Character, p. 659, in A.L. Kroeber (ed.), 'Anthropology Today', University of Chicago Press, 1953, pp. 642-67.
3 See Imre Lakatos, Changes in the Problem of Inductive Logic, in I. Lakatos (ed.), 'The Problem of Inductive Logic', North-Holland Publishing Co., 1968, pp. 315-412.
4 Jean Piaget, 'The Psychology of Intelligence', Routledge & Kegan Paul, London, 1950, p. 3.
5 Piaget, op. cit., p. 3.

Chapter 9

THE ORGANIZATIONAL AND THE SCIENTIFIC: TWO LEVELS OF DISCOURSE

Organizations are man-made. One can, by a stroke of the pen, 'create' a company, a regiment or even a country. Organizations, in consequence, are not like the events studied by the conventional natural sciences. A somewhat different approach is needed, an approach that this paper will attempt to outline. This particular approach, on expansion, will be shown to have a wider relevance than one might at first suppose.

The study of organizations demands a special kind of concept and a special kind of causality. 'Natural concepts', if I may use such a term, are categorizations or analyses of what we believe to be 'there'. We go out and study. There is no reason in principle why anything should behave in the way it does. Of course, there are reasons - and eliciting these reasons is what science is all about - but these reasons have to be discovered. They are not there before the event, nor do they have to 'make sense' in any necessary sort of way. There are no privileged causes in science.

Not so in organizations; there, causes are asserted. Consider, for instance, the use of the term 'power'. In the natural sciences such an idea is redundant; it is but another word for 'cause', to be discovered, as all causes, after the event. We diagnose; we tinker with the car or television set to see what has led to trouble. In organizations, though, one is given powers (i.e. appointed sergeant, supervisor, electrician or university lecturer); one is told - even as an organization as a whole can be told - what one's powers will be: what they will be over others ('rights'), what others' will be over one ('duties'). Just as the category 'organization' was created by man and not 'discovered' so, too, are the powers therein asserted before the event, not deduced from an awareness of the past.

Now, it is out of this very availability of organizational constructs - obedient as they are to corporate and private will - that our difficulties ensue. For how can they be defined? They must, as a result of their social origins, assume (at least in the universe of their competence) an arbitrariness that is wholly alien to the essential continuity of normal science. They must in some sense be 'unmoved-movers', 'context-independent', guarded by a boundary that permits expression outwards of the inner 'power' but shields such power from surrounding frame. This they must be in order to exert their one-way influence. How otherwise could a government act at all? Put another way, they must be what I shall call an 'inside-out' affair, different in kind from the 'outside-in' existence of the 'context-dependent' natural events.

The notion of the 'inside-out' definition - the essential property of the imposed existence - will be the pivot on which this paper will be based. Its expansion will be both more abstract and more prosaic than might be expected. It will certainly be far wider.

First abstraction. 'Inside-out' entities harbour a mystery. They must, in order to survive - for any scientific 'outside-in' explanation of the internally unknown would itself destroy the entity under discussion. This means that, if one wants simultaneously to retain one's distinctive concept and 'understand', one can only do so, as Plato did, in terms of the irreducible, 'essential', 'nature' of the entity; an 'essence' that is necessarily present and yet necessarily unintelligible in any ordinary sense.

Plato put his defining 'ideas' in heaven - he had to, for only there could the total purity of the necessary 'inside' be kept. Any expression in terms of the here and now would dilute what he was anxious to retain. It is thus somewhat as a bolt from the blue that we descend from the abstract to the prosaic, from the Empyrean to the man in the street - not to mention the man in the Clapham bus. All reputable explanation - that is, non-circular explanation, accounting for something other than in terms of itself - is explaining away. And explaining away is just what we won't abide.

'Inside-out' definitions are not just found in heaven. They are also found in any common or garden. They fit our minds, they have only seriously been challenged in the last 300 years and are still for all that very much in control - at least at the social and 'organizational' level. This is not surprising; the 'outside-in' cast of thought that reduces the unique to common constituents violates our sense of the real. The scientific approach has nothing to recommend it but its success.

It violates those basic elements of our thought - 'things', 'life' and 'freedom'. The notion of the 'organizational' - of a 'power' caused by 'fiat' - at first sight so clearly artificial is in fact far closer to our native mode of thought than any ad hoc abstraction used by science - an abstraction that can be picked up and thrown away if shown to fail in use. This affinity of the organizational with the everyday will clearly be of material consequence and so must briefly be pursued. First, a few examples of the similarities - of ways in which 'things', 'life' and 'freedom' can be said to be 'organizational' in the sense used here.

They are all three 'organizational' in the sense that they are all three independent of their context. They must be, for their very existence depends on this. We would not use the idea of a 'thing' at all if we were not able to abstract part of the world as somehow separate from the rest. The more separate, the more of a 'thing' it becomes. This can be directly observed by noticing water freeze. It starts as liquid - hardly a 'thing' - but slowly congeals to that which can be picked up and thrown about. When you can be thrown - and retain your identity in a context in which you move - you have really made the grade.

What goes for things clearly goes for 'life', and life's subjective sense of itself, which is 'freedom'. Things may have 'essences', but only Plato would bother with such an inner core; with 'life' though, this inherent bursts into obvious autonomy. When something gets up and moves around - all on its own - or, less dramatically, slowly develops or decays, the temptation to refer to inner forces - forces distinct that cannot be reduced - has not always been resisted. Indeed, hardly ever. 'Explanation' now tends to be future bent, the inner nature no longer lying dormant, but becoming ever more itself. This was essentially the message of Aristotle - things are accounted for by pointing to the essence to which they strive. This essence was called 'purpose' - by realizing their 'true' or 'natural' purposes, the living entity attains its final definition.

What goes for purposes clearly goes even more for freedom. What is 'freedom' but independence - of what is around? 'He made me do it,' we say, pointing at the offender - 'there was an external cause, and so we were not free.' The notion of freedom totally violates the 'outside-in' assumption of conventional science. It proudly flaunts its context-independence and sees virtue in its indifference to the world around. Literally - for where 'life' is defined in 'purpose', 'freedom' is accounted for in 'virtue'. 'Virtue' is true freedom - freedom wishing to achieve what is most itself - 'vice' a kind of ill health of the will.

All three of these are kin to the 'organizational'. The 'organizational' as seen in the formal role is but an extension of this kind of thought. A formal role, existing before its incumbent ('The King is dead, God save the King'), is but an abstract 'thing', given a clear 'purpose' whose fulfilment is called 'virtue' or (when not paid quite as much as it should be) 'loyalty'.

Organizations are highly complex 'things', complete with 'purposes' that are virtuous to fulfil. The trusteeship of this fulfilment is given to 'authority' - Plato's ideal made real in social form. Now this affinity of the organizational with such 'context-independent' notions as 'things' (not to mention 'lives' and 'freedoms') will give us unique problems of explanation. Unique, because they cannot be explained in a conventional way - Plato was no fool when he placed the definition of his terms in heaven.

Currently this problem is ducked. Organizations are not just taken as defining themselves - after all they are 'there' - but, on top of this, the whole of the rest of the Platonic package deal is unquestioningly subscribed to. Organizations are not just held to 'have purposes' (which is bad enough), but 'true purposes' pursued by enlightened souls who have paid the consultant's fee. This 'true purpose' is then pursued by a leadership that 'rightfully' exerts its powers. Thus the organization is suspended explanatorily in mid-air, justifying itself by its own decree, enforcing its dictates by the domestic morality of its own legitimacy.

As a way of organizing people in large numbers it has much to recommend it. We all of us - Platonists as we are - recognize the force of the self-defining authority. We all seek the virtuous freedom that 'legitimacy' makes possible. We need a moral order for it allows us to express our will - whether it be our desire to follow or to lead, to take, or, even more, to give. Without the comfort of legitimacy we are exposed - others will resent our assertions and mock our acquiescence. Without the social support of granted 'rights', we shall be ashamed of our dependence and our greed; without an authority that allows of service, we shall be ashamed 'to give'. Organizations are needed individually quite as much as socially. We are lost without the comforts of the law - and the implementation of the corporate morality we support.

But though 'organizational', we are not wholly so. We are also capable of rational thought - at least in some degree. We can think in a relational as well as an intrinsic way. 'Context' in practice is never wholly irrelevant, repeated failure can call into doubt even the best established of legitimacies.

We can see the world scientifically as well as 'organizationally'. Further, we may not need the invisible support of moral precedent - we may wish to act uncluttered by the sense of 'ought'. Both levels act on us at once, each with its exclusive explanatory demands. To do justice to each and yet violence to neither is my purpose here.

This is clearly not going to be easy. Just how difficult, in principle, can be seen if we take the very simple example of a husband and his wife. This example will show us how far apart the two accounts can be; how very different are their respective strengths and weaknesses.

The question here must be: why is there a marriage? Put brutally, why does he not leave her - or she not him? Now there can be two answers to this. Beginning with the man's position for the sake of argument, we may first point to the lack of practicable alternatives (she may be too difficult to get rid of, or, if got rid of, could be too difficult to replace); second, and quite differently, we could stress, not the lesser desirability of alternatives (in terms of divorce or remarriage) but their irrelevance. The first of these reasons for staying with her is the 'scientific', the second is here called the 'organizational'.

A scientific account is concerned with alternatives. The wife is placed in her 'context' - availability of other women, problems caused by having to look after the children if left, and so on. She is 'context-dependent', defined in a relational 'outside-in' way. The qualities of the wife here are those granted by the setting. Viewed from this point of view a perfectly desirable wife can be transformed overnight by the arrival of an alternative choice next door. This may be thought fanciful, but it is no more than happens with motor cars.

This comparison with motor cars shows us the degree of affront that phrasing relations with people in purely 'scientific' terms may give. 'People aren't machines', they are 'human beings'. I shall be accused of treating people as 'machines'.

Certainly the wife does not want to be treated as a washing (or any other kind of) machine. She wants to be loved for 'herself alone', i.e. 'valued' in a context-independent, 'inside-out' kind of way. However, she may or may not get consolation from the thought that her husband can be treated in the same way.

So far we have held the husband constant (if that's the right way of putting it) but clearly we could vary him as well. We could fill him up with drugs, take his money away from him, or, in the long term, vary his sociological, social and genetic background. Nor need we end there. Any 'solution' we might arrive at (i.e. husband, type A, with wife, type B, under circumstances C, D, E, ... etc. have a marriage expectancy of n years) itself but poses a further problem (i.e. the causes of this particular outcome). There is no end to this process in science. Today's solution is tomorrow's headache - indeed, we can note the development of a science by noting the primitiveness of its preoccupations. It is only the most evolved sciences that can ask the simplest questions.

All this is a far cry from the 'organizational' husband who might very well just stand up and say, 'I stay with my wife freely because she is the only woman for me'. Just slaughtering the idea of the 'scientific' with almost every word. For 'I' implies a separateness apart, the husband existing in some way outside the circumstances in which he finds himself - this is powerfully reinforced by the use of the word 'freely' - implying again the ability to stand outside and to impose himself upon events in an 'inside-out' kind of way; finally the statement, 'The only woman for me', whether or not it is true, implies a uniqueness on the part of the wife which can only mean, if it can mean anything, that she cannot in principle be reduced to her constituent parts.

This domestic example, albeit small-scale, shows us quite a lot about the strengths and weakness of the two approaches. The strength of the scientific approach is of course, however repugnant it may seem to us, that it allows us to predict. Whether or not we should predict if this is the price that has to be paid, is not a scientific question. Certainly over the centuries there has been a steady decline in the 'sacred', in that which it is impious to observe. There was a time when practically everything was off-limits to those that did not belong to some priestly or priest-like hierarchy. But that is by the way. The great weakness of the scientific is its inability to do justice to people's subjective experience.

Particularly, of course, experiences that stem from our dividing the world around us up into 'things', 'living things' that have 'purposes' and are 'free'. The homely example of the husband who regards his wife as the 'unique object' of his 'freely bestowed esteem' is not exceptional - he is the rule. The world of the child, Wordsworth argued, was the world of the poet; so too, it could be argued, is the world of the savage or the man in love. To a small child everything is fresh and new - even as to an adolescent, every member of the opposite sex may so appear. The poetic is not advanced or sophisticated - it is the raw material of experience. It is the prosaic that violates the uniqueness of each moment by pointing to similarities across instances and then subsumes. It is the prosaic that comes with age - and intelligence, civilization and the computing mind.

In most sciences this animistic, poetic ground to our view of the world - a view that treats of the thingness and living uniqueness of what is being seen - does not matter that much. 'Organizational' concepts such as 'purpose', even 'force', were lost years ago. In study of societies, though, such primitive apperceptions have an abiding importance.

In two senses. The first is the colour of our concepts - a colour that, as we have seen, can invade the most rational, rule-bound corridor of power. The whole idea of 'authority' as somehow deserving of respect comes here. 'Authority' is a kind of poetry of power. And much can hang on it - to the 'loving' husband believing his wife 'unique' we can set the 'loyal' employee, mindful of the 'common good'. Such 'loyalty' may be crucially important. Organizations, unlike most marriages, have to accommodate large numbers of people, each with his separate claim. It is difficult to see how this could be at all were there no abstract notion of 'legitimacy', i.e. that which has an inner validity and so commands consent.

This brings us to the second sense, and with it a return to the very beginning of this paper. Organizations depend upon the primitive (i.e. the 'organizational') not just for the colour and feel, but also for the very existence of the concepts used. Organizational concepts, to repeat, are not 'there' to be discovered by patient research, they are asserted and bolstered with a moral base. The notion of a formal 'role' with 'rights' and 'duties' pertaining to it is but an abstract 'thing', granted a purpose of its own.

The 'organizational' is necessary. But is it sufficient? Clearly not. To take the hierarchical structure of 'rights' and 'duties', currently accepted 'legitimacies' and 'purposes', as if they were determinants in some external sense obviously won't do. In the first place, of course, as we have already seen, it may not be true even at a descriptive level - the employee may not be 'loyal' and may view his 'authority' with no poetry at all; in the second place, and more important, such an approach has a very ambiguous explanatory status.

Once more we come back to the beginning. The 'organizational' is that which carries its own force. A 'thing' or 'life' is 'there', explained by its very presence. There can be a poetry of explanation just as there can be a poetry of power - indeed the two are much the same. The form it often takes is that of giving the phenomenon a name, and then saying that the name 'explains'. 'Ah well, he's in love', we say, 'and there's an end of it' - forgetting that rather than in any way helping, the name itself ('being in love') is only used as a result of what we have already seen. In organizations we do the same thing - 'Ah well, he's the boss' - as if this got us anywhere. We are merely evoking a forceful notion ('being the boss') and using its obviousness to forestall further doubt.

By a somewhat cruel twist, the very effectiveness of the organizational is that which renders it illicit. A crucial rule that any explanation must meet is that the terms used must themselves be open to further explanation. If this is not so - if we come to a point where we say we cannot go any further (like 'first cause' arguments for the existence of God - 'it must all have started somewhere'), we might as well all get down on our knees at once and save ourselves the effort and suspense.

All organizational explanations save ourselves trouble and suspense. We take what is 'there' as somehow justifying itself, forgetting that reputable explanation must concern itself with absence quite as much as presence. Indeed more so - in principle it is not concerned with what is 'there' but rather with what is not there accounting for what is there. The unique present must be reduced to the general past.

But to do this, as we have repeatedly seen, would destroy the very object of our concern. All scientific explaining is explaining away (to the extent that it is successful at any rate) and, while no one would mind water being 'reduced' to its constituents, constituents that appear to be quite different from anything in our phenomenal awareness, with people it is the phenomenal awareness itself that is the focus of concern. It is people as they 'are' 'to us' that we are interested in. We may be misguided in the way we pose the question, but that, for all that, is what we deem important.

The scientific discipline is far more drastic than most people realize - freedom, life, even 'things' must be abandoned. There are no 'things' in science, there are but relational consequences dependent upon antecedents that are themselves relationally defined. One cannot at any point - except for the sheer practicability of experimentation - escape into the bedrock of an 'inside-out' definitional certainty.

What then can be done? We cannot reduce everything to relations or there would be nothing to discuss. The notion of 'person', that amalgam of 'freedom', 'life' and 'thing', would certainly go. 'To talk about people in psychology is grossly anthropomorphic' may or may not be a good joke, but it is certainly a true joke - and so that 'meta-person', an organization, would certainly go too. This won't do - one can't get out of writing a paper on the grounds that what we are interested in does not exist. After all, even if people are deluded, their delusion is itself of concern. The 'organizational' must be retained: but must not dominate. 'Organizational' solutions, in particular, are but devices that allow us to point with pride at what is 'there', thus clothing our indolence with the unseemly garments of complacency.

Somehow these two approaches must be reconciled. Must. For anyone who has two sets of explanatory approaches can get away with anything. (If it does not work with one, you say it belongs to the other.) But how? They so basically conflict. The organizational points to the inner or the future 'real', the scientific to conditional and uncertain sequence, sequence indifferent to hope or fear.

Reconciliation in the terms that each would set is, by definition, out. Each is exclusive in its claims. There is but one point at which they both can meet - a point that neither would for a moment countenance - and that point is ourselves.

For all their protestations these two approaches have one thing in common - they are both held by men. Both are thus influenced by our private memories - 'science' is at root but memory of our past success, 'purpose' but our hope of future won.

Subjectivity gets a bad press these days - from the organizational and the scientific both. The scientific, we all know, sees its very growth as emancipation from the bias of men - no 'subjectivity' there all right. Not, anyway, as other than something to be deplored. The 'organizational', too, makes its external demands. In its abstract form it speaks of essences and purposes and God - a very high-powered form of 'reality' indeed, and of course, at the practical visual level - the level of our perception of the 'things' around - there is even less doubt it claims to represent the 'there'. 'I see it because it is "there"' is held to be self-evident, not circular.

Contrary to what might be supposed, it is the organizational that suffers most by this reduction. The 'scientific', surprising as it may sound, can remain relatively indifferent to any imputation of a subjective base. In a sense of course, scientists have always admitted it. 'Hypotheses' are finally the bases of the known, and 'hypotheses' are necessarily irrational and unjustified. That this subjective basis is ignored should, however, not surprise, for the very nature of advance attenuates its relevance. With every advance we absorb and codify our past unformulated thought. The entire development of science can be seen as emancipation from the here and now, a development of that which attains its own internal balance. Initial bias thus constantly defeats itself, only resuming pre-eminence at the edge of the known, where continued ignorance leaves scope for doubt.

But the 'organizational' has not got this inner strength. By definition, because it prides itself on the discreteness, not the interrelatedness, of the known. Once the pass is sold, and the possibility of the 'organizationally' real having its own validity is lost, then the entire edifice - or, rather, population of separate entities of meaning - must collapse. 'Things', 'people', 'organizations' all collapse, all become but what they basically must be - the subjective variously knowing itself in time.

This abstract observation is crucial. Society - organizations, laws and roles - is but a concordance of initial biases. Values are hypotheses that gain their strength through the approval, not the doubt, of others. Politics replaces experiment as the arbiter of truth.

There is a social logic of illusion, just as there is a scientific logic of disillusion. Both, though, are based foursquare upon our fragile categorization of the world outside. The 'scientific' is the subjective maintaining itself through its very consistency, the 'organizational' is the subjective indifferent to testing or disproof, resting - at least for its values - on a social ground. Despite their glaring contrast, they are finally united by a common base.

But is not the remedy then worse than the disease? What boots it if we can plot the crystallization of subjectivity into value, or the growth of its internal consistency through the discipline of organized research, if the price that we must pay is that of reliance on what both sides reject - the raw, naïve, assumptions of the half-formed thought? Worse than this, are we not selling the pass back to the 'organizational'? Back to the world of the poet, child or savage? Having so sternly resisted blandishments of either side as conclusions, it would be a sorry thing indeed if some of such conclusions were then granted the status of a necessary antecedence.

The subjective must be used as a necessary, not a sufficient base. It will not be used to 'explain', but rather to attenuate the 'explanations' of others. Without an awareness of this necessary substratum of diffidence, even scientists will succumb - the 'organizational' is not just found with children, poets and men on Clapham buses - it is far more prevalent than that. Perhaps the most organizational word in language is 'the', implying discreteness and a pre-eminent relevance - and there are always plenty of people doing that.

A PRACTICAL ENVOI

One thing that must impress the outsider to psychology is the number of competing descriptions there are of behaviour, none of which will countenance the other. This is a bit of an overstatement, but not much. Thus there can be at least three levels of description for most individual behaviour (social behaviour is more complex); the physiological/neurological level, the psychoanalytic level and the learning theory level. Given a child that cannot read, for instance, the first will speak in terms of brain damage or of perceptual difficulties, leading to the confusion of b's and d's, the second will speak in terms of unconscious aggressions and the difficulties in 'taking in', the third in terms of poor past learning experiences, the need to reward new and extinguish old responses.

Now I don't want to suggest that any of these accounts are 'wrong'; behaviour is so complex that every approach, however far-fetched it might appear, should be entertained - if it helps. What I do want to stress, though, is that many specialists see their specialism as the specialism, dispensing not helpful description but conclusive 'explanation'.

'Explanation' has a status, not unlike the objective, i.e. it is very desirable indeed. Oddly enough, this exclusive claim can be bolstered by pragmatic diffidence. 'Explanation', we may well say, 'is what works - if I can teach a child to read, where he could not read before, then I have touched the cause.'

This pragmatic basis of truth is in accord with the anti-exclusive approach taken here. However, we should not from that infer the answer or the truth. Whenever we obtain a result, it is by courtesy of, rather than due to the irrelevance of, the other levels of discourse. Granted common learning experience and common neurological condition, it can be useful to invoke psychoanalytic formulations of the difficulty; granted a satisfactory mental adjustment, and satisfactory teaching, it may well be useful to look at the hereditary factor. Simplicity of cause is something to be wondered at, not asserted. To forget this is is to turn a fine and diffident pragmatism into an exclusive preoccupation with one's own approach.

This, organizational as we are, is very easy to fall into. We must constantly interrelate to preserve our diffidence - our certainty too often starts where our preoccupations cease. (Those that have no interests in neurology rarely accord it much descriptive weight.) In this we are wholly wrong - it is only through contrast that we can attain perspective and the resilience that this brings. Those that claim too much for their approach must view all others with suspicion - where others are excluded, there is their very existence rightly seen as threat. There is no room for more than one omniscience.

Thus we must take the subjective seriously - but realize that this subjectivity must, as all else, depend upon its implications for its force. The 'subjective' and the 'objective' (to use terms loosely) must define each other.

Certainly at the level of organizations. There we can see the intentions of men take legal, moral form. The public and the private both must count. Where the latter can be said to 'cause', the former can 'define' - and, after all, causes and definitions are much the same.

Chapter 10

A NOTE ON THE DEFINITION OF SYSTEMS

In the last paper in this collection (The Organizational and the Scientific), two orders of existence were discussed, the 'organizational' that so very frequently impresses itself upon our naïve view and the 'scientific' that allows us to predict and then, with luck, control. Examples given of the 'organizational' were the existence in our lives of 'things' or 'objects', 'life', 'freedom', 'intrinsic properties' (such as 'she is beautiful', beauty resides 'in her') and the formal, organizational role. This last - being a 'foreman', for instance - was the starting point of the earlier paper and so gave this order of events its name.

Organizational concepts were self-evident - therein lay their strength and disrepute. How could one doubt that one was alive and free? Surely such assumptions speak of themselves and need no outer cause? And therein lies the rub - so obvious are they that they justify themselves. And that, in science, can never be allowed.

Scientific concepts were described in the earlier paper as an 'outside-in' affair. What something 'is' can only be the way that it responds - to that which is 'outside' and not itself. Those studying water must make it hot or cold - varying the outer conditions with which it must contend; those studying our bodies will expose them - amongst much else - to surgery or drugs. There is nothing else that we can learn - that which remains unchanged remains unknown.

Not so the 'organizational', this is known in and of itself - indeed is most itself when in repose. Those who feel 'pain', for instance (and pain is but the organizational 'life' knowing itself to its own disadvantage) see such pain as existing in itself, its quality immediate and direct. Of course we all know that pain has outer 'cause', but outer cause is not the pain itself.

Pain is a dramatic, unpleasant example of something very common in our lives - that which impinges in and of itself. The same, for example, can be said of 'things' - things are 'really seen', indubitably 'there', ready to be kicked by those that would assert their helplessness before them.

We see the world in self-sufficient terms. All around - and, indeed, within us - is that which convinces of itself. This even holds for the abstractly known. The idea, for instance, of a formal role - the foreman with certain granted powers - is but another case. A foreman, too, is 'there', something we must acknowledge unless removed. Indeed, the formal role - eponymous to the organizational form - is, but a 'thing', sensed in abstract terms.

And bolstered by a moral base - that of 'authority', the legitimating value-laden source, socially maintained. Indeed, all the organizational reduces 'is' to 'ought'. That which is 'sensed of itself' must stand apart and remain dependent on a inner quality (Plato's 'idea', Aristotle's 'form', the 'élan vital' of Bergson) to give it its distinctiveness - the sole existence it can ever have.

At every point this is at odds with science. Science reduces to a common base - it must, for it cannot deal with the unique (not in itself, that is). Science certainly cannot understand such a pre-emptive term as 'value'. An 'ought' to science - crippling to those that heed - is but another 'fact' to be explained.

These forms are logically distinct - but logic for good or bad does not wholly rule our lives (just as well, for logic is a most reactionary affair) and distinctiveness in theory is only matched by the elusiveness of what is actually 'there'. In practice, our awarenesses are hopelessly confused. We sometimes feel 'free', sometimes coerced (how could that which was really 'free' ever be anything but 'free'?); a man in love will see goodness 'in her', enduring till the stars turn back the sky - and then confess such self-evidence is less self-evident at times; even 'things', those entities whose very existence depends on their independence and distinctiveness to their surround, can exist 'to some extent', be fashioned and then left to break apart. Process congeals to structure and then dissolves.

This elusiveness and contingency of the uncontingent is crucial - for it argues the continued relevance of outside circumstance. But we forget this, 'organizational' as we are. We take what is 'there' and say it 'has to be' in some 'necessary' way and forget the context that has to underlie - a context that one day will re-absorb. Daylight is obvious - indeed self-evident - but only once we see. Those that see forget their birth and growth. The self-evident is but that which appears to have escaped its past - the relevance of anything but itself.

And this brings us to the hero of this short piece, the structuring that will allow time and the causal to withdraw, that will permit the graded elusiveness of the uncontingent in our lives - namely the idea of 'system'. System that, it will be argued, will allow the absolute and the relative, the self-evident and the dubious, the organizational and the scientific, to merge.

First - what is meant by system. This must be clarified. Being matters of degree - like all acceptable ways of seeing things - they have lent themselves to somewhat elastic use. Indeed, systems can be loosely or strictly defined, and, when defined loosely, can be held to cover almost any complex of interlocking factors. 'Loosely', the weather can be held to be a system. With the weather everything affects everything else at once - the wind affects the temperature, the temperature affects the water vapour in the atmosphere, this in turn affects the atmospheric pressure ... and so on. Sorting out which is cause and which effect can be very difficult. So difficult, indeed, that we may grasp at a term, a word, a name that (so easily is self-evidence induced) expiates our helplessness before complexity.

This loose sense will not be used here - at least not intentionally. The intention (if I may use such an organizational term) will be to use it in a strict sense. In its strict sense it will cover those areas of complex interdependence that are not only difficult to sort out, but also (and this is crucial) manifest some sort of 'resolution' to the forces that the term embraces - a 'resolution' (or 'equilibrium', or 'endstate') that has some degree of dependability and identifiability across time and circumstance.

The human body is a system in this sense. There are obviously all sorts of physiological processes that interact and that are relevant for the state of the body at any particular time. So far so good - the body qualifies as a loose system. But there is more than this - these internal forces also result in a highly predictable set of 'equilibria' or what will be called 'endstates' - endstates that will become the central concern of this discourse.

There are a whole series of endstates. Thus we can as a rule expect that the temperature of the body will be 37 degrees centigrade, that the blood pressure level, the blood sugar content will all be within definable limits, and so on. Further, we can know this even when we do not know the context, the circumstances surrounding the body. Thus, we can anticipate that the blood temperature will be 37 degrees centigrade whether or not the body is standing outside in the cold, or, on the other hand, is sweating away in the heat of a Turkish bath.

The human body is a series of self-compensating mechanisms that enable it to neutralize the environment. Now to the extent that the body can do this - to the extent that it can neutralize the cold by shivering or the heat by sweating, etc., to that extent it can be said to be a strict and not a loose system. To that extent it can be said to have what can be referred to as a 'tolerance range'. The greater its tolerance range, the more stable (the stricter) the system. A healthy body can withstand greater varieties of environment than one that has less internal strength. No one, though, can withstand the environment completely. To put it at its most obvious - no one can 'tolerate' a bullet in the head.

Now let us take another simpler example of a strict system, namely the state of a liquid in a container. The endstate here is the liquid lying immobile in the cup. This endstate has some kind of tolerance range - thus one may jog the cup a certain amount and, if left alone, the liquid will revert to its passive immobility. Again the tolerance range can be infringed - one can upset the whole cup and the liquid, rather than re-attain its old immobility, will escape the system walls and will cease to cohere.

Now comes the nub - both the human body and the liquid in a cup attain whatever tolerance range they possess by virtue of what will be termed 'underlying forces'. The 'underlying forces' in the case of the human body are the complex homeostatic mechanisms described by Cannon, the 'underlying forces' in the case of liquid in the cup are such matters as the strength of gravity, the pressure of the sides of the cup and the surface tension of the liquid.

These underlying forces are the real causal agencies - and all strict systems must possess them to attain any tolerance range that allows of continued identifiability. But - and now comes a further distinction - in the case of the human body these forces are resident to the body itself - the body carries these forces around within itself, the body is what is often called an 'organism'; in the case of the liquid, though, these forces shore up from the outside - the liquid is neutralized in equilibrium not through any internal mechanisms such as the body possesses, but because it cannot - to quote the term used above - 'escape the system walls'. The forces that act are alien and do not 'belong'. It is for this reason, indeed, that the liquid can be poured from one cup to the other, abiding by different external forces in the two cases.

Thus systems, even strict systems, can be considered to be of two types, those (sometimes called 'organisms') like the human body that carry within them their own equilibration, and those, like the liquid in a cup, where the endstate is shored up from outside. The former might be called 'systems of inner strength', the latter 'systems of no escape'.

So much for the idea of system, the formulation that will allow us to subsume the unique (organizational) present to the subsumed (scientific) past. This formulation has clearly the extremely important property of allowing time to stand still (and, indeed, reverse its flow) and thus to make possible the self-sufficient awareness that needs no past.

Time can 'stand still' because the past - itself but part of the context in which all things move - can be neutralized (i.e. not count; a system can only be a system at all by this reckoning if the same outcome can follow different antecedents). Time can 'reverse its flow', when it appears to move forward and 'become' (as in 'purpose') rather than just obey the context of what was there before.

This neutralization of time (even 'becoming' is but an attainment of the quietus of no time) is that which permist of the self-evident in our lives. For the self-evident - the self-assertive present that denies its flow in continuity - is but an endstate that, to the extent that it survives, denies its roots. What these roots may be is the topic of the next paper in this collection, where it will reappear under its Piagetian guise of 'equilibrium'.

Chapter 11

EMPIRICISM AND PSYCHOANALYSIS A Piagetian resolution

EMPIRICISM AND PSYCHOANALYSIS

Psychoanalysts and academic (particularly experimental) psychologists are not always mutually at ease. They may not read each other's papers, attend each other's conferences, or even try to see the other's point of view. In this paper I shall argue that such a situation is no simple consequence of specialized concern - those with common interests coming together to discuss - but the result of something more important. For each side feels, not just that the other side rejects it (though of course it does to some extent) but also that such rejection is in some way desirable; desirable - for the other could be a threat.

In this paper I shall attempt, first, to point out the nature of this conflict; second, to account for its occlusion - the reason why even psychoanalysts may not be as aware of it as they should; and last, to show how an acceptance of Piaget's approach could modify this divisive state of things. Piaget, it will be argued, can show how all of us - empiricists and psychoanalysts alike - can come to terms with what the other has to say.

First, the nature of the conflict between the two approaches. This may, perhaps, be illustrated in terms of the 'present' and the 'past'. (The meaning of these two words will soon be clear.) Any statement made at any time - that is any statement we can ever think of - can be seen in two different ways: we can either see it as reflecting what is actually 'there', or, on the other hand, as showing us how someone feels. The first of these, what someone sees - the contribution from the outside world - will be called the 'present'; the second, what someone 'feels' - a contribution from the inside - the 'past'. The pure case of the 'present' would be something visually wholly unambiguous, like Nelson's Column in Trafalgar Square, the pure case of the 'past' would be a dream.

Now the conflict between psychoanalysis and the rest can be summed up by saying that, whereas the empiricist (in the cover term used here) concerns himself with the 'present', that which reflects not the observer but the observed, the psychoanalyst (equally in the cover term used here) concerns himself with the 'past' - not with the observed but the observer.

Perhaps as good a point as any to talk about the beginning of empiricism is the invention of Galileo's telescope. Anyone - but anyone, provided that were adequately sighted - looking down the telescope would see Jupiter's moons - and that whatever past entrenched beliefs the observer might have held. So successful was this telescope, indeed, that the only way an observer could preserve his 'past' virginity was to refuse to look down it at all. And the empiricist learned his lesson. Wherever possible he has preferred data that speaks with its own voice, particularly, of course, those immediate data known as sensory 'facts' (after all, even communist and capitalist, whatever the past cultural influences they may have absorbed, would agree that a tiger existed if actually put in a cage with one). Somewhat lower in the empiricist's scheme of things come those constructions known as 'theories' - just because theories are more open to personal (i.e. 'past') choice; quite excluded has been the rampant subjectivity of wanton 'phantasy'.

Very different is the psychoanalyst. He is not interested in what is actually 'there'. Indeed, if everyone saw what was actually 'there', the psychoanalyst would not be in business at all. He is interested in the past, the idiosyncratic history we all have had. And he is interested in the past in a particular way - not just as a subject of public discourse (after all empiricists can study child development) but as a locus of a particular, 'private' cause. 'Private' in that it reflects not the behaviour but the feelings of those concerned - feelings (and this is a critical point) that hold their own validity. The experienced motive, the wish, what will here loosely be called 'the will' - even if unconscious - is held to be the key.

So there is our conflict: on the one hand the 'public present', on the other, the 'private past'. And the conflict does not end there, it expands with its very elaboration. With every advance in their respective disciplines, the two orders are driven further and further apart. For the empiricist, any 'cause' (that is, identifiable, lawful antecedent) is not only many- (ultimately, infinitely-) sided - an infinite number of factors converging on the consequence - but also something apart, alien and distant from that which he explains. The fear of the empiricist is always that he should be accused of that twentieth-century form of scientific heresy - 'circularity' - explaining something by recourse to itself. And this is just what the psychoanalyst does - for him causality is inward and unique: he appeals to a limited set of forces that lie 'within'. For him the relevant cause is in the motive of the person concerned, a motive defined in the experience of that very person - that which is to be explained enfolding its own point of origin. The stress on the unconscious nature of psychoanalytic causation has obscured the circularity of this position and given the notion of psychoanalytic cause a spurious independence. That psychoanalysts prefer unconscious motives is neither here nor there - for even if unconscious they remain the feelings of the person that is to be explained, feelings that, it is hoped, psychotherapy will bring to his awareness. Far more truly unconscious are the empiricist's own causes - no one can possibly have a clue as to how the injection of certain drugs can, say, make him feel differently.

These two approaches are clearly quite distinct; empiricism is 'meaningless', 'senseless', totally indifferent to our feelings (data that is emotionally impregnated is thereby suspect), psychoanalysis is 'meaningful', 'makes sense' in the most immediate way (indeed, this is where psychoanalysis after all began - it cures). And the 'senseless' and the 'meaningful' cannot be combined. It's worth saying this again to stress the gulf that - necessarily - separates the two approaches. The psychoanalyst, if he took the empiricist seriously, would have to account for how the knower would finally disappear, disabused in a tissue of contingent relationships; the empiricist would have to do the very opposite - account for the development of 'significance', the emergence of the sensed unique. Far better for each to remain apart, secure in its ruling of irrelevance.

Now it will be the thesis of this paper that this self-perpetuating division between the 'public present' and the 'private past' is illegitimate, that it impoverishes our notion of what is 'there' - an impoverishment far more serious in the social than in the natural sciences - and, further, that this division, for all its logical inevitability on its own terms, is only maintained by what amounts to a collusion between the two approaches.

Namely that the apparently blameless contention at the beginning of this paper is not true. Neither side, when they come down to it - whatever their philosophical sophistications - subscribe to the view that 'reality' can only be a reality as stated or observed by someone. Reality is taken to be 'there' by empiricist and psychoanalyst alike. Not 'as seen by someone', just 'there'.

With the result that both sides believe that there can be a final separation of the knower from the known. Thus each can remain distinct - the one personal and intimate, the other impersonal and blind. Now this duality brings great advantages. For since they are distinct, one can ignore - declare irrelevant - what cannot be absorbed. One can write off the subjective (or the objective) as of no concern. Or better still, take each in turn as it suits one - be a primitive positivist in one 'public' scientific life (and dismiss the 'private' as somehow empty) and deeply religious in one's 'private', personal life (and stress the 'private' as somehow privileged). The two can be considered, quite literally, different 'universes of discourse', that do not impinge.

And is not this course justified? Without a separate 'self' would we exist at all? And without a separate 'outside', would we not be totally alone?

Certainly our partisans - both empiricist and psychoanalyst alike - would seem to think so. They both agree (or at least the vast majority of them) that they themselves and the outside world are both 'really there' in some ontologically primary sort of way. Not only do they assert it, but, having done so - and this really is bringing out the big guns - they then declare as 'pathological' anyone who does not agree. And in this they have good precedent: the notion of the 'pathological' (or the 'deviant', the 'heretical', or the 'revisionist', you can take your pick) has been the necessary escape clause for every self-sufficient moral, political or epistemological system there ever was.

Except that this time it is doing rather better. The notion of the 'pathological' (with its concomittant assumption of unquestioned 'health') in this case performs the unlikely feat of making it possible for two conflicting approaches to exist at once.

And is, in consequence, welcomed by them both. The psychoanalyst welcomes it with open arms. As much as any empiricist, the psychoanalyst takes the notion of the external reality for granted - it is the touchstone of mental health, no less. And he does so for two reasons - it gives him a professional identity, since he is the one - or at least one of the ones - who specializes in these 'pathological cases': the 'pathological' - and pathological traits in otherwise healthy people - are his concern. And just as well too, for if his subject-matter were not special, he would find himself alongside other psychologists - and so in danger of being absorbed. (Absorbed, furthermore, by those who would question his idea of cause.)

He can preserve his explanatory assumptions intact since it allows him to lose interest in that which would, to say the least of it, put a severe strain upon his system of explanation. For how could psychoanalysis - that which stresses the inner, private past - ever account for the apparent non-existence of that private past? Ever account, for instance, for someone actually seeing Galileo's moons? How can those who specialize in distortion - and explain distortion in terms of ever earlier distortion - escape the closed explanatory world that the notion of 'distortion' implies? They do not escape or even see the need to do so for they feel no trap. That people should grow up and achieve objectivity is not seen as a problem. As of course it should be: psychoanalysis resorts to the empirically self-evident to save it from its greatest theoretical difficulty of all - how it can, in its own terms (as befits that which is granted explanatory primacy) account for its later non-existence.

The empiricist can certainly account for that. By definition - his whole system of explanation is based on the assumption that the 'public present' can override the 'private past' - that the evidence of Galileo's telescope will win out and that capitalist and communist will agree on the presence of the tiger, despite impeccably compelling inner reasons why they should reject. Not only this, but the empiricist will then go ahead and proscribe - as 'unreliable' or 'subjective' - any awareness that does not have this conclusive force. By sticking to 'facts' that which leads to convergence of observers - only facts can count.

But facts are self-defining - or rather defined by the very fact that they can be observed. And this is their great weakness. For that which is accepted without question cannot be absorbed into any wider context. 'Facts' in consequence are epistemologically alone, quite as much as the psychoanalyst's 'will'. For how can they be integrated with non-facts - for instance, theories? (This is the old problem of induction.) How, furthermore, can they be integrated with a prioris of a different kind? Not just the 'will', just mentioned, but also, for instance, numbers (or 'tautologies'). That two plus two equals four is declared equally absolute and secure, but granted this, what then is the relationship between facts and numbers? Both of these are seen as quite distinct, and, being distinct, need not be related. That which is self-evident need have no past.

And thus it is the world is divided into a trinity of primitive existences - facts, feelings and tautologies (the old distinctions of the Vienna Circle) each solitary in its inviolable sphere.

But what happens when the observer does not oblige? When someone looks down the telescope and does not see Jupiter's moons? When someone insists that two plus two equals five? This, of course, is where the psychoanalyst comes in, and since people always have a motive, whatever its causal status may be, the psychoanalyst can always find something to say. But what can the empiricist do? He cannot resort, as can the psychoanalyst, to the inner experiential wish - his whole approach stresses the message and not the listener, the enduring 'public' not the vagrant 'past'.

What he can do is - just like the psychoanalyst - bring in the idea of 'health' to save the day. Just as the psychoanalysts can use the 'obviousness' of that which does not interest him - the public present - to preserve the inviolability of his private past, so too can the empiricist, in a very similar way, invoke the private past (or something very like it) to preserve the inviolability of his public present. Thanks to the convenient notion of 'pathology', those who do not see (or will not add correctly) are written off as witnesses; their testimony is used as reflecting what they 'are' not what is 'there'. The suspected observer, being 'pathological', becomes an object of study in a special way. Something must be wrong with him (he might even be sent to a psychoanalyst): subject becomes object and the empiricist violates one of the prime articles of his scientific approach and renders that approach invulnerable.

And so something must be done - and that something is none less than the abandonment of our idea both of the public present and also of that which gives the public present its human - as opposed to epistemological - aid and comfort, our idea of 'health'. We must abandon, that is, that there is but one 'present' that all 'right-minded' men subscribe to. Drastic as it may sound, that people should agree at all must be seen as problem to be resolved, not baseline on which to build.

This suggested re-phrasing of the problem of the known is drastic indeed (most of the rest of this paper will be taken up with its consequences); far more drastic than appears at first sight, for it can be shown that it not only presents us as problem what erstwhile justified itself - the public present - it does something (indeed a good many things) a good deal more unnerving than that - it sets us the task of accounting for how we ever come to agree on anything at all. Namely, how we ever, privately - let alone corporately - come to the awareness that areas of circumstance can be called 'the same'.

And that in turn has consequences - namely, how we ever can define.

And this last consequence is perhaps the most far-reaching of them all. Begging the question - taking definition for granted - is the price we pay for intelligibility. And not just intelligibility in the ordinary sense, but any identity, any yardstick (a yardstick is but an articulated identity and hence 'criterion') whatsoever. An approach that destroys our public and then our private present would reduce us to self-defeating relativity - a relativity where, in the last event, neither we ourselves, nor 'truth' in any independent form, could ever be. And by the same token - for 'we' ourselves would not exist as we feel we do (the distinction we make, for instance, between subjectivity and objectivity - 'I will' and 'I can't help' - being now but problem area, not ground on which to build) and 'truth', even scientific truth, arrived at after discipline and research, would be but conclusions that we - as all else in causal flux - would be bound to reach, and so would have the same status as any other conclusions whatsoever. The Nobel prizewinner and the gormless idiot who does not want to know being but brothers beneath the causal skin.

And that is where we shall begin - stripped of identity, criteria or 'truth'. All these must be seen as consequence - consequence of that which is necessarily before the known. And how can that be done? Certainly not by studying 'objectivity' on its own terms, for that, too, implies distinctiveness. And all distinctiveness, whether between subject and object, between movement and rest, between necessary logic and random fact, between random fact and underlying law - all this must be seen as consequence. Consequence of that which everyone (when he has finally been defined) achieves alone.

We are indeed reduced to formless 'subjectivity' - or rather to taking as baseline what will later patronisingly be written off as 'subjectivity'. This does not mean that we can assume any personal identity beforehand - that, too, must be derived - but rather that we must plot the emergence of that distinctiveness that allows us to define - to recognise 'the same' - and so finally agree.

And someone has done just that. And that person is Jean Piaget.

We will now have a brief look at Piaget and see how his contribution (or, rather, one of his contributions for he is an infinitely fertile man) can help us with the problems we have so far met - namely the derivation of distinctiveness, of articulation, of 'the same' - of the public present that is so manifestly 'there'.

THE PIAGETIAN RESOLUTION

Piaget, as he never tires of telling us, is a 'genetic epistemologist', that is, he is concerned with the relationship between genes and epistemology, and the central point of this relationship, the link between the genes and what is known, has been the equilibrium.

An equilibrium is a state of affairs that reverses the normal course of time. With an equilibrium it is easier to predict the future than to describe the present. Whatever may be the state of agitation of water in a cup - and that state may well tax the most detailed account - one can be assured that, sooner or later it will revert to its predictable, 'equilibrated', calm.

Now Piaget has seized upon the equilibrium as the necessary precondition for the awareness of similarity. As a biologist he cannot but accept that the organism is 'active' (i.e. exists) at all times; this, though, poses certain problems. If the organism does exist (i.e. contributes to awareness), how can its contribution be neutralized? The answer is an equilibrium. It is an equilibrium that allows the active organism to achieve the passive awareness of continuity, for with an equilibrium the activity of the organism resolves itself into apparent rest.

And from apparent need of explanation. Because of this physiological infrastructure we can assert things 'are'; 'are', furthermore, quite independent of the knower. Piaget has tackled the most interesting physiological, philosophical and biological question of them all: under what circumstances do we see no problem in what - and that - we know.

In tackling this question Piaget has elaborated an exhaustive account of the entire process of intellectual development. In one span he has covered the (sensory) empirical, the theoretical and the tautological (as in number and logic). Almost everything, indeed, except for the psychoanalytic. (And that, as we shall see, for a good reason.) But that's to come.

Piaget is concerned with the development of intelligence, the way that awareness elaborates itself and so allows of a more sophisticated conditionality - an awareness that so obviously reflects what is 'really there' that it, then, needs no explanation in individual terms.

Or didn't until Piaget came along. Obviousness is the luxury of the limited (indeed, some things are so obvious to some people that it is only when someone else tells them - and not always then, of course - that they begin to have some idea of how silly they have really been) and no one could accuse Piaget of that indulgence. There is nothing, but nothing, however elementary, but that he can render it complex and abstruse.

Take the most elementary awareness of them all - the basis of the whole empirical approach, that on which they depend for any confidence they have - the ability to 'identify' - to achieve the awareness of enduring, recognizable stabilities and so to see 'what's there'. This, with Piaget, needs explanation. And gets it - in equilibrium terms.

This will briefly be described for it will, in illustration, give the entire germ of his approach. Having done this, I shall give one or two extensions of the principles involved to show their width and scope.

Nothing could be more certain to us as adults than that the world is full of 'objects', entities with some measure of invariance that can be referred to as somehow existing in themselves, independent of changes in their surround (indeed this is a precondition of their existence, that which kept on changing with changes in its surround would cease to be an 'object'). Thus, if I see a cup before me, I see a cup - and that is all there is to it (as the positivists might say). Not so with Piaget. Seeing a cup is an achievement we may not attain until 17 months or so. Furthermore, seeing a cup - to the surprise of nobody no doubt - has the properties of an equilibrium.

Because we do not see a cup. We see bits of a cup. We see it from below or from above or from some other angle. Each of these viewpoints, though, becomes for us the 'same whole cup'. Fragmentary perspectives are resolved into an emergent 'whole'. An emergent whole that has the properties of an equilibrium. The 'past' - the angle, the particular viewpoint that meets the eye - may vary if we or it should move. Not so our 'present' awareness, that does not change.

And so we say we cannot help but see. But this is an achieved passivity and self evidence, wholly dependent on our active powers. It is inference and extrapolation - even at the basic level of what we see - that makes possible order and continuity in our lives. Without this ability to equilibrate, to restore the passing to that which then endures, we would never escape kaleidoscopic flux - a flux wherein movement itself could not be recognized, for movement depends upon the continued identification of that which moves. But we do have the powers, and they convince completely. So completely, that it is only with effort that we come to realize how much activity must underlie the stabilities that frame our lives.

(Literally, when it comes to walls. Why do they stand still when we move our heads?)

Two terms can here be introduced. They are not Piaget's but will serve. These terms are those of 'content' and 'criterion' (I hope it will become clear that the use of the word 'criterion' is not quite as misleading as might at first appear; however, to keep its somewhat specialized meaning clear, the tedious resort of inverted commas will be used - as it will also for the term 'content'). The 'content' of an awareness is the particular perspective or viewpoint that actually impinges on the eye. If one is looking at a cup from below, for instance, it only comprises that part that can actually be seen. On their own, as already stressed, these 'contents' would lack coherence. But they are not on their own. Somehow they equilibrate into 'criteria'. 'Criterion' is the term being used for the 'whole', stable cup we actually feel we see. With equilibrium, time has had a stop - and that resting-place is a 'criterion'.

(Where time stands still, doubt cannot enter in. This, that an equilibrium can have a past but not a future - not as long as it goes on being the same equilibrium at all events - may in part account for the helpless certainty 'criteria' so frequently induce.)

But we need not stop at the immediately visual. Mental development, with Piaget, is the elaboration of ever more abstract 'criteria' that emancipate themselves from the 'contents' on which they rest. Three examples will be given, those of classification, measurement and the manipulating of mutually defining symbols (numbers and logic). These examples will not attempt to give any detailed idea at all of the steps by which the development is achieved, rather, all three will show - or attempt to show - how the establishment of 'criteria' goes hand-in-hand with our growing notion of what we call 'the same'.

The growing notion of 'the same' is manifest with classification. Classification allows us to group together and in grouping together to ignore the idiosyncratic. This is achieved through greater abstraction - an abstraction (that is a movement from 'content' to 'criterion') that permits the possibility of wider ranging equilibria. If a child learns of 'cups in general', then each separate cup can now be 'subsumed' and so no longer seen as different and apart. There is now more similarity and less uniqueness in his life.

There is nothing new in this. The move from 'content' 'single cup' to 'criterion' 'cups in general' is no different from the move from 'content' of particular perspective to 'criterion' of 'seen whole cup'. There too there was a loss of uniqueness in his life. Before the cup was 'conserved' in Piagetian terms (i.e. in this language, the 'criterion' was derived) each separate perspective must have spoken with insistent poetic force.

The next example - measurement - is very similar to classification. Indeed a measure is but a purified, monothematic 'class'. Most classifications make various demands - thus a 'cup' must a handle, be something you can drink out of, be not more than a certain size, and so on. Some classifications are simpler, so simple, indeed, that they have but one base. When such 'criteria' can be varied along the quality (called 'dimension') that defines them, we have a 'measure'.

It is presumably a task of supererogation to point out that measures allow us to see 'the same' where erstwhile uniqueness stood. A thermometer allows even the quean's ante- and the queen's bed-chamber to be in certain respects the same. They both have warmth in varying degrees. Indeed, with a measure there cannot be differences at all unless they be of the same 'dimension'. Measurement is but another and more searching form of 'recognition' - the ability on which all classification rests - a recognition that allows of graded awareness of similarity.

Finally we come to symbols - logic and the use of numbers. Here 'criteria' take the final giant step to total independence. For symbols now can define each other and so achieve an equilibrium apparently quite separate from lesser happenings in space and time. At least Pythagoras and Plato thought so, they considered such free-standing 'criteria' were so obviously 'really there' that they could not be accounted for in 'content' earthly terms.

Yet numbers, too, are based on past experience. They are but abstractions from past situations that can be variously recombined to the extent that they do not belong in their implications to specific situations. They are the interplay of 'criteria' dependent on each other for the equilibrations in which their implications permit them to participate (i.e. three equals two plus one, equals one plus one plus one, etc.).

All this is very abstract. The only really important point though, is Piaget's contention that such 'criteria' - 'criteria' that now define each other (three equals two plus one, two equals three minus one, etc.) and so appear autonomous and outside time - are themselves awarenesses achieved in time and but the last example of the whole process of development. This development has, arguably, biological roots and witnesses the consequence of activity upon the contents we all have met.

So much for a Piagetian account, taken at something like blitzkrieg rate. How, one might ask, can such a very abstract, rarified - and compressed - account as this help us with the problems we have met? Indeed, are not the issues raised by this recital so difficult and so abstract that we were better off before it began? At least we were bewildered in a fairly uncomplicated way.

Well the liberty to choose one's own shortcomings is (or should be) a basic civil right and so will not be questioned here. However, for those inclined, it might be pointed out that Piaget with his account of development has shown us in principle how the public present can be the inheritor of the private past, how the individual can become aware of that which will be seen as being 'the same' - and so become a baseline that apparently can define itself. Without the idea of equilibrium and of emergent 'criteria' it is difficult to see how this feat could have been achieved. It is equilibria that underlie the similarities of classification and of measurement (where two aspects have been classified as 'the same' in certain respects, there has there come a resting point from varying antecedents). It is equilibria that manifestly underlie those mutually defining definitions we call numbers. With numbers, to repeat, 'contents' and 'criteria' are interchangeable and the free-standing equilibrium - grotesque thought - has been achieved.

So far this has only referred to the individual on his own, the solitary development we all experience in growing up. By an identical extension of the argument, we can see how a public, not private, present can be achieved and how the individual 'agreeing with himself' through his privately derived 'criteria' can come to accept stabilities that others share. This is not just because others may have the same genetic equipment as ourselves so that unless there is a fairly drastic difference in environment (being brought up in round huts so that we don't see the Müller-Lyer illusion, for instance) we shall come to the same conclusion as others do, but, of more interest and moment, because more abstract and elusive, agreements can be considered in the same terms. A discussion that results in 'agreement' is but another example of the emergence of a superordinate 'criterion' that then subsumes the 'contents' of the various individuals' contributions on which it rests. We all chip in our 'content' point of view and 'consensus', or whatever it is, emerges. When it does. Note, further, that by this account, those of different abilities will not achieve similar agreements and so will not live 'in the same world'. This, of course, is manifestly the case.

This point - that of the derivation of a possibly idiosyncratic public present - may be as good a point as any on which to consider some of the implications of the Piagetian approach for the thesis argued here. The most obvious is that it undermines empiricism - at least as here described. Empiricism that, it was argued, depended for its whole force upon the separation of the public present from the private past, is now held to be consequence of that very private past! Furthermore - and this is also damaging - a consequence not 'obviously' arrived at. Empiricism prided itself on its 'obviousness' - that was why 'facts' were 'facts' - but this 'obviousness' is now argued to have a conditional, inferential base. Indeed public 'facts' are no longer qualitatively different from those private 'hypotheses' that were once put below the salt. Worse still, they are no longer finally distinct from those wanton 'phantasies' that were quite excluded from the feast. For what is a phantasy but an awareness that has not yet achieved articulation, giving us thereby an insight into the unequilibrated ground?

But, it could be argued, equilibration involves disciplined interaction with the world around. As such it must clearly be superior to impulsive phantasy. This is true, but a 'fact', disciplined though it may be, need not necessarily be veridical for that reason. This is not just for the practical reason that people may not agree, but because of the logical reason that the whole idea of a 'criterion' before the event is undermined. Once that happens, there is no abiding timeless on which to rest and nothing can be assumed with final confidence. Not even the existence of 'objectivity' itself, let alone 'subjectivity', 'logical necessity' or 'health'. All we are left with is the constant re-confirmation of a past assumption (to the extent that it is reconfirmed, of course). All standards before the event imply an escape from that arbitary, conditional and to some extent predictable sequence we call 'time', and, by his notion of an equilibrium, Piaget has shown us how the timeless 'criterion' can be achieved.

TWO FORMS OF KNOWING

Is all over then bar the shouting? (Not that there has not been a fair amount of that.) In one sense, yes. Once one has admitted that the present is consequence - and taken the statement seriously and not considered it as something too abstract and academic to warrant weight - then everything that has been said (which is no more than that any distinctiveness that can be treated as the object of thought is achieved) should presumably follow.

Should. But this is really but a glimpse of the promised

land - that most freely available refuge of those that do not come down to earth. What has not so far been tackled at all is 'how'. And once we look at this, difficulties arise.

For two forms of 'knowing' can be inferred from Piaget, both of which can be argued to have disastrous consequences - the second form of knowing even more disastrous than the first. Still, it will be on these two forms of knowing that the rest of this paper will be based. And it will be this second, virtually nihilistic impasse that will provide the basis for the reconciliation of the empirical and the psychoanalytic, the unconditional and the relativistic in one scheme of discourse.

These two forms of knowing are the psychological - that learning follows the 'reconstruction' of an 'anticipation' - and the biological - that learning results from the 'accommodation' of the organism to 'unassimilated' contingency. First, the psychological form of learning - that learning results from the 'reconstruction' of an 'anticipation'. Several points can be made about this formulation: it is what is called a 'feedback formulation' and as such very common; it is 'necessary' and yet incompatible with elementary awareness; and, it involves the idea of 'criterion' in a different form. These points, which have fairly considerable implications, will be somewhat expanded on.

It is a 'feedback' formulation since it argues that the organism must be active in order to learn - there must be an 'anticipation' before there can be a 'reconstruction'. (Incidentally, the term 'anticipation' and 'reconstruction' will not here be used, but 'feed out' and 'feedback', written FO and FB for short.) FB formulations are, of course, very common (cf. 'set', 'expectancy', etc. besides, 'anticipation') and can be argued to be 'necessary' in that they embody the fairly elementary assumption that we participate in all we know - and do so by virtue of being alive at all. After all, we don't learn everything, see everything, or want everything. Being alive at all argues a continuing identity - and hence selectivity - in our ability to react.

But now the difficulties start, for although necessary, it is not compatible with elementary awareness since elementary awareness can manifestly give us experiences that are not dependent on any antecedent anticipation, expectation or hypothesis whatsoever. This brings us back to Galileo's telescope and the apparent 'existence in itself' independent of the observer that the empiricist stressed.

Some of the difficulties of the active organism being passively aware and certain possible solutions in the form of equilibria have already been mentioned in the earlier section. More of possible solutions later, for the moment what may clarify the dilemma at this stage will be the introduction of terms, reference to which will be made later.

These terms are the '+0' and '+-' forms of knowing. Our being passive before the data argues a '+0' form of knowing - that something can really exist, '+', and conversely that something need not exist - that there can be '0'. Our being active before the known argues a '+-' form of knowing for what matters is not what is 'there' but whether what is 'there' is more (+) or less (-) than we expected. From the point of view of the '+-' active form of knowing, 'two cups' could be '+1' (i.e. one more than we expected) or '-1' (i.e. one less than we expected).

The same goes for 'minus two cups'. If one thinks one has lost two cups, one may have lost one more than one expected (-3) or one less than one expected (-1). And so, if the reader will forgive the pun, positivism is nonplussed. It is nonplussed since '+1' depends for its positive quality not on something actually existing, but on something being 'one more than expected'. From this point of view, '-1' can be just as positive as '+1'.

The '+-' form of knowing lacks any absolute zero point, for '0' is not objective but rather what we happen to expect. We could hardly have anything more 'psychological' as a basis of the known. Indeed there can now be an infinity of different 'knowns' in any situation depending on where the initial anticipated '0' point might be (thus '+2' (or '-2') cups could be one more, two more ..., one less, two less ..., than expected).

So the impossibility of an active knower being passive before the data can be re-phrased as the impossibility of the relative '+-' and the absolute '+0' forms of knowing existing side by side. If we do accept that learning does consist of anticipations and reconstructions of a '+-' kind (where '0' is what we expect) how can we ever arrive at the awareness of a '+0' world wherein objects can exist in themselves and '0' has an absolute status? It is very difficult to see how we can.

For all that the attempt will be made; in the meanwhile, before proceeding, it may be worth pointing out a further incompatibility between the '+0' and the '+-' forms of existence. This time the incompatibility resides in the nature and locus of the 'criterion'. The term 'criterion' was introduced to refer to the emergent awareness of the 'whole object'. As such it was contrasted with the 'content' - 'content' described the fragmented input that actually met the eye (the 'perspective'), the 'criterion', the 'whole', 'conserved', 'object' of which we were aware. Now this can be linked to what has been said above - for a 'criterion' residing in an object outside us implies a '+o' form of existence - we acknowledge the 'object-in-itself' - outside; but the '+-' form of knowing argues that the 'criterion' lies in the seer not the seen. The 'criterion' indeed has now become the '0', that is the FO 'anticipatory' personal basis of any FB 'reconstruction'.

Thus any account that starts from a FO-FB, anticipation-reconstruction '+-' basis must not only account for the emergence of a '+0' world in itself that impinges willy-nilly, but must also account for how the 'criterion' can be moved from observer to observed. Indeed, if we are indeed to credit Plato, from the eye of the beholder to heaven - the only place where a non-personal 'criterion' could feel quite at home.

Before proceeding with the second and even more disastrous form of knowing, a couple of additional points might well be made.

The first is ancillary to the above - the '+-' form of knowing not only has difficulty in becoming the basis of the '+0' known, it has also difficulty in accounting for what might be called the

'1 + 1 = 2' form of knowing, namely that inherent in the manipulation of symbols. Numbers, which define each other and can never be escaped (since they are in no fixed place), are even more autonomous than 'objects'. At least Pythagoras put them in heaven some 200 years before Plato thought of adding ordinary 'things'.

The other point is rather different. It is just that in a sense we have been here before although in a different way. The difficulty of shedding the FO 'criterion before the event' and achieving the FB 'criterion in the perceived' is none other than the difficulty the very different approach adopted by the psychoanalysts encountered. These have been excluded for a while and we shall not return to them until later, still we can see that they were taxed on this very point - that of not accounting how 'psychic reality' (which has affinities with the FO - 'criterion before the event' just discussed) could ever, on its own terms, account for its subsequent non-existence. Both cases present clear parallels: how can the knower ever become irrelevant to what he knows?

But the difficulties we have found ourselves with our psychological account pale into insignificance when we come to the second, biological approach. As befits a genetic epistemologist with a background in biology, Piaget sees knowing as the outcome of process, a process that is biological at its roots and reflects the unceasing rhythms and regulations of organic life, rhythms and regulations that are necessary for the maintenance of the separate identity of the organism in question. In order to maintain the processes that permit continued self-regulation, the organism must rhythmically transact with the world around - take in, transmute and then exude. We must take in food, digest and then excrete. In doing so, the organism affects not just itself but the environment as well - wheat once fed upon becomes manure. Indeed, organism and environment are, in this scheme of things, interdependent - the influence of one must act upon the other and so in due course react upon its source. If people stopped breathing they would stop exhaling and this latter would affect the oxygen in the air. Conversely a change in climate can influence the resources available to the organism, this in turn affecting the organism's contribution to that environment.

An organism that has achieved stability and balance with the environment is said by Piaget to be 'adapted'. Adaptation is the point of repose in which transactions of a particular form can reciprocally maintain their interaction.

It is in this setting that we can look upon the known. Knowledge like all else is but a commodity that can be transacted, only in this case the transaction takes on a more complex form - for what the organism takes in is awareness and what the organism releases is activity.

In a sense, of course, all output from the organism can be seen in terms of activity - excretion and exhalation, after all, are acts - and similarly all input can be seen in terms of knowledge, breathing involves some filtering by the organism of what is breathed; with knowledge, though, this reciprocal effect of assessment upon activity is vastly increased. An organism that was only capable of reflexes would have no need to 'know' in the sense that we commonly use the word at all.

The process of knowing may resemble the process of breathing in certain critical respects but in one central respect it differs. For knowledge and activity can enrich each other: indeed knowledge can elaborate itself in its very activity. When presented with a problem of breathing, for instance - perhaps because we are at too high a height - we can breathe faster, but that is about all the accommodating we can do. With 'knowing', though, in an unknown dangerous place, we can not only look around more carefully (the analogue of breathing faster) we can actually - under certain limited conditions - change the structure of the way we know.

If 'to look around more carefully' is similar to breathing faster, altering the 'structure of the way we know' would need as its equivalent something like changing the way we breathe - such as by growing gills if we found ourselves under water. Of course, over the aeons of evolution this has happened to lungs. Evolution, too, permits of structural adaptation - or 'learning'. For 'learning' is the ability to alter the way that we react, an ability, in consequence, justified - from the organism's point of view - by the success of that adaptation.

The forms that such learning can take and the conditions necessary for it to take place is Piaget's principal concern. This will not be pursued here. What will be mentioned, though, is how, in principle, this process of adaptation - or rather re-adaptation - can occur at all.

It can occur when the organism can 'notice' changes in the environment and then 'do something about it'. At this point two Piagetian terms must be introduced, those of 'accommodation' and 'assimilation'. 'Accommodation' occurs when the organism modifies its response to meet an environmental change - growing gills is a major structural accommodation, hurrying up to catch a train when you suddenly realize you have less time than you thought, is a minor behavioural form of accommodation. 'Assimilation', the companion term, determines the form that the accommodation will take. We can't grow wings on realizing we are late, we have to go on using the legs we've got. The environment is 'assimilated' by being absorbed into the resident processes of the organism - we humans assimilate through lungs, fish through gills.

'Adaptation' in Piaget's terms is an equilibrium between accommodation and assimilation. An organism is 'adapted' when it has come to terms with an environment (has 'accommodated' to it) and so been able to absorb that environment into its patterns of response (i.e. 'assimilate' the environment). Threats to adaptation can come from two sources, the environment and the organism itself. The environment may change and the organism may have to come to terms with that change. Of more interest is disequilibration coming from within. The intellectual development of an organism as it grows up can be looked upon as a series of internally determined disequilibrations imposed upon the organism through its greater capacity to 'notice'. These disequilibrations are then accommodated to through the elaboration of existing assimilatory processes - we become more aware of the complexities of the world around us and come to terms with them by adapting the forms of awareness we have already achieved. This assimilatory development can be indefinitely extended - at least it can cover our awareness of maths, logic and science (come to that, it can account for Piaget himself) but, however elaborate it may become, it has its roots in what is virtually a hereditarily determined biological response to the world around - a response anchored at all times in the structure of the organism that makes it possible - and is enriched by it.

Which is, of course, why certain species can 'learn' more than others.

So much for the (bones of the) biological, process form of knowing. Why, it might be asked, should its consequence be 'even more disastrous' in its implications than those of the psychological, FO-FB, +-, form of knowing?

Because, in brief, not only does it suffer from the same disadvantages in an even more acute form, but, in addition to that, presents us with a whole new panoply of meaninglessness - a meaninglessness where, it must be admitted, minor matters like 'disadvantages' are of but passing concern.

First, 'the same disadvantages in an even more acute form' - 'assimilation', that steers the activity of the organism, bears a close resemblance to FO (and, come to that, to the psychoanalyst's 'will' as well), just as 'accommodation' bears a clear resemblance to the earlier FB. Now not only will 'assimilation' have all the same difficulties in accounting for the apparent existence of a '+0' world around us as did the earlier form of knowing, but this very activity of the organism - the FO and 'anticipation' on which all depends - is thereupon itself downgraded to being but part of the wider process of 'adaptation'. As such, 'anticipation' is quite as influenced by 'reconstruction' as 'reconstruction' is by 'anticipation'. Indeed the process form of knowing, when successful, quite undermines both FO and FB - the bases of both psychoanalysis and empiricism! - for both these terms are now descriptive conveniences carrying no final causal weight. One can no more have an anticipation (or FO) without some form of response (or FB) - or conversely - that one breathe in without breathing out - or conversely. A factor that cannot be avoided is never decisive in itself. It is only a factor that cannot be that can have an unambiguous effect.

However, to do justice to the 'process' form of knowing - and to catch a glimpse of 'whole new panoply of meaninglessness' it must be admitted that it is not interested in the 'truth', 'objectivity' or anything that implies that what we know is 'really there'. It is not interested, for knowing is now a practical affair, not concerned with 'truth' but something quite different - our ability to survive.

The way we know is but part and parcel of the equipment that we possess. As such it should be judged - and has been by evolutionary history - not as being 'right' or 'wrong' but as being helpful or unhelpful, quite a different matter. This is not to say that knowledge cannot be 'right' or 'wrong' but rather that the fact that we as a species think something is 'right' or 'wrong' need have no conclusive force: it merely suits us (or perhaps it would be more right these days to say 'has suited us') from the point of view of our survival to think the way we do. Different species survive in different ways and so no doubt 'know' different things. This goes for ourselves as well: the sights, sounds, colours and poetry we all recognize are those that enable us to live. It is insufferable arrogance to assume that they should be more.

Certainly an organism can 'accommodate' and so improve its consequent response, but such improvement - when it does occur - would still be a self-centred affair, even more dependent on the ability to assimilate than on the necessity to accommodate. 'Even more' for there is no reason why learning 'should' occur. Some species just suffer - and we have no idea how much we ourselves are suffering. Change when it comes (and it usually only comes when it must) is filtered through the past - given the same changes, different species will 'adapt' in different ways.

Ways that will thereafter determine their varying 'criteria' of success: we may as a species have transformed the world; in another sense we may have been incapable of asking ourselves questions that we were unable to answer. The spirit of an age is seen in the questions that are not asked.

So much for the 'even more disastrous' implications to which the biological, process form of knowing can reduce us. This 'virtually nihilistic impasse' will here be taken seriously and given pride of place. Other forms of knowing - the '+-' psychological way of knowing and the '+0' empirical way of knowing (as well as the psychoanalytic way of knowing) - will be considered but variants (strictly speaking, aberrant variants) of this accepted baseline. How such an uninspiring baseline (the idea of 'adaptation' is not exactly exciting) could become progenitor of presumptions more perilous than itself will be adumbrated in a moment. In the meanwhile the reader should be warned that in what follows the Master might not agree: the consolation of success before the event is lacking.

But then, with any luck, success will not be there. This observation is not facetious, but, as the reader will see, germane to this thesis. Part of which is that success has always had far too good a press. Anyone can succeed - if he sets his sights low enough. In the workings of our bodies we can witness a success story that puts our mental and social fumblings to shame.

But the price of success is inflexibility. Numerous species are 'perfectly' adapted - but only so long as there surroundings tolerate such perfection. Like some gorgeous, decadent, self-confident aristocracy they must ride on the backs of others. Others - in this case an environment - that one day may not continue to provide. Success has always had far too good a press, for we only see those cases that do in fact survive: the history of evolution is littered with species whose success has been their undoing.

With which insurance policy behind us - on the infinite desirability of failure - a thoroughly decadent attempt will now be made to succeed.

THE APPROACH ADOPTED HERE

The thesis can be simply stated: despite its 'utter meaninglessness', the biological, process assumptions (hereafter called 'process assumptions') will be given pride of place. The psychological, '+-' assumptions and the psychoanalytic 'will' assumptions (which will be discussed in greater detail later) that we all recognize in our daily lives will be considered but maladaptive, disequilibrated variant of the process assumptions. Psychology, in other words, is maladapted biology. Only not quite, since the growth of articulated intellectual awarenesses - the conservations and constancies that end up by our attaining what we call the public present - will be seen as a form of re-equilibration. Awareness of the public present, then, the starting point for the empiricist and end point for Piaget, is re-adapted biology.

Now for a further important point. As the organism becomes re-adapted (by grasping the nature of outside equilibria, etc.), so does it become aware of the causal forces that operate upon it. An organism that is totally non-adapted (presumably at birth, before it has had any chance to digest the onrush of new input that bombards it) would have no idea - from its own feelings - of what were the causal agencies at work.

We start, in other words, with feelings we can't believe and progress to further awarenesses that we can - or we can more. A few words about these earliest feelings - with their necessary descriptive qualities and necessary explanatory limitations - may not be out of place here, for such feelings, it will be argued, will provide the ground and backdrop of any articulation we can achieve.

These early feelings will almost certainly be those of 'omnipotence' - the belief that there is no distinction between FO and FB, between 'must' and 'is', between 'will' and reality. How could we believe anything else before we had become aware of outside regularities that could refute? But, of course, this would not mean that omnipotence for one moment should be believed on its own terms as carrying causal weight. 'Causality' refers to necessary antecedents, not FO insistence. FO insisting on its own explanatory self-sufficiency is, indeed, itself but another example of that illusory self-sufficiency summed up by 'omnipotence'.

Refutation - the loss of 'omnipotence' - comes from accommodation - of meeting the world on its own terms, not ours. Or rather from 'adaptation' - the mutual interdependence of FO assimilation and FB accommodation. Three main headings will be taken to show how adaptation could ensure, these three will be those of 'visual objects' (and will subsume the constancies and conservations that end up with the public present), the adaptation implicit in the grasping of logical relations (logic and numbers) and finally, briefly, 'structures'. The cake will not be cut in the same way as before (when visual objects, classifications, measures and numbers were dealt with) but it is hoped that the conclusions will be the same.

OBJECTS

We will begin with the public present - the first of the three categories of events which will now be discussed. The '+0' world of the public present is an adaptation - and that can only be when FO and FB are in balance. In other words - despite all aesthetic FO experience of being helpless before the facts (so reminiscent of our experience of being helpless before our 'will') - FO depends on FB quite as much as FB on FO. Indeed 'helplessness' ensues when equilibration can go no further - when initial FO, hypothesis assumption can no more be modified by accommodation to further FB - and when the FB we would 'like to see' can no more be modified by FO desire.

What we call a 'fact' is where FB input determines the FO hypothesis by which it will be adjudged - just as the FO hypothesis informs (literally in-forms, gives form to) the FB that will be experienced.

This suggested sequence, though exceedingly simple, has the advantage of accounting for the hypnotic power of the public present, while still retaining the essentially 'meaninglessness' of the 'process approach'. The public present has the hypnotic power - even for the Inquisitor - simply because such awarenesses represent awareness in equilibria. Any awareness where the FO is not 'free' must leave us helpless.

But this does not mean that our consequent awarenesses are any less 'meaningless'. They are still 'meaningless' - at least in the sense of not being 'veridical', of not seeing what is 'really there' - since the consequent 'adaptation' is itself quite as dependent on the organism's FO as it is on the environment's FB. Other species, with different FOs and FBs would see different things. What would be our view of the world - and of ourselves! - if we had eyes on the ends of stalks that could look around corners, and, worse still, see each other? We cannot escape the contribution we make to what we see.

Our apparent passivity but argues successful equilibration - the still water in the cup that never moves. Unless the cup is shaken - unless we get brain-damaged or suffer in some way. Then we can suddenly become aware of how much we have been contributing to our apparent anonymity.

Still, although 'meaningless', it is perhaps not too simple-minded to see the growth of our articulated awarenesses, not just as more and more causally effective - in that FO and FB become more intimately intermeshed - but also more 'veridical' in the sense that the equilibria established need less and less subsequent readjustment. How far this can be finally taken is, of course, unknowable; in the meanwhile, we can note that the preconditions of the effective influence of the FB on FO are plausibly those of where the child indeed meets an equilibrium -

an equilibrium that gives him consistent failure - that is, constant FB to varying FO.

Imagine a child lying in a pram with some rattle tied across the pram in front of him on a string: however that rattle is hit - whatever the nature of the FO - the rattle will rattle and after a while stop - FB will be the same, unflinchable in its inevitability. FO 'omnipotence' will have been disabused.

Where FB can be independent of any one FO, there can FB attain its own identity and no longer be assimilated to ignorant FO 'omnipotence'. The greater the range of FOs, the more this will be the case. When the child, a bit older, sits up in his pram, he may seize, suck, bang, throw and drop the rattle - go through a whole repertoire of (presumably) inherited initiating activities - and the more ways in which he 'explores' the rattle or whatever it is he is interested in, the greater identity that rattle can have.

And so an equilibrium is established - the rattle assumes its own identity in a '+0' way, and the inner 'will' - psychic reality, omnipotence - to that extent is curbed. And by the same token - a precondition of anything being acknowledged 'in its own right' (and not just an extension of a play in which we are the sole actors) is that it cannot be wished into something that is not itself. And that will occur when the outside is to some extent equilibrated. A child playing with a pair of scales can become aware that - under certain conditions - the weights he puts upon them can cancel each other out - and, in cancelling each other, reflect their indifference to his 'will'.

From this kernel, the '+0' 'factual' world - and eventually the public present itself - can be derived. Put another way, this learning by accommodation to equilibria (i.e. that which, like all equilibria abides - the rattle that goes on being a rattle) allows underlying causal 'process' to resolve itself into the empiricist's spiritual base - namely the present.

For the empiricist there is only the present. The 'here and now' is the only final real. The present is a prison that cannot be escaped (and the changing colour of its prison walls is 'time'). Any observation is necessarily in it: it is only because a fact is wholly 'present' (pun) that it is trustworthy at all. To set off, like Piaget does, to define the present in terms of the past, is to enter a quagmire of infinite regresses (since the past that determines the present must itself be known in the present) from which no articulation could escape.

And yet the 'present' seen in these terms (and the whole '+0' absolutism - something either exists or it does not) is, of course, outside time. It is only because events abide and do not change - i.e. allow time to flow past them - that the empiricist can speak with confidence at all. Time is the great diluter. Plato was quite right to place his defining ideas in heaven. The gods do not age.

Hence the power of talking in terms of equilibria - whether of the knower or of the known. With equilibria, the flux can articulate itself. If there were no equilibria, all would be changing flux, if there were nothing but equilibria, nothing would ever change. Equilibria allow us to calibrate that which is not itself.

NUMBERS

They also allow us to define mutually defining relationships, logic and number (though only number will be commented on here). This whole area (the second of the three main headings being dealt with here) has always been peculiarly intractable to the empiricist. By his own book, as we have seen, he can only talk in terms of the 'present' - and numbers, are not 'present'. Or rather they are everywhere and nowhere at the same time, necessarily true and yet invisible. As a result they have always been dealt with with a kind of respectful disdain. Pythagoras, as we have seen, sent them to heaven 200 years before Plato did the same for more mundane identities, and ever since they have had a kind of quasi-religious status - like God, all-important and profound and yet also, like God, somewhat removed from the nitty gritty of the hard graft of science. Not quite certain what to do with them - they have been regulated to the limbo (i.e. pending tray) of 'tautologies', cursed with the stigma of 'irrefutability'.

There are no such problems in the Piagetian scheme of things. Since all awareness depends on the memory of past activities, and there never is a clear-cut 'present' that speaks with unambiguous voice, there is no baseline that can exclude. Numbers are but the consequence of another form of equilibration.

A re-equilibration not due to failure - or, at least, not immediate failure. So far we have considered the derivation of the '+0' world of the self-evident 'fact'. That derivation was based four-square on failure - variation of FO was neutralized by consistent FB response (however the rattles were hit, they always settled down again after a while). But we do not always meet consistent responses in our exploring of the world. To a fairly considerable extent the world we live in (and the infant's world) is within our control - that is, determined by the organism's FO initiative (clearly cognate with the active '+-' way of knowing) and not the environment's FB response. Thus the child can put paid to his rattle on a string (and their 'inevitable' FO reducing re-equilibration) by breaking the rattle or the string. A bit later he can turn a piece of plasticine into all sorts of wonderful realities; or again he can cry out, express hunger and pain and so bring about (he hopes - this is no doubt critical for mental health) his mother's presence. In all these ways, the child does not have to accommodate unilaterally. In the contrary, he can bend reality to his will.

This creative, emergent aspect of the reality that surrounds us - the houses we have built, the very life we have carved out for ourselves upon this planet - has almost been totally ignored by the empiricist and left, in consequence, to those who derive from Marx and Hegel (such as Sartre and Laing) to explore. And no wonder. The empiricist is concerned with the enduring - that which cannot be wished away - not the magical. And our sense of control - and successful control at that - over the daily realities we have to deal with is magical by any standards that do not beg the question. And it is magic - creativity aware of its own achievements - that underlies our grasp of numbers.

Which 'magic' we must now explore. However, before doing so, a certain number of prefatory definitions are in order. This is not just that numbers themselves must be defined more closely, but so too must 'identity', for numbers exemplify in its purest form a new kind of identity.

Namely 'identity-in-context'. So far, we have only considered 'identity-in-itself' (these terms are not Piaget's, by the way). Identity-in-itself - the identity we have considered - is that which, by definition, resists context. The supreme form of an identity-in-itself is the visual object. A visual object is only identifiable at all to the extent that it resists the context that surrounds it. Hence - quite unlike the results of 'creative' abilities - they have always been the bedrock of the empiricist's approach. Each of Galileo's moons, for instance, went on being 'there', resisting context in a bloody-minded way in spite of all the oaths, prayers, conjurations and dismissals that were brought to bear on it. It went on 'being itself' or, as we might say these days, 'doing its own thing'.

But, of course, (and our own 'magical' powers are being left out of it altogether for the moment) lots of environment is less principled and bends with outer persuasion. In other words, it behaves 'lawfully' as we patronizingly put it. This brings us to the new form of identity - identity-in-context. Identity-in-context is quite different from identity-in-itself - entities are now defined not in the way they resist external changes but in the way that they conform to them.

Thus we can have the 'class' (i.e. 'identity') of metals that respond to magnetism and the 'class' of metals that do not. This kind of identity is different from the earlier identity-in-itself in that it is not an absolute. Thus, not only can this identity be a matter of degree (some metals needing more magnetism than others) but can also be a matter of conditionality - two objects being the 'same' if one considers their reaction to condition X, but different if we consider their reaction to condition Y - water and oil are both liquid but they respond differently to fire.

Thus the whole notion of 'identity' (with identity-in-context) becomes diluted into a matrix of possible consequences. What something 'is' (in identity-in-itself terms) being but the residual unaccounted for, the timeless (i.e. unchanging) Platonic defining ideal.

And time is all there is. Or is it? At this point, an important and quite new idea must come in, that of 'reversibility'. 'Reversible' is an adjective given to those changes that can be undone. Thus water freezing is 'reversible' since water that is frozen can return to its non-frozen state - and vice versa - without affecting in any permanent way its identity-in-context, the way it responds to outside contexts (water has been freezing and unfreezing - and boiling too - for a very long while without apparently being affected by these transmutations). But compare the process of freezing to that of burning! Burning really is a goal of no returns. Once burned, burned.

This does not mean that that which is burned achieves an identity in itself - ashes can be done things to, used in the garden and so on - just that the original pre-burning state cannot be recaptured. Time has moved on.

Now reversibility (or rather irreversibility) has a complex, assymetrical relationship with identity. Put baldly, irreversibility has the wider span, for, although all irreversibles do not have identity-in-itself, anything that has identity-in-itself is irreversible.

Ashes have been irreversibly transmuted; but ashes have no immediate identity-in-itself. Ashes, as has already been said, can be used in the garden to help in the eternal cycle of change. But, although the irreversible need not have identity-in-itself, the objects that have identity-in-itself must be irreversible - visual objects (our prototype of that which has identity-in-itself) for instance, are all irreversible and cannot be changed to what they are not. Hence, of course, their hypnotic power and the weight put upon them by the empiricists.

Now for a further complication - although irreversibility is a precondition for identity-in-itself, irreversibility itself, absurd as it sounds, can be a consequence of - reversibility. Thus, by extension, reversibility (as well as irreversibility) can be the basis of an identity-in-itself.

Let's assume that water has a limited repertoire of reversible existences (this assumption is certainly wrong but as an illustration it will serve) and that all that can happen to water is that it can be frozen, unfrozen, boiled and unboiled for the rest of eternity, then the triad ice-water-steam - a triad of reversibles - becomes itself a complicated form of irreversible - an irreversible that cannot be 'done anything to' and so has identity-in-itself. Water as water has no identity-in-itself and can change but water as ice-water-steam has identity-in-itself and cannot change.

Thus identity-in-itself, although only a sub-category of the irreversible, can nevertheless owe its existence to a set of reversibles. If all there ever can be is ice-water-steam - then, at whatever point in eternity we look in (and we can look in anywhere, the outcome in the long run will be the same) ice-water-steam is all we shall find and, in a sense, no change will have occurred at all. And hence no time will have passed. This higher order identity-in-itself will be called meta-identity-in-itself.

Thus can identity-in-itself come in through the back door of reversibility. As long as the snake eats its tail and our end is our beginning then, however complex the intervening process, there is a unity in everything that can be.

Or is there? How far this can be taken will be commented on later when we come to structures. Certainly on the face of it, the argument is overwhelmingly seductive. Before being seduced, though, a yet further complication besets us. Perhaps in the nick of time to save us from a fate worse than being subsumed.

That complication is the following: that the reversibility that can lead to meta-identity-in-itself need not be based on any underlying identity-in-itself whatsoever. The snake not only eats its tail, it is also suspended in mid-air.

So far everything has been based, in the last resort, on identity-in-itself - Jupiter's moons, for instance. These identities-in-themselves can then be shown to have identity-in-context and, on occasions, to be reversible. To the extent that they can be reversible, can the identities-in-context themselves achieve a meta-identity-in-itself. In other words, we begin with water (identity-in-itself), then see how water changes with heat, etc. (identity-in-context), then see how the set of changes (water to ice to steam, etc.), if they change back, can become the meta-identity-in-itself of ice-water-steam. That is what has been said. What is now being said is that the basis of this progression - the identity-in-itself of water, etc. - can itself be dispensed with. And can be dispensed with in that sheer reversibility - not based on any underlying identity-in-itself - can achieve its own higher order meta-identity-in-itself.

And the most comprehensive example of this autonomy and what we have been leading up to all along is number.

'Fact' - the obtrusive 'self-evident' - has been argued to be never pure, but always admixed (at least in any articulated form) with the knowers powers of integration. But facts, for all that, retained some alien FB base - some input from the outside world we were not adapted to. With numbers, though, we go one further and the activity of the observer - present in all we see and know - achieves its own equilibration. Numbers (as such) exist only in the minds of men.

Or so it would appear. Numbers, after all, are entirely self-defining and are suspended in mid-air. What is '2'? 1 + 1. And what is '1'? 2 - 1. The circle is complete. And furthermore quite detached from anything else. Each number has zero identity-in-itself, but numbers as a whole, taken as a package deal, have an invincible meta-identity-in-itself.

And how is this derived? The empiricist, as we have seen, has no answer. If we were honest he would be a Platonist. For Piaget, though, the problem does not exist. For numbers, like all else, are the result of activity. Only this time activities that are spread in time not anchored (as with our last example of the visual object) in the here and now. Numbers are but a form of ordered memory. And memories have a curious immortality.

Numbers are spread in time (hence their odd quality, already referred to, of being everywhere and nowhere, of being necessarily true, and yet quite invisible) and that which is spread in time can also achieve an equilibration (only, of course, at the cost of losing immediate identity-in-itself). This equilibration, too, can be irreversible - numbers, once achieved, need not then turn into anything else.

Thus, in order to understand numbers (and here we come to the whole point of this long preamble), we must understand how people learn them. And so we come at last to our infant who has not yet - despite this complex argument - achieved mastery of number one (optional pun).

The awareness of numbers is achieved through abstraction. As indeed, with Piaget, are all awarenesses (even the awareness of the visual object implies an abstracted 'criterion', emergent consequence of more 'concrete' 'content'). Abstraction, though, in this case, of a particular kind - not that of 'objects' but of 'acts'. Numbers summarize the implications of what we have done.

Numbers are based on the 'magical' abilities of the doer - on the child's ability to control and manipulate his environment. This activity allows him some measure of escape from the intrinsic qualities of the present (since he can change the present) but does not (since the child's control is but limited control) enable him to escape some, at least, of the consequences of those acts. Time, which gives way to our initiative, all too often catches up with us and shows us the consequence of what we have done.

Numbers summarize some of the delayed consequences of creative acts - those that can be ordered in degree. And, more particularly, can be undone. Activities, too, can sometimes be 'reversed'.

Not always, of course. So far, the great weight has been on 'irreversibles' - that 'done' that cannot be 'undone'. The perception of visual objects, for instance, has this quality - 'contents' merge into 'criteria' and there lock - what is seen cannot be unseen. (Hence, indeed, its resilient identity-in-itself.) But the same does not go for all forms of activity. Some activity is cyclical - like breathing - some activity has a wider inevitability - like that of maturing and eventual decay - and some activity can be undone.

The child can build a tower of bricks and knock it down. We can all of us come home again at night, get divorced, even commit suicide. All these reversals are a way of bringing back the past - to the time when there was no tower, had not left home, been married or been born. It is out of such bringing back that we can escape the self-justifying flow of process, and learn to compare the consequences of our acts.

If we are a child, we can do more than knock down towers. We can collect our marbles in a pile and then scatter them over the room again. We can bring together and then separate. We can add and then subtract.

It is out of such activity - of taking together and then spreading apart (and building and knocking down towers is another form of doing just that) that numbers are born. Even number one, basic identity, can be thought of as that which cannot be taken apart. We learn that 'two' - 'one' + 'one', the result of an act of bringing together - has features in common with the results of other such acts of bringing together - whether such acts concern such empirically different contents as bricks, sweets or teddy-bears' legs. In every case, where 'two' has been realized, another 'one' can give us 'three' - and 'three' is different from 'two' (and also 'three plus one', or 'four') in that 'three cannot be split in two.

And so on. Very soon a different form of reversibility emerges - not what might be called the 'voluntary reversibility' of knocking down bricks (the term, of course, is descriptive) but the 'imposed reversibility' implicit in the degree of articulation already achieved. Voluntary 'reversibility' refers to what is done, 'imposed reversibility', to what is necessarily learned.

'Imposed reversibility' can be seen as ground determining its own figure. (The reader should be warned that once more these are not Piaget's terms.) If we know that there are thirteen cards in a suit at bridge, for instance, then we know that if we can account for ten of that suit in three hands, that the three remaining cards must be in the unknown hand. The implications rebound off the framework that has been achieved - and 'failure', offset by 'voluntary' activity, returns through the back door of the inescapable consequence of 'implication'. You are 'free' to eat your cake, but, having eaten it, are not free not to have eaten it. You are necessarily minus one - at least as regards cakes.

So here. A child will learn that, if he has four and takes one away, he will be left with that set of implications we call 'three' - and need not look, after a while, to confirm. Thus does framework slowly assert its own autonomy. Indeed it ends triumphant and dictates a form of reality, quite unachievable by direct empirical approach. The allusion is to the number 'nought' - an absolute consequence of a logical necessity, a necessity itself based on experience.

This grasping of necessity is greatly accelerated by the ability to 'internalize' our acts (an ability, called by Piaget the 'symbolic function', that emerges between one-and-a-half and two years). We need no longer actually eat our cakes and knock over our towers, now we can begin to imagine what would happen if we did. 'Flout 'em and scout 'em,' say Shakespeare's underlings in 'The Tempest' (and we are all Time's underlings), 'thought is free.' With this freedom we can envisage the timeless consequence of acts that could not be done. Consequences that could themselves be starting points and so contribute in turn to the wider framework that defines, and is defined by, those relationships we call 'number'.

(For those interested, this can be rephrased in 'content' and 'criterion' terms. Each number can be looked on as a 'criterion' - or equilibrium - that subsumes its varying 'contents' - 'contents' that are themselves 'criteria' of varying 'contents'. Thus 'six is a 'criterion' - or equilibrium - subsuming 'content' five plus one and 'content' four plus two, etc., and five is a 'criterion' - or equilibrium - subsuming various 'contents', one of which is six minus one. Where 'content' and 'criterion' are thus mutually defining, the circle is closed and equilibration is complete.)

And thus does 'adaptation' once more return. Only in a very curious way. Not, as with visual objects, where FO and FB equilibrate, but rather where FB, bending back upon itself in time (through the good offices of memory), defines itself quite independently of any FO supposition. With numbers it does not matter where you look. And so the psychological '+-' world of anticipation and reconstruction - and activity, such as knocking down towers - is quite left behind.

Only to be revealed again by those who study not the nature

but the genesis of our awarenesses. And those who study that (and look at children like Piaget has done) will realize that these two - 'nature and 'genesis' - cannot be kept apart.

STRUCTURES

This evolution of the meta-identity-in-itself, we call number has a bearing on the last form of equilibration that will briefly be considered - those of 'structures'.

So far we have had examples that have either been very concrete or very abstract. The 'very concrete' equilibrium was, of course, that of the visual 'conservation', the 'abstract' equilibrium, the one we have just discussed, that of 'number'. The question to which we can now briefly address ourselves is whether there could be a form of equilibrium in between - that was neither as concrete as the one nor as abstract as the other, but just as 'equilibrated', just as 'necessary' as what we see or how we add.

The answer to this question - an issue of contention at the moment - is a modified 'yes'. Or rather a 'yes-but'. 'Structures' (as these middle range equilibria from now on will be called) can emerge whenever the initial observations can themselves be modified by the conclusions that they have made possible. Put in the terms used above, whenever the visual hard datum of the identity-in-itself leads to the development of assumptions that then modify our view of that datum. This, of course, happens all the time - the identity-in-itself of water, is seen also to possess the identity-in-context of being changeable to steam or ice; this, in turn, leads to the meta-identity-in-itself of 'ice-water-steam'. This meta-identity-in-itself can be argued to be a 'structure' since we now see that what we first started with - the 'necessary' fact of the existence of 'water', with all its context-resisting identity, is now 'really' (or 'usefully to be considered but' - or whatever other form of triumph or apology we use to gloss over the miracle) but part of a wider identity.

Structuralism is the consequence of definitions becoming consequences. Whenever this happens - and it is constantly happening - we are put in an impossible dilemma from which there is no escape. Except, of course, evasion - the usual resort before the extremely high status of some of the advocates of the structuralist position (such as Piaget himself) made it impracticable.

The consequence of definitions becoming consequences is very serious since it means that the time-bound datum (identity-in-itself) becomes absorbed by the time-free (because always enduring) assumption (the meta-identity-in-itself) that it has made possible. And it is not just the identity-in-itself, but also identity-in-context that is absorbed. The 'event' of water turning into ice, for instance, (water exhibiting its identity-in-context) is but part of a process (water turning into ice and steam) that has always happened and always will.

Thus is the hard data of science trivialized by the assumptions it makes possible - assumptions that constantly grow as science progresses. As the present of the identity-in-itself is progressively absorbed by the reciprocally defining - and hence, enduring, meta-identity-in-itself - the natural sciences tend to become as emancipated from the here and now as numbers. Numbers, of course - implications wholly shorn of the adventitiousness of the identity-in-itself - are the limiting case to which all structures tend. Parmenides - who argued that there could be no change - laughs again.

Not least, because the arguments for this progression cannot be refuted. Not, that is, from the Piagetian perspective - subsuming the identity-in-itself into the meta-identity-in-itself is no different from subsuming a 'content' into a 'criterion' (a meta-identity-in-itself is clearly a 'criterion' writ large) and so necessary for the awareness of any articulated sensory datum whatsoever. The object must be conserved before it can be observed.

'Structures' are but another example of equilibration - of data reciprocally defining each other and so escaping their several pasts. The only escape from structuralism is a Platonism that insists that the identity-in-itself cannot be reduced. It may or may not give the empiricist consolation to note that his staunchest ally in this matter - equally adamant about not being 'reduced' - is the psychoanalyst.

So much for the 'yes', now the 'but'. Structuralist knowledge has all the necessary strengths and practical weaknesses of knowledge after the event. It may be able to swallow its own tail and then suspend itself in mid-air - but only after someone has put it there. Piaget, structuralist though he is, and stressing the necessary self-equilibrating quality of an equilibrium once arrived at, though he does, is also the child psychologist who plots the painstaking steps by which this subsequent emancipation is achieved. To deny the logical force of the structuralist position (unless, of course, one becomes a clear-headed idealist of some kind) is silly, but to adopt a superior attitude towards those that are still earthbound is perhaps sillier still. Certainly it is more sterile - kicking away the ladder that has enabled one to get up to where one has, is condemning oneself to never getting any higher.

(And not just that, but, it can be added parenthetically, to being factionalist as well. Equilibria, as we have seen, appear to have no past, and the avowal of an unqualified structuralism by specialists - such as linguists or sociologists or psychologists - is a marvellous way of creating a new identity-in-itself at the subject level - thus cutting off that area from being subsumed. Structuralism in sociology, for example, is a great defence against those narrow-minded reductionists, quite incapable of seeing the larger view - and it is true they are incapable of seeing the larger view - we call 'psychologists'.)

Only when all relevant data have been absorbed can there be a final restructuring and equilibration of the achieved. When that happens, there will perhaps not be the compartmentalization of knowledge as we know it now. 'Perhaps' because we shall never know when - or whether - that that time has come.

Anyway we may not be interested in those lofty altitudes. There is, after all, plenty to talk about besides the absolute. Our lives may be lived at a very low level of discourse and of no interest in the wider scheme of things, but, for all that, they are the only lives we are likely to get. There may be only fifty-two cards in the pack and every hand we get may be a sampling of those fifty-two, nevertheless our particular hand (i.e. 'life') may present us with problems enough - as well as an identity which, limited in our horizons as we are, we tend to cherish.

THE RELEVANCE FOR PSYCHOANALYSIS

Now, at long last, the relevance of the above contentions to the psychoanalytic approach. To summarize what is to come, the approach adopted will be extremely critical of the psychoanalyst's causal assumptions (of explanation in terms of the 'will' or 'psychic reality') but, despite this, very appreciative - far more so than any unreconstructed empiricist would ever be - of the descriptive usefulness of the language he uses. Indeed, in large measure, this language will be held to be neither bad nor good but inevitable - and of far greater scope than might at first seem plausible.

It might, at first blush, be thought that the psychoanalyst would welcome the Piagetian thesis. Has it not undermined the psychoanalyst's arch-enemy, the empiricist? and has it not done so by insisting - just as the psychoanalysts do - on the explanatory primacy of the 'private past'?

The answer to this question is, of course, 'yes', but this is a 'yes' that brings but little cheer to the psychoanalyst (unless the spectacle of seeing the empiricist - always so ready to rubbish the psychoanalyst of being 'subjectivist' - himself reduced to a subjectivist base, is enough to keep him going). Little cheer since the 'private past' is not necessarily the inner 'will'. Indeed, the whole Piagetian progression is one of emancipation from, not continued thraldom to, the inner will. In other words we start riddled with egocentric phantasies - but we end up at the end of the day, contemplating those impulse - and random - free awarenesses we call 'structures'.

Unless something goes wrong. What now requires explaining and what should be attempted is not, as the psychoanalysts contend, the persistence of primitive impulses in later life (adult neurotics being described in terms of early impulses) but rather the loss of these very impulses. We should not ask why neurotics are still crippled by their past (not in the first instance anyway) but - and this is a much more powerful question - how it is possible that any of us ever can escape.

As we do. For the psychoanalyst to turn his back on the developments we make and to insist that the area he is left with - those that do not develop as others do - can be treated on its own, with its own set of laws (the 'will', etc.) that are quite enough in themselves, is to behave like an old, blind emperor still claiming total power, not 'recognizing' the provinces he has lost.

Just as the empiricist loses the explanatory primacy of the '+0' 'fact', so too does the psychoanalyst lose the explanatory primacy of the '+-' 'will'. Both 'fact' and 'will' are now but staging posts in a process of adaptation - the latter ('will') primitive and deluding in its explanatory force, the former ('fact') equilibrated and deluding in its explanatory self-sufficiency. Once we adopt a 'meaningless' biological approach - an approach that does not recognize the 'self-evidence' of 'fact', 'will' or 'health' (be that health physical or mental) - we can no longer escape facing up to the more important questions.

Such as the one mentioned above - how it is possible that we should ever escape the immature - shed our imagined feedback of 'phantasy' and adopt instead later, more sophisticated, awarenesses.

A pitifully small attempt to answer this question has been made in this paper (in the assumption that equilibration is the consequence of constant FB to varying FO, the child playing with his rattle) and no more will be done here. It may be worth noting before moving on, though, that there is no reason in principle why the answer - when we do get it - should be anything like we expect it to be. It is quite possible, after all, that we have wrongly defined the problem - with the result that we would not recognize the answer if we saw it.

So far, the process approach has been hostile to psychoanalytic assumptions. That, however, is not the end of the story. Although it has been critical of explaining people in their own terms (in terms of what the people themselves feel about things) it not only fully recognizes (infinitely more than would any empiricist of the hard school) the necessity - or rather, inevitability - of taking peoples' feelings seriously (of which more anon) but, further, it can help elucidate - or at least cast new light on - the psychoanalyst's own problems.

Perhaps the best example here is that of the derivation of the ego - surely one of the psychoanalyst's great weaknesses. The ego can now be seen to be an equilibration, that is a resolution of disparate tensions, not a unitary concept in its own right; an equilibration, furthermore, that marches pari passu with our other equilibrations. Just as we learn to 'conserve' objects outside ourselves and see them whole, so we learn to 'conserve' impulses inside ourselves and feel them whole. The two are almost certainly mutually dependent - were there no stabilities outside we would surely be hard put to it to integrate our inner conflicts (or at least inner incoherence); conversely, it is plausible to argue that, were there no inner basis of incipient resolution, it would be more difficult to come to terms with outer stabilities.

An ego, that is, can be looked upon as derived and the Piagetian approach can give us a form (that of equilibration) by which the derivation could be achieved. This again helps us in the phrasing of psychoanalytic problems since it suggests that processes such as 'projection' and 'introjection' are not - at least not in the first instance - as their names suggest, based upon the existence of the antecedent ego (I have an ego - or whatever - and then 'introject' into it, etc.) but rather processes that precede the development of the mature ego. From this point of view, residual projection and introjection in later life can be looked upon as islands cut off from wider experience by the rising tide of equilibration.

An equilibration that may itself define the impulses (by now tempered with the graded failures and successes they have experienced) that remain. It is quite possible that impulses cannot recognize themselves and can only be known in opposition to that which is not themselves - that is, when a certain degree of structure has been attained.

As it is not when we are first born. These very early experiences, too, can be looked on helpfully in Piagetian light. Equilibration, like all articulation, implies delimitation. Before equilibration has been achieved, all must have seemed an absolute - absolute desirability, absolute despair. Hence the ruthlessness - absolute insistence on his demands - of the very small child. Hence, also his guilt - for guilt (and here we come to another Piagetian term) is based on the assumption of irreversibility. 'Reversing' has to be learned - first practically and then in thought. Before such ability has been achieved, each impulse and act (and, of course, at first the two are not distinguished) must have a final consequence. But we do grow - emotionally as well as mentally and physically (after all the most emotionally retarded psychopath is a veritable pillar of moderation compared to the extremism of the young infant) and an acknowledgment that this process somehow or other occurs makes possible a quite new (and more optimistic) view of mental illness.

Freud, for instance, noticing the great difficulty people had in free associating argued that this drift to coherence was in fact a defence - the underlying pain thereby being repressed. But from the Piagetian point of view, it is perfectly possible to look on this excessive coherence in a different way - not negatively, as arguing a move away from underlying motive, but positively, as arguing a move towards maturing structure.

Once granted that the move towards structure is 'natural' like growing up (i.e. due to forces we can at that level assume are there) then, to say that people do not free associate because they 'will' not do so (since they are anxious to avoid pain), is like saying of someone who is physically but not mentally mature, that his physical maturity - which is after all all the poor man has - is a 'defence' against his mental backwardness.

In other words, painful feelings are not necessarily 'repressed' (an explanation, anyway, that leaves a large question mark behind it as to what could be the source of such repression) but can also be left behind, relics of a failure in normal development. Once more, what has to be explained is not (in the first instance at least) the persistence of the old but the emergence of the new. The new can no longer be taken for granted - as it was all too much, for instance, with the ego.

And the new cannot be explained by what is already (experientially) 'there'. The new is explained by what is not yet (experientially) 'there'. There is no reason why we should experience the causes that bring about our maturation any more than we can experience the causes that are responsible for our eventual senescence.

The psychoanalyst has (apparently) been content to leave these questions unanswered because of his insistence on the surprising relevance of the 'will'. Even passively experienced awarenesses - like being the innocent victim in a car crash - can, it is stressed, be illuminated (and the patient relieved) by a reference to an active, not passive will. ('You wanted to attack him and saw the crash as retaliation.') From this it has been assumed that the active feeling must have been the cause.

But - to repeat - there is no reason why we should be aware of the causes of our (even unconscious) reactions. Even if the active impulse is 'there', buried in the unconscious, this need not urge that the impulse is primary. Indeed the impulse could itself be perfectly well the consequence of the crash. After all, it had to come from somewhere.

If the psychoanalyst dislikes this analysis, he may (or may not) take comfort from the thought that a directly analogous suggestion was made for the empiricist. He, too, had his absolute - not FO of the inner 'will' but the FB of the outer 'fact'. This 'fact' stood alone - quite as alone as the psychoanalyst's 'will'. For both psychoanalyst and empiricist, though, it is being suggested that FO (that in the one case had granted independence to the FB fact through its passivity and in the other case asserted its dominance over the FB fact through investing it with the 'psychically real') is itself influenced by that very FB over which it had had such varying fortunes. In both cases, it is being suggested, some form of equilibration (mutual influence of FO and FB) ensues. In the latter case, though, it must be admitted, in a rather primitive way - for the FO to assume 'responsibility' and, hence, guilt where it itself was but passive victim, argues an as yet imperfect grasp of (rather than, as the psychoanalysts themselves would imply, indifference to) external relevance.

Masking all this, and rendering confusion worse confounded, has been the great red herring of the unconscious. The unconscious, being remote, reeks of primitive 'cause' and so endows - as said at the very beginning of this paper - its findings with a quite spurious finality. That the unconscious should thus be considered as some sort of a First Cause is but a comment on the psychology of the psychoanalyst - or, perhaps, his patient. Perhaps, at the end of the day, the psychoanalyst pays the price of talking a language his patient can understand.

A far greater moment than the distinction between conscious and unconscious is that between FO neutralized into equilibration and FO as yet unequilibrated and 'free'. FO neutralized is witnessed in our learned articulations - the constancies of vision, the conservations of intelligence, the abstract equilibria of numbers and the necessary equilibria of wider structures; the FO as yet unequilibrated is seen in the impulse and willed desire that has not yet run its course; it is seen in 'purpose' and in the insistence that precedes reason.

In other words, the psychoanalyst's 'will'. The relevance of psychoanalysis - far more than it can give us an insight into the unconscious, or even (at this heartless, theoretical level) than it can be therapeutic in its effects - is that it gives us an insight into the nature of the unequilibrated will.

A will - if its own insistence be credited - that totally misleads; but, for all that, is inevitable and the basis of our conscious lives. It misleads because - according to this biological, process approach - it only exists as a separate entity at all under conditions where it cannot be believed. It is only when the organism ceases to be adapted that FO and FB break apart, no longer fused in mutual definition; FO then, severed from the equilibrating restraint of FB, can dream its own dreams of what reality should be.

And this happens to us all at birth - that violent disruption that reduces us to awareness and to need. But then, bit by bit, equilibration is restored; FO is once more modified by FB and, its illusions being lost, acknowledges what is 'there'.

Equilibration is where psychic reality stops. There is no 'purpose' in the way we see (Galileo's inquisitors saw the moons despite all inner 'will'), there is no longer any motive in our awareness that one plus one equals two (and it took Piaget to show that once there had been), and once we achieve wider structures - well then there is no observer (and so no illusion) left at all - all being subsumed in wider, necessarily equilibrated, constancy.

The way we see, the way we count, the way we disappear in structure - all this was impulse once. An equilibrium is cause cancelling itself out; and, in this case, that cause (in its psychological form) is the inner 'will'.

But, of course, this 'will' - equilibrated in large part though it be - does not retire. It cannot, since the relationship between FO and FB is not symmetrical. FO precedes FB - it has to because the organism is 'alive' (i.e. self-regulating) at all - and, however elaborated in structure it may become - underlying FO is necessarily antecedent - and so 'there'.

Forever being equilibrated, forever being renewed. We recognize this FO as 'free will' - that inheritor of our infantile omnipotence - as insistent to us (however jaundiced, apathetic or intellectually convinced to the contrary we may be) as pain. This free will does not express itself in random terms (as it should if it were really 'free') but (with adults) fuses with those relatively structured courses of action we call 'purposes'.

'Purposes' - disciplined but still assertive 'will' - informs all but the most adapted of our acts - leaving behind as legacy those summaries of our aspirations and successes we call 'definitions'. It is hardly possible to define at all without references to past uses - or past hopes. A 'cup', as we have already seen, is 'something we drink from' (that is, 'something we have managed to drink from'), a 'paper' (such as this one) is 'something that has been written' (definitions by purpose do not imply success!), a 'church' is a place where people 'pray' to God (and so needs to be 'consecrated' to 'act' as one).

It is virtually impossible to exaggerate the importance of this form of definition. After all, it forms the basis of that extension of the non-animistic we call 'science'. 'Science' is but the articulated outcome of men's enterprise - an enterprise that sees the 'control' of 'independent' (sic) variables, the establishment of 'functional' relationships and, frequently, indeed, seeks to establish 'cause' - this latter implying that absurdity, a unitary source (clearly a mirror of a purposive cast of mind - there is one source of purpose, so there must be one source of cause).

This purposive base of science is all too readily forgotten. We are both pushed and pulled towards presumptions of anonymity. We are pushed because purpose is in our blood and creeps all too readily into what we know. We have none of us wholly escaped our self-centred past - so self-centred, indeed, that it was quite unaware of its own relevance.

But there is a pull as well as push. There is the lure of anonymity for those who would presume they do not count - for only thus can they insist that others must agree. A devastating blow, indeed, to many a scientist's pride would be to suggest that his observations are but a reflection of his point of view. The high priest of that twentieth-century version of the Holy Ghost - 'objectivity' - would be revealed as guilty of the twentieth-century version of mortal sin - 'subjectivity'.

This need not happen of course - a grotesquely patronizing remark in a paper like this which, after all, is parasitic on what others have established - but it well can. Scientists are human too, and all of us, unless we are alert to the motivational dimension of what we see as 'there', are all too prone to be seduced into assumptions of personal irrelevance.

Particularly, as we shall see, in the social sciences. Before coming to the next and last section of this paper, though, it must be stressed that the psychoanalyst, by giving us some insight into the motivational and pre-articulate base of what we later take as 'there', can provide an admirable corrective to our presumptions of personal impotence.

To throw away the insights of psychoanalysis because they are not fully equilibrated - where nothing else by definition, at that primitive stage of development can ever be attained - is like committing suicide because we have no hope of being immortal.

Or, rather, pretending that we are not alive.

THE NATURE OF THE SOCIAL PSYCHOLOGICAL

Finally to the social field. Politics may be the art of the possible, but so is life. We can now have a look at the way these three approaches - the empiricist, the psychoanalytic and the Piagetian - can cope with those individual and corporate attempts to deal with the problem of living we call 'society'.

The attempt poses certain unique problems since the 'social' is an area in retreat. The social used to embrace the whole of knowledge - nature was seen in terms of 'personalities' and 'spirits', each of which had their 'will'-ful characteristics. The weather, for instance, used to be dominated by these personalities - Zeus getting angry and throwing his thunderbolts, Apollo driving the chariot of the sun across the sky, Artemis chastely contemplating her somewhat frigid life on the moon.

All these were 'people' (of a sort), to be cajoled, bullied or bribed. Certainly not to be looked on in any cool, dispassionate way - they were far too involving to be viewed with such alienating detachment.

One day, though, the intimacy of poetic involvement was callously left aside, men began the exploration of the arbitrary and the detailed. Man, that is, began to measure. Science, the expansion of the impersonal and the indifferent, supervened.

Praying for rain, in other words, was dropped, - the social was absorbed by the scientific.

But, what if praying for rain had worked? What if Zeus could have been bullied or cajoled? - or had the long-term advantages (in future sacrifices) of a good harvest pointed out to him? Then, Zeus and the rest would still be members (albeit apprehensively respected members) of that wondrous frame of discourse we call 'society'.

Society is where mythology is still alive.

Mythology is the epistemology of the unequilibrated 'will', the set of assumptions - read into the world around - of those whose impulses are unequilibrated and so 'free'. It is the way of knowing of those who still have hope, who still presume that the will itself can bring about what it would see.

It sounds ironic (if not obscene) to regard the world of the primitive in all the squalor of its naïvety as a heroic world where all is possible. But so it is in a way. Who knows? The sun may be propitiated if not seduced. Not so with the sun as seen by science. The price paid for entry into the natural sciences is the rejection of all such hope and talk of 'will'. Meterology only became a science when will was dropped.

Science outlines a tragic world where we must acknowledge what cannot - not can - be done. But in society we still have hope. Society is the venue in which we express our will. As do others - others that appear as mysterious to us in many ways as ever savage thought the sun.

The normal course of science - the denial of the will is not open to us here. Somehow we must do justice to the will - place it in a context that will illuminate without eliminating that absolute. And this must be done while respecting the regularities in society we can in fact establish. In society itself - as opposed to the 'experimental control' of the empiricist's laboratory and the 'clinical control' of the psychoanalyst's setting - will and necessity, heroic and the tragic, jostle side by side.

Above the gods in Olympus sit the Fates. Above the 'will' lies the inevitability of final defeat - the victory of that meaningless continuity outlined by science. I shall now try to show how this amalgam of triumph and failure may be approached in Piagetian terms.

PSYCHOANALYSIS, EMPIRICISM AND THE SOCIAL PSYCHOLOGICAL

But society is even more difficult than mythology. It is even more difficult since, in society, there is a third factor in the equation - as well as integrating 'fact' and 'will', there is also that meta-will, called 'value'.

'Value' might be termed a 'meta-will' in somewhat the same way that a 'criterion' is a 'meta-content' - it subsumes the will, even as 'criterion' subsumes 'content'. But it does not do so in any emergent sense - 'criterion' arising out of 'content' - but, on the contrary and quite differently, it asserts a 'criterion' before the event of what that will should be.

In a totally unscientific way. This 'criterion' is imposed in the name of an arbitrary, self-sufficient, mysterious source, here to be called 'authority'. 'Authority' is not only qualitatively distinct from, it is also superior to, those whom it holds away. Compared to authority, ordinary people have very low status indeed.

And may well be 'worthless'. Authority is the custodian of value, and failure to obey the prescriptions of value casts doubt on the moral not intellectual qualities of the individual, thus giving us a quite different meaning to 'right' and 'wrong'. To say that the Battle of Hastings was in 1067 is factually 'wrong', to break a value is to be wrong in a different way - the wrongness of crime and sin. Not least - and this brings us to one of the oddest features of value - because those who obey the law are, or should ('must' is more important than 'is' in this form of discourse) do so 'freely' (another meaningless term in the eyes of science); furthermore this obedience can induce, if not a sense of euphoria, at least an easy conscience, while breaking the prescriptions of value gives - or at least should (again 'should') - give a sense of 'guilt', 'shame' and general lack of self-worth.

The anaesthetic of value can deaden men to emotional and rational considerations. Emotionally, our spontaneous feelings of compassion can be suppressed by telling us it is our 'duty' (value being precise in its demands) to kill the enemy, or, to take another example, our feelings of shame at accepting financial help from others can quite evaporate on being told that we have a 'right' to certain returns (after all, it is our 'property'; the difference between 'property' and 'theft', Proudhon might like to know, is that we have a 'right' to the former - 'rights' are the demands that value allows us to make); rationally, value can abstract us from the economic world of constrained optimal choice (where a worker, for instance, takes the job that gives him the best return for the least effort - 'constrained' since he only does so as long as no better alternative presents itself) and place us in a position where certain demands are made upon us ('duty') and certain returns made to us (the 'due' reward), demands that we are expected to accept with 'pride and joy' ('I'm proud to volunteer for my country') and returns we are expected to receive with gratitude ('it is the least I can do for my country'). Thus values have the power to abstract us from ordinary causal considerations - context and self can be declared irrelevant. And all this, it will be remembered, at the behest of an inscrutable hypnotic power - 'authority' - that can blight reason and compassion.

This stress upon the intrinsic makes possible a surcease from rational behaviour, namely 'consensus'. 'Consensus' is the word being used for the agreement of two or more people on values. Thus those who 'consent' to the same values can enjoy a conflict-free relationship - 'conflict-free' since each 'willingly' (values, as we have seen, have the ability to create 'willing' obedience) that which the other accepts as 'right'.

And consensus - one of the two most important relationships (at least on the wider scale) - creeps into every crevice of our lives.

But although values are important values are not all. There is jam tomorrow as well here today. Human beings, being intelligent, can plot and plan. In other words a quite different form of relationship is also possible. One that depends not on consensus between man and man, but on the exploitation of man by man. This form, for want of a better term, will be called the 'instrumental'. This, too, must be described.

The central feature about the instrumental outlook is that a course of action is accepted or rejected not on the grounds of its intrinsic 'rightness' but in terms of extrinsic cost. And 'cost' can be defined as the resources (in the widest sense - it could include effort, money or humiliation) that must be made available. With the instrumental approach, economics - in the widest sense - replaces value as the determinant criterion.

The instrumental outlook stretches, of course, far beyond the social. Indeed it is not primarily our social orientation at all - it reflects but the expansion of relativity and the logic of choice (as opposed to the value stress on the moral and the intrinsic). Whenever we go into a shop and look for the best buy (the best return for outlay) we can afford, we are behaving in an 'instrumental' way. Indeed we are behaving instrumentally whenever we make a decision on pragmatic rather than moral grounds.

'Best buys' are unexceptionable - unless we are in a slave market. But we are all of us in such a market, for we all of us have our price. And our price will depend, not upon - and here we take a giant step away from consensus - others' co-operation but our need. The greater our need, the less we will settle for: you can always overcharge a starving man.

The defence of those who need is choice. Childhood is a prison because we have no choice. Blessed are the monopolists, for they shall not be diluted by their fellows. The resultant, net, price will depend on the intensity of desire (which will put the price up) times the range of choice (which will bring the price down). A frigid woman stranded on a desert island with two highly sexed men is in a strong position - as would such a man be if the positions were reversed. If she came to like it or if another girl who was prepared to undercut her should be washed up as well, she would have to bring her price down: blessed are the meek for the less you want something, the less you will have to pay for it.

One's bargaining position can be looked on in terms of 'economic power'. 'Economic power is quite different from the hypnotic power emanating from a revered authority. Economic power is the resultant of a situation, not the intrinsic property of a compelling source - be that source a person or a god. One's 'economic power' does not depend upon oneself alone - a firm's 'economic powers' stranglehold over its workers can be lost over-night if another firm opens next door. Those that want to retain economic power do so, not as in the value world by making themselves more magical and more irrefutable, but, on the one hand by advertising (or 'creating a demand' as it is so correctly called) so that people will want one's products more, and, on the other hand, by restricting competition - through import tariffs, cartels, restriction on entry to the professions and trade unions.

Now it will be contended that values and economics, the intrinsic and the instrumental, despite their total incompatibility (by definition the intrinsic and the relational cannot exist side by side; they cannot since 'intrinsic' means 'independent of context' and 'relational' means 'dependent on context') are the two main strands inextricably interwoven that determine the nature of society as we know it. Society as we know it is an amalgam of principle and pragmatism, of authority and choice. We prey upon each others' dependence and we join with those same others in protective ritual.

Before illustrating these points, it must be stressed that it is not being denied that there can be other relationships between people than those of price and value. Between individuals, there can also - manifestly - be 'affection' (unreasonable - because independent of consequence - positive regard towards them) and 'compassion' (awareness of - as opposed to exploitation of - the other's vulnerability) but, except for compassion to some extent (at least we appear to be a more compassionate society than we were a hundred years ago), these tend to be personal rather than public relationships. Publicly, even if we cannot go the whole way in describing the social scene in terms of moral and economic considerations, we can go a very long way indeed. Sensitive individuals, too compassionate to exploit those near them are perfectly prepared to do so, time and again, as members of a distant group. Particularly when value considerations come to the aid of economic advantage (as they so often do) and persuade us that the stability of society - or whatever - depends upon it.

Back now to instrumental and value considerations. To illustrate the way in which these incompatibles interpenetrate, three brief examples will be given. These will be those of wages and prices, of war, and of unbalanced power relationships between people.

If any area is an open area for economic forces that area is presumably the market. When goods are scarce prices go up, when plentiful, they go down; so too with workers (and, as already seen, many workers keep their price high by keeping themselves in short supply). Having said this, though, it would be quite wrong to write off wages and prices as purely the product of market forces - the market indeed may itself be due to value considerations. There can be quite a strong idea of a 'fair day's pay' and a 'fair price' - even if it is not as explicit today as was the old medieval idea of the 'just price'. The word 'extortion' has a clear value meaning to it (a value meaning which is central to the thesis argued by that arch 'economic-power' man Marx); again, the term 'bribery' has a strong value implication - a 'bribe' is an illegitimate - i.e. not prescribed - payment. Finally, as we all know, the whole issue of 'differentials' suggests that certain people 'ought' to get a certain amount - otherwise 'justice' is not done ('justice' has no meaning in economic terms). The worst conflicts over wages occur when men feel that this moral 'ought' has been disregarded. It is not so much because one's heart is pure that one's strength is as the strength of ten, as it is that one feels that one has been done down.

He who does not pay the 'right' wage and breaks the consensual (value) contract, shall be proscribed. Then shall there be war.

War is an example of the naked use of economic power or 'coercion'. Again, though, what has been said about economic power holds here: the more one is prepared to spend, the more one will buy. The reason why the North Vietnamese were able to keep the Americans at bay was because the Americans were not prepared to suffer - American casualties were far more painfully felt. If someone shows he is prepared to go to any lengths at all, he will very often win. To want something badly enough will lead others to put their price up. It will also mean one gets more in the end: cursed are the meek for they shall be easily satisfied.

But, they are also considerable prescriptions in war. In the good old consensual days before the Industrial Revolution turned all to pragmatism, there was an elaborate code of warfare. Most of that has gone now, but not all. There is still some possibility of moral protest. And also, of course, moral commitment. What else kept the North Vietnamese going?

War leads us naturally enough to 'unbalanced power relationships between people'. The very clumsiness of the wording shows us the lengths one has to go to to get away from value connotations in this area. Certain men may have more 'power' than others - they may be in a position to control. This control, though, (at least in the pure case cases used for illustration) may have either a value or an instrumental base. The pure case of an instrumental control of one man over another will here be called 'coercion' and the man who exercises such coercion a 'despot' (for want of a better word, 'tyrant' would do as well). 'Let them hate so long as they fear', said Lucius Accius about 100 BC. He, presumably, was a despot and his despotism lay, not so much in the stringency of his rule (though it was presumably pretty tough) as in his indifference to the willingness or otherwise of his subordinates to 'co-operate'. Presumably they were unwilling - at least is is being presumed here - and so Lucius Accius relied solely on the persuasive power of external economic sanctions; or, not to put too fine a point to it, on his ability to terrify them into obedience.

The nature of the control, in other words, is defined from below. Compare Lucius Accius's position with the director (hereafter called 'leader') who is granted the 'right' to lead by those who then obey. Such a man can enlist the 'co-operation' - or 'causal participation' - of those who are granted inferior powers.

A 'leader', in other words, can be part of that consensual association of those who 'co-operate' in a group. Differential position in a hierarchy is no necessary bar to a subordinate's acceptance of another's 'rights' - even when those 'rights' extend over the subordinate himself.

So much for the distinction between 'leader' and 'despot', a distinction that shows us the encroachment of value into the heart of differential power.

And, conversely, the encroachment of power into the heart of value. For anyone who has read half a page of history knows that today's tyranny can become tomorrow's legitimate monarch. William the Bastard's ruthless rule - ruthless because the Anglo-Saxons gave him no 'co-operation' - crystallized in time into the impeccable legitimacy of Richard II, the king who was 'not born to sue but to command'.

This did not prevent Richard II losing his throne - presumably because he foolishly disposed of the economic powers he had. At every level these two incompatibles interpenetrate, are qualified, and so, of necessity, of degree. We obey the boss because he can reward and punish. And also because he is, after all, 'the boss'.

And the result of this amalgam is society as we know it, society that has by now become a 'fact' and achieved the status of objectivity. That which is reacted to becomes reality, reality sometimes of the most inexorable kind: the army may be based on myth, but once they've shot you you are just as dead.

So there it is. Even an unreconstructed positivist would be silenced by being shot. Out of an amalgam of primitive fear, magical control and exploitative strategem, society as we know it - with all its demands we must be 'socialized' to accept - emerges. The question that remains is how it can be accounted for.

On the face of it, it is the psychoanalyst who has the most to contribute, whether we are concerned with the magical or, even, odd as it sounds, the instrumental. Psychoanalysis is none other than the analysis of the unequilibrated 'will' - the inner mysterious (and therefore powerful) that defines itself. (A will that, we hope, loses some of its hypnotic power when rendered less mysterious in interpretation.) The central magical belief in 'authority' is but the projected 'will' - a projected impatience that insists that others believe 'our' values and so gives us a vicarious triumph. The 'ought' of principle is but the inflexibility of the infant given a public gloss. 'Consensus' on values is but the collusion of those who use each other to recreate that earliest world of omnipotence before 'is' and 'must' could be distinguished. What, after all, is ritual - so often the reconfirmation of consensus - but a way of shutting out the daylight?

Even the instrumental can, be illuminated by psychoanalytic consideration. Instrumental behaviour is but the application of intelligence to desire. At its base it implies that men are yet unequilibrated and so still seek. They still have 'purposes' which, they hope, the market will fulfil. At least psychoanalysis does justice to this inner driving force and so recognizes -

which most empiricists seem unwilling to recognize - that 'economic power' is no more 'scientific' (in the sense of belonging to the natural sciences) and just as 'social' as magical powers: the sun does not bargain with the sea.

But the Stock Exchange is, by and large, a very rational and disciplined affair. This is the great weakness of the psychoanalytic approach when taken from an ambience of its own choosing - the clinical solitude of the inner will - and set amongst the wider framework of that will's expression. Once this is done - once we look at the vicissitude of the 'will' in the wider setting, it becomes blindingly obvious that the 'will' - that absolute that precedes all - itself can have a history. And having a history is part of time and so no absolute.

This is so obvious that it hardly needs spelling out. What, after all, is 'socialization' but bringing people up to want to do what we want them to want to do? The imposition of one will upon another, in other words. And it works (or it works quite often). Again, on the wider scale, it is perfectly obvious that the emergence of consensual 'values' can be lawfully plotted. According to Marx, by reference to economic context - not that Marx himself would be immune (for instance with his theory of value) from psychoanalytic illumination. But even if we are not dialectical materialists, even if we can see that there can be 'triumph of the will' that lasts a good deal longer than the Third Reich (the Jews' survival of two thousand years of persecution is a rather better example), in the long run we have to admit the reciprocal impact of reality upon desire.

Even to say that people's wants 'depend on circumstances' is dangerous for the pure psychoanalytic position, since it implies that wants have histories. And if ever wants had histories it is today: inflation is as intractible as it is since wants themselves are ever being increased. What today is accepted with 'gratitude', tomorrow is demanded as a 'right'.

But if it is hard to see how psychoanalysis in its pure form could resist dilution, it is equally hard to see how the empiricist could deny the private basis of what is later public. Inflation, indeed - which shows the reciprocal effect of desire upon reality - is, once more, a good example.

But the ghost of Galileo lingers and the prospect of the self-evident 'fact', independent of the observer or men's desires, remains. Not, in fairness, only with the social scientist. The damage done, though, by this illusory hope is far more serious in the social sciences than elsewhere (in the natural sciences it only matters on the edges of the known) for it blinds the social scientist to the nature of his subject-matter. Which, to repeat, is that qualitatively distinct and more primitive arena, that ante-room of science, here called 'mythology'. We can be as sophisticated as we like about the methods used, the 'how', but, unless that 'how' transforms the 'what' - that is what is being talked about - and drains it, as it has done in the natural sciences, of all trace of 'will', at the level of mythology (at least as here defined) we remain.

And do so by virtue of the subject matter. No doubt one day mythology will be escaped, all human behaviour will be stripped of purpose and desire - and so reduced to biochemistry or something similar. But, if this were to happen, there would be no social psychological problems left to deal with. Blood corpuscles do not worry about the price of bread - nor come to that, whether the arguments being advanced here are justified. At the level with which social psychology is concerned - the behaviour of recognizable 'people', 'like us' - its non-scientific basis must be acknowledged.

Ironically the subjective basis of social psychological phenomena has been obscured by the very thoroughness and consistency of that subjectivity. When everyone is equally involved, that involvement achieves a certain inevitability. And that involvement is due to our having been brought up - every one of us - as a person amongst people.

And so, not just learning a set of values, instilled in us by our parents, or even learning a language whereby to communicate to others (though, clearly, a paper could be written on that alone) but, far more importantly, learning a language of purposive behaviour.

Wilful ourselves, we learn to interpret wilfulness in others. A wilfulness that has widespread relevance in our understanding of the everyday. Sentences such as, 'I'll try my best, but you know what he's like' or 'It was perfect, he never knew he was being done', are 'meaningful' to us and no doubt (perhaps with a little training) could be consistently - and so, we tell ourselves, 'objectively' - recorded. However, this consistency should not allow us to forget that our observations, however 'reliable', are based on empathy. One must know what is meant by 'trying' (which implies 'an inner will', 'doing its best'); or what is meant by 'what he's like' (which implies qualities which inhere 'within' an individual); or 'It was perfect' (which is a reaction to success - i.e. fulfilled will); or 'He never even knew he was being done' (which implies ignorance of another's will).

That recognition should depend on shared experience has two dangers. The first and least important is that we may, ourselves, not have had the experience in question. If one has never 'tried one's best', then 'trying one's best' is a meaningless term. Perhaps it is to some psychopaths. And we need not know that we do not know. As Macduff said of Malcolm, 'He has no children.' Every act of communication is an act of shared privacy.

Of course, by and large we appear to share experiences and so get along fairly well. (Perhaps that is what 'culture' is all about.) This does not mean, though, that our awarenesses of the social scene begin to be as 'objective' as our awarenesses of the 'natural sciences' - where the relevant awarenesses are based on such elementary sensory capacities as the ability to look down a telescope.

In the social sciences our perceptivity depends upon ourselves in a far more subtle way. Malcolm could not console Macduff because - fortunately for him - he had no idea what it was like to lose his whole family.

But this is only the lesser danger. The greater danger is

that, out of the very agreements that we do achieve, we should blind ourselves to the essentially purposive nature of what we are describing. Agreement between observers cannot itself take the social sciences out of mythology.

Of course any generalizations we do achieve are welcome. That is not at issue. What is at issue is that we must remain aware of the basis of these generalizations - namely, very largely (though varying from area to area), shared willed experiences. The psychoanalysts are often taken to task for being 'unreliable' and disagreeing amongst themselves. But if we do participate, as argued, in what we observe, it should occasion no surprise. Some people, clearly, would be better at it than others. (Just as some people play the piano better than others - no one would say that no one plays it well because others play it less well.) To regard 'reliability', under these circumstances, as the touchstone of 'objectivity', is not only to impoverish our data by our insistence on the lowest common denominator of observers, it is also - and more seriously - to delude ourselves as to the status of that data.

If we do not acknowledge the subjective basis of much of our interpretation of the world, we arrive at an odd inversion of the infant's mind. The infant, who cannot reconcile himself to intrusion of adult FB, sees the world 'omnipotently' and so argues, 'must', therefore 'is'; the social scientist, if he cannot reconcile himself (in his desire to achieve a purely objective science) to the enduring relevance of FO argues 'is' therefore 'must', and so fails to see the parochialism - because bolstered by like mindedness - of his conclusions.

There is no escaping the subjective basis of our awareness of social phenomena. Certainly not by taking refuge into the sophistication of the subsequent analyses we make. Indeed, to insist that vulnerable data be as well established as the methods used to process it, is to expect a child to be turned into an adult by asking it to pay taxes.

Or trying to spend one's way out of debt. We have to accept the difference between 'leadership' (in the terms used here) and 'despotism' (a distinction hardly ever, if ever, made by those who insist that all observed phenomena be equally 'there') - messy and inadequate though that distinction will be most of the time. Data in real life is messy and inadequate. Even the definition of a 'group' that expresses the nature of the relationship instead, as so often, sheer proximity ('you four around the table are a "group"') is messy and elusive - critically important though it is.

In the social field, 'purposes' are lived out, 'achievement' is possible, and, if one 'fails' there may be 'extenuating circumstances' (imagine the sun having 'extenuating circumstances' for not shining!), people may 'co-operate' (what does that mean in strictly scientific terms?) or are reduced to 'conflict' (i.e. there is a clash of that mythological property, 'wills'), 'institutions' are 'set up' and given 'powers' (try those two on a hard-headed natural scientist!). This is the ground out of whose moving base of fusing and conflicting 'wills', the wider fabric - and the private relationship - attain the degree of stability they may have. When anyone insists that the social sciences are just like any other sciences, try imagining the 'people' concerned to be the sun and moon. Try imagining the sun and moon 'co-operating' or having 'attitudes'. As, of course, they were once thought to do.

The problem has always been in the past of knowing how to do justice to the 'will' without being overwhelmed by it. Once this potent, mysterious source is let out of the bottle, how can it ever be contained? Psychoanalysis clearly, has not succeeded - it has been quite taken over by this unique and - once acknowledged - 'inevitable' force. Would not the same fate await ordinary social scientists once they listened to the siren voices of 'purpose', 'meaning', as ordinary understood, or 'health'?

As long as the 'objective' and 'subjective' are seen as qualitatively distinct, this might well be the case. If the only alternatives are the blind progress of the planets around the sun on the one hand, and 'the life force' that variously manifests itself in 'desire', 'purpose', 'authority', 'value', 'function', 'hope', 'co-operation', 'conflict' - not to mention 'formal role', 'institutions', and codes of 'law', 'rights' and 'duties' - on the other, then, clearly for anyone who accepts that social psychology has a human face, the temptation to take the plunge into psychoanalysis or one of its watered down derivatives must be great indeed. If, however, the dilemma is less starkly put, it may be possible to preserve our sense of balance whilst retaining our acknowledgment of the reality of the willed.

But to do that, the human and the 'meaningful' and the scientific and the 'meaningless' (or rather 'non-meaning' for in science the term 'meaning' itself has no meaning) must be both seen as a matter of degree. And that can only be done if, like Piaget, we move away from the problem of the 'known' and look rather at the nature of the 'knower'.

THE SOCIAL PSYCHOLOGICAL AND THE REVENGE OF THE MYTHOLOGICAL

Knowledge is no better than the person who knows it. All knowledge has a personal base since, where there is no one there to know, the problem would not arise. Death, in other words, resolves all doubts. What we call 'blind objectivity', is what we have come to see as such. To talk of 'objectivity in itself' is, from this point of view, a form of idealism - that is an inference turned into an absolute.

Once we accept the personal basis of the known and see the 'known' to be an equilibration of the will, then all these problems fall away.

Since objectivity becomes an achievement and a matter of degree. Once it is granted that we are born self-centred, certain only of the manifest insistence (not even nature) of our desires, and with no clear awareness of the world around and that, bit by bit, by integrating FBs, we achieve that equilibration and degree of balance we call 'objectivity', then the objective and the subjective, the willed and the inevitable, can exist side by side. They can do so, of course, because, because these antinomies are no longer qualitatively distinct.

'Of course', since this is but a re-statement of the thesis of this paper. This entire paper has been based on the assumption that the public present is the heir to the private past: what can now be further inferred, and what has not so far been elaborated, is that the equilibration that underlies 'objectivity' may itself be a matter of quality and degree.

We need not just 'equilibrate' on meeting that refractory input we know as the 'objective', we can also equilibrate when we meet - another person.

And this form of equilibration would be a far cry indeed from the accommodation to Jupiter's moons, whose cold certitude has always been the epitomy of 'objectivity'. 'The universe is not hostile, nor is it friendly. It is simply indifferent,' wrote my namesake J.H. Holmes. Not so are our relationship with people - that can be hostile and friendly alright, and it is on its hostility and friendliness that our mental health very largely depends.

In society we can equilibrate with those 'like us' who are just as hopeful of success and in need of re-assurance and as prepared to be deluded as we are. And with them - unlike the 'universe' - we can agree on a kind of social contract on what constitutes reality.

In the natural sciences we have to meet reality on its own terms. Not so in society; what will be called 'social reality', is the result of a kind of collusion or, less invidiously put, 'co-operation' in which we can persuade each other on what is actually there. In the language of this paper, of course, it will be seen as an 'equilibration' in which one man's FO becomes another's FB. And the circle is complete.

This formulation of the problem - whereby we can provide each other with what is 'there', so that what is 'there' can have an inter-personal as well as impersonal base - is only possible with the gradations implicit in the FO-FB approach. If we see the world as absolutes as either objective or subjective (respectively pursued by the psychoanalyst and the empiricist), then each can define the other: 'objective' is that which is not subjective (and so the social scientist insists his subject matter is just as 'objective' as any physicist - after all, he is talking about other people's feelings, not his own!) and 'subjective' that what is not 'objective' (so that the psychoanalyst will assume a separate causal 'will' at any point where the context no longer seems to provide a complementary patterning).

This formulation, on the other hand, can be quite complex enough to satisfy the most subtle interplay of value, desire, reason and acknowledgment of the outer real; of feelings being asserted into fact (as in a revolution) and facts decaying into aspiration and regret ('the king across the water').

Three examples will be taken to illustrate this thesis, the simplest of all - which will be called 'social expectancy' - and then the more complex ones, both of which appear to break the closed circle of socially defined reality, those of 'value' and 'fact'. That 'an independent fact' is not baseline but precarious achievement, will be the last point made.

First, the simplest example, that of 'social expectancy'. This goes as follows - 'My acceptance of the real depends on what I expect your acceptance of the real will be.' This very simple formulation (which might be defined as 'anticipation of the other's reconstruction') can take us a long way. Money is a good example - I will accept money from you, if I am persuaded that you - and others - will take it back from me. Reciprocally, of course - and conversely - you will accept money from me if you expect that I - and others - will take it back in turn. We 'co-operate' and determine, through our mutual anticipations of the other's response, what the other's response will be.

Anything further from Galileo's moons can hardly be imagined. They do not suffer from 'crises of confidence' - when the whole process goes into reverse - nor can they bring about the 'self-fulfilling anticipation' of the charismatic leader who has the power - like modern advertising - of convincing potential followers that others have already followed.

Compliance, indeed - the whole mechanism of social control - is another good example. 'I as citizen will heed the establishment and not the revolutionary because I expect that others will obey the establishment as well.' Blessed are those in positions of power because other people will presume that they have it.

And, once they are presumed to have it, the whole apparatus of elementary sanctions can come into play, giving the whole tissue of expectations enormously greater force. Once the firing squad has fired, those left are persuaded that members of the firing squad expect each other to obey. Cursed are those who threaten and fail to act, for they shall be as an emperor taking off his clothes.

This pattern of expectations is very frequently (if not always) stiffened by considerations of 'value'.

Values, at first sight, appear to contradict the argument. For, surely, they are first believed in and only then agreed. Not so by the thesis advanced here. Even values - which, if anything, appear to have an 'intrinsic existence' (and so appear to preceede awareness) will be argued to be (at least in the form that we meet in society) as much a form of 'the social real' and the result of men's co-operation as anything else.

This appears paradoxical for values, anchored as they are in the self-sufficient, mysterious, arbitrary (and, hence, unscientific) source known as 'authority', can turn our minds away from pre-occupation with the other's response and allow us to find peace in the solitude of our convictions.

But this solitude - and apparent indifference to the demands of others - is only possible where others help. It is the presence of others (either in the present or in the past - or both) that allows us to preserve this conviction of a 'higher reality' - a higher reality that, by the view advanced here (which allows the psychoanalytic approach descriptive weight), reflects the earliest insistence of our FO desires, so that (like a new-born child that has yet to accept what might be called the 'outer inevitable', the world on its terms, not on ours) we imperiously demand that a certain outer reality 'should be'.

We can turn to ceremony to provide a clue. Ceremony grants each man solitude, for where the other can be anticipated - and this is the critical point which will also come up in a different form in a moment with 'facts' - the other can be ignored. That which can be predicted, need no longer 'be'. Not, at least, in the sense of providing us with that refractoriness of the outside, the resolution of which - the digestion of 'contents' into 'criteria' - that is the basis of our intellectual growth. With ceremony, inward-looking world of the intrinsic, 'content' is not transcended but preserved. For in this closed world, each participant provides the other with a FB that allows that other to retain the illusion of his FO omnipotence intact. Values, too, depend on the support of others.

And the active FO-FB formulation can cope with confirmation and intellectual arrestation quite as well as with refutation and intellectual re-adjustment - and, hence, growth. And no other formulation can.

But values have yet another feature - they are polarized around 'authority'. It is through authority that we express our nostalgia for past illusions. It is in obedience to authority - and ceremony is but a striking and extreme example of this - that this latter-day predictability, and hence solitude, can be re-attained. We must preserve the weakness as well as impatience of the early child.

This adumbration of the absolute can also be cast in FO-FB terms: 'authority', the social stiffener of value, is what those more powerful than ourselves believe.

Or what we believe they believe. 'Do it because I wish it', and 'Do it because God (the boss, 'other people') want it', are quite different messages. The first implies the parent's assertiveness, the second, much more difficult to shake off, his submission. Parents, however bullying they may be, can only exist in one place at a time, and eventually will die; but the shadowy object of a parent's reverence (and an impressive parent at that, who 'should know best') may be anywhere - at any time - at all, and so quite impossible to declare irrelevant.

And for 'parent', read 'those with more power' in later life. No doubt, with adults as well as children, 'transactional power' - the power to satisfy our needs. (In childhood, it must be remembered, we are imprisoned by our dependence.) Thus, maintenance of values, will, by this argument, depend on the continuance of an élite - or corporate 'authority' - that then continues to believe. If the élite should drift into cynicism (or, perhaps, more to the point, be seen to do so) or lose its 'power' (its control over resources), others will no longer co-operate with their credulity - for it is only that which those with more power and knowledge than us fear, that preserves the magic of its mystery intact.

Hence the oddly egalitarian nature of even the most hierarchical ceremonies or societies. Even the Queen, as we saw, salutes. Ceremony witnesses the committal of the powerful - and hence the weak.

A committal that, by this approach, need not be. Where parents - or the élite - assert themselves as themselves and not as God's messengers, there will the powerful other be revered - but only so long as they are actually 'there'. It is in these terms that the force of 'respectability', 'public opinion', 'honour' - what might be summarized as 'shame' - can be accounted for: the fear of being seen by the seen, not the unseen.

That which is socially preserved is socially derived, and values too - and lack of values - can have an idiosyncratic history. According to Marx, an economic, 'transactional' history. This is possible - there would certainly appear to be a drift to value where common interests favour both hierarchical and reciprocal control - psychologically, though, the process looks like Marxism in reverse. Instead of achieving a 'synthesis' from the underlying transactional thesis and antithesis, we start with the unassailable certainty of the synthesis (omnipotence, the cloudy 'ought', value in all its forms) and then achieve the relativity of a dialectic.

Once values are seen to have a past, all the logical problems of the relationship of values to non-values disappear. That belief in value can be a matter of degree, that belief in value can be re-inforced by - or weakened by - purely instrumental considerations is no longer absurd, once values lose their integrity and are but part of the texture from which all awarenesses are derived.

And so it is in later life, we still avow the part 'fact', part 'value', part fact because value (other people's values, after all, even when we are not impressed by them, are 'real') and part value because fact (our acceptance as 'right' what cannot be escaped) known as 'authority'.

But if values are socially anchored, surely 'facts' are free. With facts, if anywhere, we can escape the oppressive influence of those around and come to conclusions independent of our fellows. Was it not facts - Galileo's moons that upset the medieval cosmogeny and asserted the possibility of the unwelcome irreducible?

But although science - the elaboration of the unwelcome 'fact' - can disrupt society, society can reabsorb; there can be a revenge of mythology on science, a revenge that comes about through the very adaptation that science makes possible.

Namely, the withdrawal of the 'unwelcome irreducible', a withdrawal implicit in the entire biological, process point of view. (And not, it might be added, in any other.) This point of view argues, not just the derivation of the known (which is bad enough for those who accept the public present on its own terms) but the pragmatic derivation at that; knowledge, rather than being a reflection of 'absolute truth' (or whatever), is a resource that may (or may not) help us to survive. And survival, in the last resort, means adaptation.

Hence the 'whole panoply of meaninglessness' that this approach implied: that which is 'adequate for survival' at one time need not be so at another.

And that last sentence, inoffensive though it may sound, is lamentably reactionary in its implications - namely, that science and society can deprive us of the need to know.

The need to know - the very existence of psychology, as opposed to physiology - was argued to be due to the break down of adaptation that had occurred at birth. Knowledge was the digestion of the unexpected: had we remained in the continuity of the womb, 'knowing' would not have been necessary. Or possible. But we learn. We resolve the competing contents that assault us into a 'criterion' that is then seen to endure. We achieve a growing awareness of outer identity (through, it was suggested, receiving constant environmental FB - to varying FO initiative) that breaks the assumption of our omnipotence (i.e. that there is no need to know) and gives us an identity of our own.

But, once known, there is, indeed, no need to know. Knowledge, too, can be equilibrated. We can move away from the decision-making implied in our dealings with an uncertain future and rely on the capital of memory - a totally different basis of the known. Memory, indeed, might be described as incipient physiology - the reliance upon continuity, not judgment. A continuity that may well approximate to 'value'. We are all prone to become mentally middle-aged and develop a kind of idiosyncratic bureaucracy of the known - in which precedent and memory replaces decision making and doubt.

This 'withering away' of the psychological need not happen. Learning, as we all know, can lead to an awareness of what there is to learn. Learning, for all that, though, can hold within itself the seeds of its own decay.

A decay that can assume ominous proportions when it happens on a social scale. Society, too, can become middle-aged, dominated by the corporate memories of its established continuities. And that which is but a passing inconvenience - and then only for other people - on a personal scale is a far more serious matter when it happens in society. The presence of others, in other words, that can lead - by providing us with conflicting points of view - to the development of our intelligence - can also render the use of that intelligence, not just unnecessary, (though it can) but suspect.

Society can render our intelligence unnecessary because society can relieve us of uncertainties. Life in society today is clearly a much safer and more comfortable affair than it was before we became organized into groups. Perhaps the amount of intelligence that we possess - far more than most societies seem to need - dates back to a time when each was alone before uncertainty.

And this discrepancy between what society needs and what society gets - clearly a potentially explosive discrepancy - may well get greater. And do so through the advances that only society - in the form of organized research - makes possible. There is no reason why one day, for instance, there should not be invented a car that never fails. Once that happens, the skills of car repairing, manufacturing and designing can fade away. It is easier to repeat than to invent. Any society that does not change will, almost certainly, need ever fewer skills to maintain itself.

Prediction of the future is the least profitable of exercises. 'When men foretell,' as a Japanese proverb has it 'the devil laughs.' One thing is fairly certain, though - and that is there is no reason to assume that economic growth - nowadays taken quite for granted - is here to stay. And it is economic growth - with its implications of economic choice (and hence, almost certainly, political choice and even political revolt) - that has been the framework of society for at least the last six hundred years, if not a good deal longer. And if ever the economy does cease to expand - and it is difficult to see how it can go on expanding for ever - the self-equilibrating properties referred to here, may well come into play.

And these self-equilibrating properties will not just go for the skills of car making and the general appurtenances of life, but for the very content of the known. Knowledge itself can be equilibrated.

Knowledge can lose its base in doubt, once knowledge is assured. Knowledge after all (at least from the process, biological point of view) is no better than the knower - and where the knower does not understand, that knowledge will decay.

And the knower may not understand because the knower may not have to. Yesterday's intellectual breakthrough, only possible to the daring mind (like, for instance, the decimal point) can be used pragmatically by those who have no idea at all of the originality once needed. Once the formula is assured, the formula need be no longer understood. Once the reasoning cannot fail, the conclusions of that reasoning - in so far as they are necessary at all - can be learned by rote. And that which is learned by rote - blindly assimilated with no awareness of the context that made that knowledge possible and shows its limitations - is all too easily considered 'inevitable', and being inevitable necessarily 'right'.

How far this debasement of the known can go, is of course, anyone's guess. But there is no more reason in principle why there should be indefinite scientific growth than there is that there should be indefinite economic growth. And, once the development of science stops, at whatsoever level of complexity it may be, the skills required to maintain that science will drop.

And the possibilities of alternative explanations will withdraw. (By definition - since the growth of knowledge is but the elaboration of alternatives.) And, where the daylight of uncertainty is removed, 'is' will once more drift back to 'must'. Value will creep back, this time far more powerfully entrenched - for it will be socially enforced.

There is no reason why a priesthood of scientists should not arise, laying down as unquestioned 'truth' that neither they nor others have the courage of imagination to deny. And this drift into a legitimacy of knowledge (with science reduced to a form of ceremony) need be no one's 'fault', but rather the operation on a social scale of the drift into bureaucracy described above. Values after all - corporately insisted on memories - constantly accrete through that most pervasive of authorities - an authority to which we are all subject and need not be imposed - the past.

A past that is most oppressive on those who do not share it - that is, the young. But we all of us - even the young - may be tempted as well as pushed into considering what we have acquired as 'right'. The young have too much to gain, the old, too much to lose. We value, all of us, the approval and certainty - and anonymity - that orthodoxy can bring. With orthodoxy - triumph of value over fact - we not only can achieve success, we can also disclaim responsibility for what we know.

And so we drift into intolerance. Tyranny is but certainty in action, and once we cannot help what we now know is right, others become the object of correction, not debate.

And orthodoxy is a tyranny in which all can join.

Some men know more than others (the growth of knowing has been the subject of this paper). But we can none of us be sure. We see reality as through a plate of glass. At first we only see our own reflection, but growing awareness, bringing with it its own light, slowly allows us to see beyond.

But we can never be sure that we are not looking at ourselves.

INDEX

alienation, 101, 104, 106, 108, 117
Aristotle, 126, 135
authority, 9, 12, 14, 16, 29, 30, 34-7, 38, 40, 43, 44, 48, 62-4, 67-9, 72, 91-102, 103-17, 135, 173, 175, 177, 181, 183-5, 187

Bergson, H., 135
bureaucracy, 25, 83, 186, 187; see also ritual

caste, see class society
cause, 7, 124, 133, 139, 169, 171; see also power
class society and caste, 2, 3, 15, 16, 17, 22, 26, 32-7
communism, see Marx
competition, 25, 41-4, 89
conflict, 58, 115, 180
consent and consensus, 8, 13, 14, 37, 51, 64, 114, 148, 173, 174, 176-7
co-operation, 7, 41, 42, 177, 180, 181, 183
Copernicus, 6
creativity, see originality
criteria, measures, measurement and standards, 58, 81, 100, 106, 107, 108, 112, 117, 119, 122, 145-8, 151, 154, 156, 162, 163, 172, 173, 184, 186
cross-cultural data, 1, 118-23

decisions, 23, 54, 57, 174, 186
definitions, 106, 122, 133, 143, 164, 170; see also identity

economics and economic power, 174-7, 178
ego, 167, 168
empiricism, empiricist, 1, 2, 5, 120, 138-42, 153, 157, 158, 165, 169, 178-81, 182
equilibrium, equilibration, 144-71, 181-7; see also system

facts, 8, 139, 141, 143, 148, 156, 158, 161, 167, 169, 178, 183, 184
fascism, 91-3, 98-9, 100
followership, 9, 13, 14, 16, 24, 35, 43, 67; see also consent
free will, freedom, 98, 107, 125, 126, 128, 130, 134, 135, 156, 169, 170
Freud, S., 2, 4, 5, 17, 18, 27, 29, 39, 41, 60-2, 65, 68, 86, 93, 100, 101, 168

Galileo, 6, 139, 141, 149, 170, 178, 183, 185
groups, 9, 11, 15, 39, 44, 49-51, 53-7, 60, 69, 80-90, 91-100, 180

guilt, 69, 168, 173

Hegel, G.W.F., 110, 158
holding concept, 120

identity, 143, 151, 157, 159-66, 186; see also definition

leader, leadership, 1, 9, 12, 13, 14, 16, 24, 26, 29-43, 54, 61-6, 67, 70-3, 79, 85-6, 95-6, 114, 126, 176-7, 180, 183
legitimacy, 3, 8, 29, 34, 37, 39, 116, 127, 129
logic, 4, 8, 100, 143, 144, 146, 153, 155, 158

Marx, K., and Marxism, 2, 91, 94-7, 98-102, 110, 111, 176, 178, 185
measures, measurement, see criteria
morale, 1, 3, 75-90
morality, 8, 12, 62, 67-74, 84, 86, 92-3
mythology, 171-2, 180, 181-8

norms, 18, 83, 87; see also groups, morality
numbers, 142, 146, 147, 158-64, 165, 169

organizations, organizational, 3, 124-33
originality and creativity, 7, 100-2, 124, 158-9, 162
ownership and property, 1, 3, 46-59, 114, 173

Parmenides, 165
Piaget, J., 2, 4, 5, 6, 29, 39-41, 101, 110, 111, 113, 121-2, 138-88
Plato, Platonism, 7, 120, 125, 126, 135, 146, 150, 151, 158, 159, 165
politics, 7, 8, 131, 171
Popper, K., 120
power, 7, 13, 34, 50, 51, 53, 57, 62, 70-3, 85, 86, 89, 99, 124, 129, 180
Primal Horde, 4, 8, 9-12, 60-74, 93-7
professions, 6, 53, 55, 85
property, see ownership
psychoanalysis, psychoanalyst, 1, 7, 138-42, 153, 165, 166-71, 172, 177-8, 181, 182, 183; see also will
purpose, 25, 83, 89, 126, 128, 129, 131, 137, 169, 170, 177, 179, 180, 181
Pythagoras, 146, 151, 158

ritual, 6, 25-7, 33, 34, 35, 36-7, 38, 48, 65, 69-74, 81-4, 89, 175, 177

science, 7, 8, 91, 97-102, 103, 112, 114, 116, 118, 119, 121, 124-33, 134, 135, 164, 170, 171, 172, 179, 185; see also social science
shame, territoriality, 91, 97, 98-100, 114, 173, 185
social class, 1, 2, 3, 6, 9-45
Social Contract, 13, 61, 93; see also Primal Horde
social science, the social psychological, 103, 112, 114-17, 171, 179-81; see also mythology
society, 7, 8, 9, 107, 114, 131, 171-88
standards, see criteria
structures, structuralism, 5, 135, 152, 156, 160, 164-6, 168, 169, 170
system, 1, 134-7; see also equilibrium

territoriality, see shame
time, 118, 135, 137, 144, 147, 148, 157, 158-66
trade unions, 6, 55-7

unconscious, 139, 169

value, values, 2, 3, 5, 7, 114, 131, 132, 135, 172-4, 175, 177, 178, 179, 181-8

will, 5, 7, 8, 116, 139, 142, 153, 155, 157, 166, 171, 177-81; see also psychoanalysis

nted in the USA/Agawam, MA
gust 14, 2014

5049.131